April 5 2018

For Brian,

You can (o)count on
the fact that this
will be a great
read.

Enjoy the books,

Harry Rubin

The GOLD COINS of NEWFOUNDLAND

1865-1888

How Newfoundland came to possess
a spectacular mintage of gold coins

HARVEY B. RICHER

Library and Archives Canada Cataloguing in Publication

©2017 Richer, Harvey, author
The gold coins of Newfoundland: the fascinating story of how
Newfoundland came to possess a spectacular mintage of gold coins
/ Harvey Richer.

Includes bibliographical references and index.
ISBN 978-1-927099-87-2 (hardcover)

1. Gold coins--Newfoundland and Labrador--History. I. Title.

Design by Sarah Hansen

Published by Boulder Publications
Portugal Cove-St. Philip's, Newfoundland and Labrador
www.boulderpublications.ca

Printed in Canada

HG660.N49R53 2017   332.4'04209718   C2017-901930-9

We acknowledge the financial support of the Government of Newfoundland and Labrador through the Department of Tourism, Culture and Recreation.

We acknowledge financial support from The J. Douglas Ferguson Historical Research Foundation.

We acknowledge the financial support for our publishing program by the Government of Canada and the Department of Canadian Heritage through the Canada Book Fund.

TABLE OF CONTENTS

LIST OF TABLES

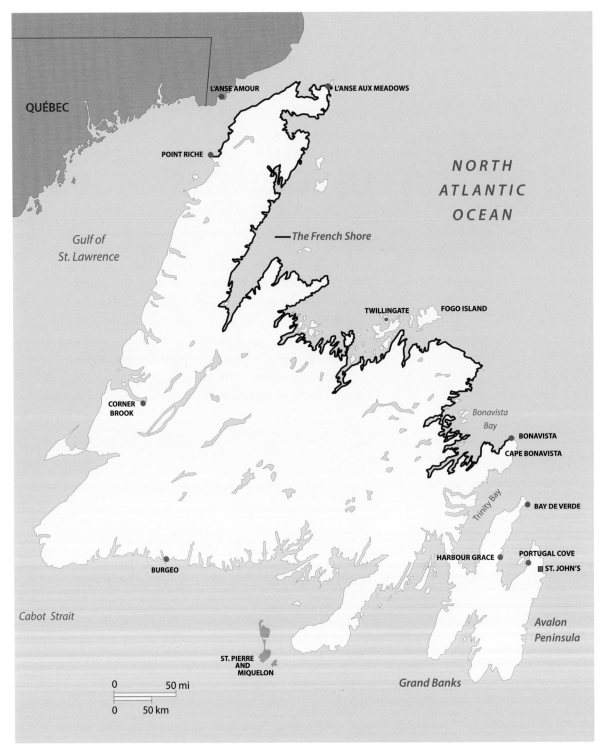

A map of Newfoundland indicating the locations specifically mentioned in this book.

ACKNOWLEDGEMENTS

Authors often write long notes of thanks to those who helped in the preparation of their book. I had hoped to avoid this, but there are a number of individuals who contributed to making this particular effort possible. Foremost is my wife, Klara, who was a constant source of encouragement in both the writing of the book and the acquisition of certain coins that constitute my Newfoundland collection. The staff at The Rooms, a cultural facility in St. John's that houses the provincial archives, museum, and art gallery, were wonderful during my several visits there, particularly Jessie Chisholm, Maureen Wade, Melanie Tucker, and Charles Young. Additionally, staff at Memorial University, particularly Joan Ritcey and Linda White, were extremely accommodating. I spent part of a very fruitful day chatting about Newfoundland history with the well-known Newfoundland historian James Hiller at Memorial University. James also read an early version of Chapter 1 and made numerous helpful comments. Another wonderful Newfoundland connection was Erika Steeves, who provided decisive editorial oversight. Rob Danay, a good friend and lawyer, agreed to read an early version of the entire manuscript and made a number of useful suggestions, some of which I actually followed.

Museum curators are often the sources closest to invaluable information about their collections. In the writing of this book, three were of prime importance. Chris Barker is assistant curator at the Royal Mint Museum at Llantrisant, Wales. He first made me aware of an extremely useful book by William John Hocking, *Catalogue of the Coins, Tokens, Medals, Dies, and Seals in the Museum of the Royal Mint*, and then later provided an image of a coin in their collection that I did not believe existed. Thomas Hockenhull, the curator of modern money at the British Museum, answered numerous questions and provided a complete listing of the museum's Newfoundland $2 gold coin holdings. Paul S. Berry, Chief Curator of the National Currency Collection of the Bank of Canada, responded promptly to my numerous queries concerning its Newfoundland $2 gold coin collection. Mark Ferguson, manager of collections at The Rooms, allowed me to view their collection of Newfoundland gold coins on a visit there in June 2014. Other collectors and dealers also provided stores of useful information. The owners of a Private

Canadian and the Perth, Kingston, and Southern Cross Collections provided both permission to use images of their coins in this book and information about their acquisitions. Several Canadian coin dealers were also useful sources of information, including Brian Cornwell, Geoff Bell, Joe Iorio, Chuck Moore (most unfortunately, recently deceased), and Sandy Campbell.

Detailed research is part of the writing of almost any book but certainly was a key element for this particular one. The librarian of the Royal Canadian Numismatic Association, Daniel Gosling, was of enormous help in tracking down a few obscure references. Fellow author Rob Turner inspired me with his wealth of knowledge acquired while writing his several excellent books. He also provided a key document from the UK National Archives that was important in understanding the 1865 $2 coinage. During the summer of 2014, I hired three University of British Columbia history students (Jennifer Cassie, Jason Fernando, and Sarah Thornton) to do archival research. Some of this involved searching through several miles of microfilm of 150-year-old newspaper stories to find (or, in some cases, not find) the rare gem of information. Keith Bunnell, reference and collections librarian at UBC, was most helpful in getting us started with the microfilm research, and with me personally when I was just embarking on this work.

The J. Douglas Ferguson Historical Research Foundation provided support for the publication of this book. Their assistance is gratefully acknowledged.

- Vancouver, British Columbia
Spring 2017

PROLOGUE

After the American War of Independence concluded in 1783, British North America consisted of Canada (what is today Ontario and Quebec), New Brunswick, Nova Scotia, Prince Edward Island (at that time called St. John's Island), and Newfoundland. Further west, Britain also controlled the enormous territory of Rupert's Land, which encompassed much of what forms present-day Manitoba, Saskatchewan, and parts of Alberta, as well as some of the Northwest Territories. Figure 0-1 indicates these British possessions at the end of the war.

One might have assumed that the British system of currency would prevail over this enormous territory, whose most heavily populated area stretched almost from the eastern edge of the Prairies to the Maritimes. While each of the British colonies was required to keep its accounts in pounds, shillings, and pence, the colonies decided on their own values of the various coins in circulation. The most prevalent coins were those from Britain and France but there were also some from Portugal and Spain and their Latin American colonies (Mexico, Peru, Colombia). Popular among the latter was

the Spanish silver dollar (or 8 reales), whose value tended to depend upon the location of exchange. The variation could be large, differing by almost a factor of two between various North American locations and Britain. The ratings were always higher in North America, reflecting efforts to attract and retain gold and silver coins in the colonies.[1] Such a system was ripe for currency manipulation, thus negatively affecting the conduct of commerce.

US coinage also tended to circulate widely in the British colonies, particularly after the US-Canadian boundaries were fixed in the 1830s. The volume of trade between the two countries increased dramatically after this time, so it eventually became important to fix the value of the US dollar (in both gold and silver) in the local currency. The US $10 gold coin was to circulate in Canada for $10 Canadian while the British sovereign was fixed at $4.8667. Both of these, together with silver coins, were accepted as legal tender within pre-Confederation Canada.

In Newfoundland, coinage was quite scarce even until the late 1700s. Much of the colony's commerce was carried out through the truck credit system, whereby local merchants outfitted fishermen in the spring (generally at exorbitant prices) and were repaid in the fall with dried codfish (usually at deflated prices). As commerce expanded, however, the same mix of coinage found in other British colonies began appearing. In September 1836, a prospectus for a St. John's branch of the London-based Bank of British North America was published in the colony. Opening in St. John's in February 1837, the bank drew severe criticism for operating in its own interests, which were often contrary to those of the local populace, and it eventually closed in 1857. Two local banks opened for business in the mid-1850s,

largely in response to the poor service provided by the Bank of British North America. The Union Bank of Newfoundland, established in 1854, held the government accounts that had been in the hands of the older bank. The Commercial Bank of Newfoundland was established in 1857 in response to fears that the Union Bank would have a banking monopoly in the colony. Both banks produced their own currencies, denominated at first in pounds but later in dollars.

Even with these improvements, the amount of coinage in circulation was insufficient to satisfy the demand. For everyday commerce, what was particularly required were low-denomination coins

1783

■ Great Britain
■ Spain
■ United States

Figure 0-1: British North American possessions in 1783 (in dark blue). British claims in British Columbia are not included on this map.

(Image: Wikipedia Commons)

Figure 0-2:
A Rutherford
Brothers halfpenny
token ca. 1840.

(Image: Courtesy of Heritage Coins)

such as British pennies and halfpennies, bronze five- and ten-centime pieces from France, and Regal Irish coinage. Responding to the need, local merchants began importing tokens. Prominent among these were those distributed by the Rutherford brothers, who established themselves as merchants in St. John's and Harbour Grace in the 1840s (Figure 0-2). Their design (a suspended sheep carcass on one side) came from a British trade token and actually had very little relevance to Newfoundland.[2]

In 1857, the province of Canada adopted its own system of decimal currency with the minting (in London) of a set of coins consisting of a bronze 1¢ coin and silver 5¢, 10¢, and 20¢ coins, all dated 1858 (Figure 0-3). New Brunswick had its own pre-Confederation coinage also, with bronze ½¢ and 1¢ coins, first produced in 1861, and silver coins, in the same denominations as Canada, minted in 1862. Nova Scotia never had silver coins minted for it, but had a release of bronze ½¢ and 1¢ pieces dated 1861. Prince Edward Island did not join Confederation in 1867, but waited until 1873 (Figure 0-4). It had a single mintage of coins, a 1¢ piece in bronze, dated 1871. None of the

other provinces produced official coinage meant for circulation before they joined Confederation. British Columbia, which joined Canada in 1871, did produce pattern (experimental) $10 and $20 coins in both silver and gold that were dated 1862. The gold coins were minted in New Westminster, British Columbia, while the silver ones were produced in San Francisco. The design had been developed by Albrecht Küner, an experienced engraver, who had also designed various US gold coins for private companies during the California Gold Rush. His surname is prominently displayed on the reverse of the British Columbia coins below the wreath (Küner F[ecit]) (Figure 0-5). Minting of these coins was largely a response to the discovery of gold in 1858 along the banks of the Thompson River near Lytton. This set off the Fraser Canyon Gold Rush, and, as in the California Gold Rush, a mint was established to provide a medium of exchange since virtually no coins were circulating in this region at the time. After a small number of coins were produced, variously estimated at about five to ten in each denomination in each metal, the New Westminster mint was closed and no more coins were produced.

Figure 0-3: A sampling of the first coins produced in Great Britain for each of its various colonies in North America.

Top row: Canada 1¢ and 20¢ coins, both dated 1858. Middle row, left: New Brunswick 1861 ½¢ coin.
Right: New Brunswick 1862 10¢ coin. The obverse of this coin (effigy of Queen Victoria) was later used for the obverse of the Newfoundland gold coins after "NEW BRUNSWICK" was ground off and replaced with "NEWFOUNDLAND." The reverse was used to make a pattern (experimental) Newfoundland $2 coin after the denomination and date were removed and replaced with "2 DOLLARS" and "1864." This rare coin is discussed more fully in Chapter 6 and illustrated as the front coin for this chapter.
Bottom left: Nova Scotia 1861 1¢ coin. Bottom right: Prince Edward Island 1871 1¢ coin. This is the only coin of those illustrated here that was not struck at the Royal Mint in London. Rather, it was manufactured at the Heaton Mint in Birmingham.

NEWFOUNDLAND'S DIFFERENT COINAGE HISTORY

The numismatic history of Newfoundland is different from that of the other provinces, mainly because it did not join Confederation until 1949. Like the other provinces-to-be, it began producing (at the Royal Mint in the United Kingdom) its own coinage in the early 1860s, but since it would not join Confederation for another eighty-five years, it came to have a much richer and more extensive coinage history than any of the other British colonies, producing coins up to 1947. The Royal Mint (with some subcontracting out to the Heaton Mint in Birmingham, England) was the exclusive manufacturer of Newfoundland coinage until 1917; starting that year, and intermittently thereafter, some were struck at the Ottawa Branch of the Royal Mint. The Canadian Mint was used exclusively during the Second World War in order to avoid the risk of shipping coins across the Atlantic.

Not only did Newfoundland, like the other provinces, request from London bronze and silver coins but in eight nonconsecutive years between 1865 and 1888 it asked London for a supply of gold coins. It is apparent from the documents discussed in this book that these requests were always granted. This is remarkable because Newfoundland

Figure 0-4: Map of Canada in 1867 indicating the regions in red that joined initially to form the new country. The states that had already joined the United States are shown together with some territories that had not yet formally joined the US.

(Image: Wikipedia Commons)

Figure 0-5:
An example of the
British Columbia
$10 coin that was
struck privately in
New Westminster in
1862. This coin was
not authorized by the
British government.

(Image: Courtesy of PCGS)

was the poorest of the British colonies in North America in the 1860s, and significantly less wealthy than virtually any other locale on the continent at that time. For example, in much of Canada and the United States during this period, the average farm wage was about 50¢ per day, but room and board were generally included. Nonfarm salaries averaged about $1 a day, whereas a constable in a small village away from St. John's made about a dollar a week![3] So why did the colony request – and Britain agree to – gold coinage for Newfoundland? And why were none minted after 1888? These are some of the main questions explored in this book.

While some of the information for this exploration has come from the Newfoundland Provincial Archives (The Rooms in St. John's), most has been obtained from the UK National Archives, which proved to be a rich source of the correspondence between the Royal Mint and the Newfoundland legislature during the period when the coinage was being planned and executed. The complete correspondence between the Royal Mint and the Newfoundland government related to the new coinage of 1865 was also obtained.

The subsequent years of coinage production are generally also included with correspondence between the governor of Newfoundland, the legislature, the banks, and the mint, which are available almost through the end of the nineteenth century. There are, however, some frustrating gaps in the information. I hired a professional archive researcher who lived right next door to the UK National Archives to try to find specific details not available in the correspondence. Her search yielded some new and interesting information, but a number of unanswered questions remain.

Another theme in this book is the effect of the coinage on the Newfoundland populace. How did average Newfoundlanders react to the handsome coinage produced for them, particularly the artistically beautiful gold coins? Did this increase pride in their colony? Did it help with commerce by providing a stable currency with a known exchange rate? How difficult was the transition from the British system of pounds, shillings, and pence to the decimal system eventually adopted by the colony? These are difficult questions to explore as the answers are often buried in the psyche of the inhabitants and thus not easily quantified. But there are ways to probe these issues; a useful approach is through an analysis of contemporary newspaper articles, which are used extensively throughout this book.

My goal was to write a book that would interest historians, the general public looking for a good historical narrative, and, particularly, numismatists desiring new insight into the gold coins of Newfoundland. Towards this end, the historical and numismatic aspects are interwoven throughout the book since they are intrinsically and essentially linked together. Nevertheless, certain chapters are clearly more focused on one or the other of these themes.

CHAPTER 1

· ·

A Brief History of Newfoundland

Newfoundland has had both a rich political history as well as a virtually unique natural history. We explore both in this chapter.

NATURAL HISTORY

About 4.7 billion years ago, the sun and its retinue of eight planets formed in the outer reaches of the Milky Way galaxy. This number is eight and not nine (as you might have learned in school) as Pluto is no longer considered a planet – it was demoted in 2007 to the status of a minor planet and I am proud that I voted against Pluto at the meeting in Prague that reclassified it. This change of status for Pluto was necessary because by 2007 numerous objects about the size of Pluto, and a few even larger, had been discovered at roughly Pluto's distance from the sun (forty times that of Earth).

The solar system is dominated by the sun and its most massive planet, Jupiter. The chemical composition of this system consists largely of hydrogen and helium with a few percent admixture of the heavier elements such as carbon, nitrogen, oxygen, neon, and iron. Gold, from which the

Newfoundland coins we discuss in this book were coined, is only about one hundred billionth as abundant as hydrogen. Where did this gold come from? The current model for the evolution of the universe begins with a big bang 13.7 billion years ago in which only hydrogen, helium, a small amount of deuterium (also called heavy hydrogen as it has a neutron in its nucleus as well as a proton whereas normal hydrogen only has a single proton), and lithium are produced. Many of the heavier elements have to be manufactured in the hot, dense interior of stars where nuclear reactions provide the real alchemy of the ancient scientists: they turn light elements into heavier ones. Carbon, oxygen, and iron are produced in such reactions. Gold is a much heavier element than any of these with 79 protons and 118 neutrons in its nucleus. Astronomers believed that gold could be produced rapidly in nuclear reactions that occurred in supernovae – exploding stars that are at least ten times more massive than our sun. However, recent discoveries suggest another possible formation mechanism. A research paper published in 2013[1] suggests that gold may come from a more cataclysmic event:

the collision of two extremely dense stars called neutron stars. These amazing objects have about the same mass as the sun, but they are typically only 10 kilometers in radius whereas the sun has a radius of 700,000 kilometers. This means that their densities are enormous, perhaps a few hundred trillion times that of the sun – an unimaginably large number. The huge energy released by a collision of these objects allows gold to be formed in the ensuing rubble. Very recent observations using the Hubble Space Telescope indicated that several moon masses of gold were found in the debris of such a collision.

Some time, then, before our solar system formed, a huge collision between two neutron stars took place near the gas cloud that was to eventually form the system in which we live. It polluted the gas, which then later collapsed to form our sun, the earth, and the rest of the planets, comets, and asteroids that now make up our solar system. Eventually a minuscule fraction of the gold produced in this cataclysmic event was mined on Earth and coined into the spectacular Newfoundland gold coins we treasure today. In this way, the Newfoundland $2 gold coins are intimately connected to the history of the universe.

The early history of our solar system was both chaotic and somewhat unpredictable. Most of the material in the collapsing gas cloud ended up in the sun, which now has more than 99.8 percent of all the mass in our system. Jupiter has about half of the remaining mass while the earth contains less than 0.001 percent. We are puny indeed! Within about 30 million years after the collapse of this gas cloud, the solar system had largely formed with its star (the sun), its planets, moons, asteroids, and comets. For an extended period of time, the earth and all the other planets were bombarded by remaining material that had not as yet fallen into the sun or planets. Earth was so battered by this process, and so much heat was released in these collisions, that it actually melted and became largely a liquid. We know that this happened because the earth is now differentiated; that is, the heaviest elements (iron, for example) are found closest to the earth's core, with the lightest elements near the surface. Such a process can happen in a liquid (throw some sand in a pail of water and it will sink) but not with a solid (throw some sand on a frozen pail of ice and it will not sink). As this bombarding material was swept up, the energy dumped into the earth decreased over time and it re-solidified.

The solid surface of the earth is not a monolithic structure. It consists of a number of plates (currently thought to be about ten) that move around driven by density variations in the earth, convection from the hotter interior, and the earth's rotation. This complex process, commonly referred to as plate tectonics, remains to be worked out in detail. The motion of the plates is extremely slow, about a centimeter per year on average (by contrast fingernails grow at about four times this rate), which is why it took so long for the idea of plate tectonics to become generally accepted. Where plates meet, interesting geology takes place. Mountains are pushed up, plates are pushed under, volcanoes occur, and earthquakes are common. The motion of these plates over billions of years have shaped the continents. Just imagine, a centimeter per year for a billion years amounts to ten thousand kilometers. Continents are easily changed and altered over periods of time significantly shorter than the age of the earth but very much longer than the human experience.

Newfoundland hosts one of the great demonstrations that plate tectonics is, in fact, occurring. Located in the western part of the

Figure 1-1: This photograph, taken by the author, was shot at Tablelands in western Newfoundland. The terrain on the left does not support extensive vegetation as it was pushed up from the earth's interior by continental drift.

province, between Trout River (a charming fishing village) and Woody Point in Gros Morne National Park, are the Tablelands.

At the Tablelands, photographed in Figure 1-1, the terrain on the left of the valley is distinctly different from that on the right. On the left, the appearance is that of a barren desert while on the right we see a large amount of vegetation. What is thought to have occurred here is that the rocks on the left were pushed up from deep below the earth's surface several hundred million years ago. These rocks do not contain the chemical elements required to support abundant vegetation and that is why this part is so desolate.

Because of the continuous motion of the plates, the continents come and go and rearrange themselves over time. About 200 million years ago, the continents likely formed the supercontinent of Pangaea, as illustrated on the map on the following page. Note that what is to become Newfoundland is thrust up against Europe. Over this long period of time, the continents separated into distinct land masses and the Atlantic Ocean opened between them.

Thus, the connection between Newfoundland and Europe (including Great Britain) began many hundreds of millions of years ago and continued into the modern era's voyages of discovery and ensuing colonial history.

POLITICAL HISTORY

Following the last ice age, the ice covering North America slowly melted and the continent began to transform into what it resembles today. The ice covering the island of Newfoundland and the Labrador coast is believed to have melted relatively slowly, disappearing around 11,000 years ago.[2] Roughly 12,500 years ago a movement of humans from Asia crossed over the Bering Strait while the two continents were still connected, and slowly moved eastward.

NATIVE SETTLEMENT

The first human settlement of modern-day Newfoundland and Labrador is believed to have taken place around 10,000 years ago. This distinct group of people left no skeletal remains. Their

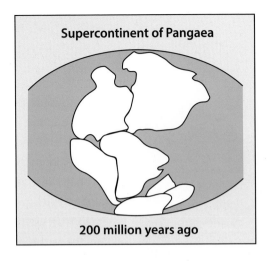
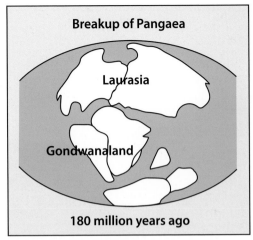

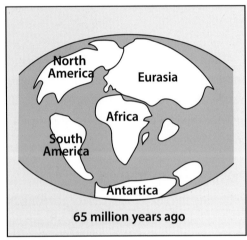
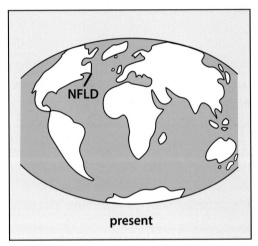

Figure 1-2: Continents on the earth from 200 million years ago through to today.

existence is therefore based on the discovery of weapons and tools, including polished stone axes and adzes, antler toggling, sealing harpoons, bone daggers, spear points, red ochre and graphite pigments, which are believed to be unique to these Native peoples.[3]

In 9000 BP (before the present), the Maritime Archaic Indians migrated northward into Labrador from the south shore of the Gulf of St. Lawrence. This group is thought to have reached the island of Newfoundland by 5000 BP.[4] These indigenous peoples lived across areas stretching from northern Maine to the northern coast of Labrador, and from Newfoundland up the St. Lawrence River to modern-day Quebec City.[5] On June 19, 1978, the government of Canada recognized the L'Anse Amour burial site in southern Labrador as a National Historic Site.[6] It remains the oldest known burial mound in North America and confirms that indigenous peoples did

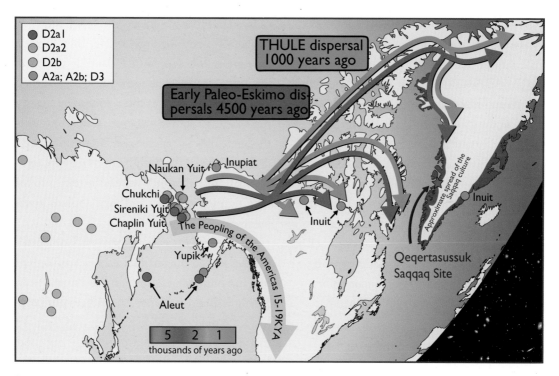

Figure 1-3: Native migrations into the northern regions of the New World. North America is the central landmass in this figure with present-day Russia to the left and Greenland to the right. Newfoundland is the small island at the lower right of the image.

(Image: Courtesy M. Thomas Gilbert et al., *Science*, June 27 2008, Vol. 320, pages 1787-1789)

inhabit the land over 9,500 years ago. The circular burial mound at L'Anse Amour was eight to ten metres in diameter and formed by a "low mound of large stones."[7] Underneath the mound lay the burial chamber where the relatively well preserved skeleton of a twelve-year-old child rested, along with a number of artifacts.

The L'Anse Amour site contained a walrus tusk, a harpoon head, painted stones, and a bone whistle. The buried body had also been covered in red ochre and wrapped in either skins or birch bark and laid face down, with the head pointing west.[8] This intricate burial evinces a degree of cooperation

and respect for the way in which the child had died or a belief in the afterlife or some form of rebirth. The items buried with the child served a purpose of some sort, likely to aid the child in his or her next journey, and they hint at the nature of the Maritime Archaic Indians' religious or spiritual beliefs that required such an elaborate burial.

Paleo-Eskimos moved into Labrador around 3800 BP, and onto the island of Newfoundland around 2800 BP.[8] Historians believe that these indigenous peoples originally came from Siberia, having rapidly crossed the High Arctic and adapted to the frigid climate while venturing all the way to

Greenland in just a few generations (Figure 1-3).[10]

Archaeologists have noted a significant cultural shift in Labrador and the island of Newfoundland starting around two thousand years ago. Location of settlements and raw materials being used changed abruptly, and the style of artifacts took massive leaps forward.[11] It is generally thought that a new group emerged – the Beothuk, who were descendants of the Paleo-Eskimos.[12] When the Vikings established a settlement in L'Anse aux Meadows in about the year 1000, they encountered an indigenous group already inhabiting the area, which historians believe may have been the Beothuk. These Algonquian-speaking hunter-gatherers had a population of roughly one thousand people by the fifteenth century.[13]

The Beothuk, and the later Thule people, were the indigenous peoples who encountered the Europeans – first the Vikings and then the sponsored expeditions of explorers such as John Cabot.[14] Fewer than one thousand Beothuk populated Newfoundland upon contact with the Europeans.[15] The Beothuk people managed to avoid complete annihilation from European diseases and displacement, and did not become extinct until 1829.[16]

EUROPEAN SETTLEMENT

Newfoundland, otherwise known to the British as "New found Isle lands," has had a long and complex history of interaction with Europeans.[17] The Vikings who ventured to the island of Newfoundland and the Labrador coast from Scandinavia in the ninth and tenth centuries found little land that would have been appropriate for their already developed farming practices. The mentality of Europeans during the era of territorial expansion and colonization was largely to find land that would accommodate their previously established way of life. They appear to have given little thought to adapting to the way of life of the peoples who were already living there. Evidence suggests that the Vikings who reached the Maritime shores made no real effort to settle the land. They left quite soon after initial contact, desiring instead the mountainous regions and high latitudes that they were accustomed to for their farming practices and their animals' grazing habits.[17]

In subsequent centuries, various European peoples visited the territory each year in order to fish and hunt whales through the summer season.[19] As hunters and gatherers, the indigenous peoples had no notion of private property and did not feel that it was out of bounds to scavenge any goods left over from the semi-permanent settlements abandoned by the Europeans. Although the Europeans returned annually to the island, the indigenous peoples did not believe that this gave them any rightful claim to the land. In constructing homes, the Norse custom was for dwellings to be very far apart from one another, as Scandinavians appreciated substantial personal territory. Hence the discovery at L'Anse aux Meadows, where the Viking dwellings were in close proximity to one another, suggests that any interaction with the Native peoples was probably aggressive in nature.[20]

In 1497, John Cabot claimed the island of Newfoundland for the English king, Henry VII. Thus, Newfoundland remains England's oldest colonial acquisition (although some historians argue that this distinction actually belongs to Ireland). Cabot and his crew of eighteen West Country men had actually been searching for a shorter route to Asia.[21] In the fifteenth century, the English crown was desperate for colonies, as the

Spanish and Portuguese colonies in Latin America had brought riches that contributed substantially to the economic health of these two monarchies. Lagging behind on the colonial front, England was becoming a smaller and less significant player in European politics.

Cabot appreciated that the Grand Banks was a superb resource. Although he subsequently claimed Newfoundland for England, it is not clear why he believed he had a right to make this claim, since Portugal had already claimed it in the Treaty of Tordesillas in 1494.[22] João Álvares Fagundes, a retired officer from the city of Porto, had been granted permission by the Portuguese crown to govern various parts of Newfoundland and the present-day islands of Saint Pierre and Miquelon.[23] However, as Newfoundland possessed almost nothing compared with the riches found in Latin America and generated little through what would become known as the Columbian Exchange, the colony was not of great importance to the Portuguese,[24] who, more than anything, wanted to keep the English crown in its place and ensure that it was aware of its insignificant status in world politics.

After Cabot returned to Bristol, England, there was no great celebration and little or no public recognition of his accomplishments.[24] He had not discovered any gold or prospects of profitable trade that would have greatly enhanced England's economic power.[26] His reward from King Henry VII was modest: "August 10, 1497. – To Hym that found the New Isle, £10."[27]

COLONIZING NEWFOUNDLAND

Following the defeat of the Spanish Armada in 1588, Queen Elizabeth I set about enlarging her empire. Greater financial backing for the Newfoundland fishing industry was provided,[28] and in 1610 King James I granted a royal charter for the entire island of Newfoundland in order to encourage permanent settlement of the territory, in the hope that not having to rebuild settlements annually would increase profits.[29] This royal charter marked the first real attempt by Europeans to "settle" the area, in contrast to annual attempts to exploit its resources, ravage the coast, upset the local people, and return to civilized England. The indigenous peoples who already inhabited the territory were deprived of their rightful ownership, in part due to their pagan worship but also in view of John Locke's argument regarding property – that one could claim ownership of a parcel of land only if "proper use" was made of it. Europeans viewed "proper use" as farming, not hunting and gathering.

European Newfoundland began as an international fishery, which eventually spawned local settlement, official and unofficial. In due course, the English and the French shared the land but began fighting over it from the late seventeenth century as part of their larger international contest. Official recognition of British sovereignty over the island of Newfoundland came in 1713 with the Treaty of Utrecht. Labrador was added in 1763, when New France disappeared except for Saint Pierre and Miquelon and the shore of Newfoundland from Cape Bonavista around to Point Riche, commonly termed the French Shore.

Many problems arose in attempting to colonize Newfoundland, primarily that skilled men appeared to have little interest in moving to a place where they would be separated by an ocean from their friends and family, and forced to endure frigid and long winters in a desolate place. Few women are recorded as having made the treacherous journey across the Atlantic, which eventually made for a very low birth rate.[30] The first few men and women who made the journey also noted that their local economy depended completely on the health of the fishing industry and the international market price for fish. Thus, the population of Newfoundland grew slowly throughout the seventeenth and much of the eighteenth centuries.[31]

There is evidence that in the sixteenth century French explorers began encroaching onto Newfoundland and Labrador territory.[32] War broke out between England and France in 1690, and with both European powers gaining assistance from regional indigenous tribes, the situation in the Maritimes became even more precarious. Overwhelmed at home, London provided no supplies, arms, or trained military men to the colony. Thus, while England profited from its control of the island's economic activity in times of prosperity, in times of desperation – when the burden of having an overseas empire was acutely felt by officials in London – Newfoundland was left to fend for itself.

Beginning in the mid-eighteenth century, Newfoundland's population experienced unprecedented growth. The European settler population, which totalled ten thousand in 1750, had climbed to sixteen thousand by 1764,[33] and Newfoundland fishers earned higher wages than skilled and unskilled labourers in Europe.[34] Their working conditions were known to be almost inhumane, however, with captains refusing them any form of rest for days on end in order to maximize their catch during fishing expeditions. During the off-season, some fishers began engaging in fur trapping in order to see them through the long, bitter winters.[35]

The late eighteenth century also saw a large influx of Irish settlers and migratory workers into Newfoundland. Ships from the West Country of England would stop in Irish ports such as Cork to pick up supplies for the voyage to Newfoundland; eventually they began taking on Irish labourers, some of whom then settled in the colony. Despite its harsh climate and working conditions, Newfoundland did not rate much lower than Ireland itself as an Irish homeland. Catholics in Ireland could not hold public office in the eighteenth century, and were prohibited from buying land beginning in 1704.[36] Famine devastated the country in 1741, killing thousands. Eventually the situation turned violent and by the end of the century various laws began to be repealed, although Catholics remained at a definite disadvantage with Anglican England's control over Ireland.[37] The influx of Catholics into Newfoundland made its predominantly Anglican and Protestant population anxious.[38] Protestants feared the loyalty of Catholics to the Roman papacy or to an enemy Catholic government, such as the French.[39] If the Pope were to demand that the Irish wage war or turn on the Protestant inhabitants of Newfoundland, would his word trump the local government's laws?[40] In addition, the pro-Stuart rebellions in Scotland in 1715 and 1745 aggravated existing prejudice against Catholics and the Irish in general. Meanwhile, Catholics in Newfoundland were greatly angered by the fact that they were not permitted to freely practise their religion. Beginning in the early 1740s, the Newfoundland government demanded an oath of loyalty and allegiance from Irish settlers, but many simply refused to comply. Over time, however, Irish labourers – 35,000 of whom had settled in Newfoundland by the early nineteenth century and who typically accepted grisly jobs that few others would take – became an essential part of the colony's fishing industry.

The relationship between English settlers, migratory fishers, and French settlers remained tense throughout Newfoundland's entire colonial history, sometimes erupting in violence. In 1696, French forces and their indigenous allies invaded Cape Breton, the northern tip of Nova Scotia just across the Cabot Strait from Newfoundland, and managed to capture St. John's. In 1763, the Treaty of Paris reinstated the rights of the French to fish in Newfoundland waters between Cape Bonavista and Point Riche.[41] This further frightened the Protestant settlers, who believed that war with the French meant war with the Catholic Irish.[42]

THE ECONOMY IN LATE-NINETEENTH-CENTURY NEWFOUNDLAND

Newfoundland's status as a migratory fishing stopping-off point finally gave way to true settlement. The French Revolutionary and Napoleonic Wars helped this along. The economy of Newfoundland now rested in the hands of its inhabitants, but the situation was increasingly complex. Britain refused to provide the necessary subsidies and funds to support Newfoundland, leaving it up to the residents to find money to pay for public houses, church and road upkeep, and so on.[43] The American Revolution also changed the mindset of the colony, which now traded with Americans who were free from British control and had become their own masters. The American motto "no taxation without representation" also rang true to a certain extent in Newfoundland, since ever-greater taxes on businesses and economic transactions began to anger residents.[44]

Whereas poorer people benefited from seal hunting, fur trapping, logging, and building of boats for the resident fishers, investment in fishing also took the form of purchase of large schooners that were able to venture further offshore. The financial risks, together with the credit advanced for many entrepreneurs, put residents in quite a predicament.[45] Wealth and power began concentrating in the hands of a select few while most of the population struggled to survive.

Diversifying the economy became a popular idea at the time, as reliance on international fishing prices and dependence on Mother Nature had often left Newfoundlanders in precarious situations over the centuries. Following the end of the Napoleonic Wars in 1815, the risky nature of an undiversified economy became clear. The high fish prices of the war years fell and operations were curtailed substantially. Attempts were made to unionize, but merchants were unwilling to pay labourers the higher wages they had earned during the war and these attempts quickly failed.[46] The situation became so dire so quickly that the Court of Sessions ordered all unemployed labourers to report to St. John's in order to be removed from the island or else be flogged or imprisoned.[47] The order was quickly reversed, however, as it was clear even in relatively lawless Newfoundland, where the governor often acted as a dictator, that one could not imprison someone for being poor. This attempt at forced eviction showed how terrified officials were of an impoverished mass of men and women without financial subsistence.

In 1797, William Waldegrave was appointed governor of Newfoundland. He maintained that the existing naval government was sufficient to provide for the residents of the colony if they extended more civil authority for poor relief. Waldegrave felt that real property rights or colonial status were unnecessary.[48] His views accorded with those of

Figure 1-4: A fortune in dried codfish on a Newfoundland dock ca. 1900.

(Image: The Rooms, Provincial Archives, St. John's.)

many members of the British Parliament, who had never visited Newfoundland but considered themselves experts on what level of support and independence was necessary. The local people remained focused on the growing economic inequality between the majority, consisting of impoverished servants and labourers, and the select few wealthy merchants.[49]

The larger merchant firms, centralized in the main ports and the only institutions able to take the financial risks, had the most up-to-date equipment for profitable hunting and fishing. The wealth of the island thus became further and further concentrated, resulting in a growing gap between the haves and the have-nots.[50] In the early nineteenth century, murders occurred when neighbours' livestock encroached on each other's vegetable gardens, and women came to blows over topsoil disputes.[51] The economic situation in Newfoundland was dire and no one seemed able to do anything to improve it.

GROWING INEQUALITY

Throughout the eighteenth century, bartering was the rule, with dried codfish mostly used as the medium of exchange (Figure 1-4).[52] Spanish and English coins began appearing throughout Newfoundland as a result of constant travel to and from Europe. Although it was legislated that the accounts of the colony were to be kept in dollars and cents after January 1, 1865, it was not until 1877 that the law was actually enforced.

In 1834, an act was passed that permitted the Newfoundland Treasury to issue treasury notes ranging in value from £1 to £100 (Figure 1-5). The Newfoundland Savings Bank opened in 1836, thanks to legislation enacted by the newly installed

Newfoundland House of Assembly. The bank was fully owned by the government of Newfoundland. The London-based Bank of British North America opened in February 1837 in St. John's, and closed in 1857. The Union Bank of Newfoundland opened its doors in 1854, followed in 1857 by the Commercial Bank of Newfoundland, which was primarily used by merchants located in St. John's. Decimal coins, originally just in the form of bronze 1¢ pieces, were made available to Newfoundland residents in late 1864.

In the mid-nineteenth century, Britain controlled foreign relations for the colony, as it did for the empire as a whole. This made it particularly difficult for Newfoundland, whose economy was based on international fishing prices and exports of goods. French and American fishers, whalers, and sealers were still being given access to key Newfoundland coastlines due to treaties that Britain had negotiated without Newfoundland's input.[53] In 1865, there were eight foreign consuls in Newfoundland, from Spain, the United States, Prussia, Hamburg, Portugal, Brazil, France, and Italy – jurisdictions with active fisheries and hence interested in close association with the colony.

The free trade agreement with the United States, signed by Newfoundland in 1855, proved insufficient to increase exports to that country, much to the disappointment of many Newfoundlanders.[54] This was at least partly due to the outbreak of the American Civil War. In 1871, the Treaty of Washington reinstated the United States' legal right to fish off the Newfoundland coast. Government-funded projects, such as local road construction throughout the major cities, were implemented in the hope of relieving poverty, providing employment, and reducing vagrancy. Such projects benefited the growing numbers of Irish settlers in Newfoundland but provided little more than a Band-Aid solution to the greater, unresolved problem of economic frailty within the colony.[55]

In 1864, Premier Hugh Hoyles began seriously considering Confederation with the rest of the British North American colonies as a positive step towards economic diversification and stability in Newfoundland. Although this went against the nationalistic policies of earlier politicians, Hoyles sent delegates to Quebec to discuss the terms of unification.[56] His plan did not come to fruition, however, and neither did the idea of constructing a railway, which some politicians

Figure 1-5: An 1850 Newfoundland £1 replacement note (printed to replace a faulty one). This note was not actually issued as it is unsigned and undated.

(Image: Courtesy of Heritage Auctions)

argued would bring about the colony's economic diversification and health.[57] In 1865, the public debt of Newfoundland amounted to £197,505, about 151 percent of its GDP that year (compared with about 25 percent for Canada at the time of Confederation and 66 percent for Canada as a whole in 2013).

Throughout the nineteenth century and into the twentieth, politicians and economists struggled constantly over the issue of preservation of the environment versus short-term profit. The issue of economic stability through union with Canada versus sovereignty and Newfoundland nationalism was another consistent theme. Newfoundlanders felt that joining Canada would enable Canada to become politically dominant in Newfoundland's internal affairs; on the other hand, the colony's dire economic situation meant that politicians had few real choices in terms of nationalistic sovereignty.

In 1894, the Newfoundland banks defaulted and the situation became desperate. The banks had neither substantial cash reserves nor diversified portfolios, which would have provided greater security for their investments. Instead, they had been more interested in generating wealth for their investors than in building strong financial institutions that could have helped develop the colony; the Union Bank, for example, had paid a large dividend of 8 percent to its shareholders in 1867. The Great Fire of 1892 decimated St. John's and forced insurance agencies to make large withdrawals, although, ironically, this actually helped the economy by injecting $7 million for rebuilding of the city. Late in the century, there was also an overall decline in fish exports. The banks had not foreseen any of these events and had therefore not made adequate arrangements.[58]

In 1895, Premier William Whiteway turned to Canada and Britain for immediate financial assistance, even proposing to have Newfoundland become part of Canada if Canada and/or Britain took over Newfoundland's debts.[59] However, both countries refused to provide sufficient funding, forcing Robert Bond, then Colonial Secretary and later leader of the Newfoundland Liberal Party, to use his personal assets to back large loans to the Savings Bank of Newfoundland (the one bank that did not fail in 1894) in order to stave off the colony's financial collapse.[60] Newfoundland was by no means out of danger as a result of Bond's arrangements, since these loans were not flexible or subject to renegotiation without a great deal of arm-twisting. Forgoing its nationalistic aspirations, it adopted the Canadian currency due to its greater stability and the prospect of strengthening the economic future of the colony.

THE DRIVE FOR CONFEDERATION WITH CANADA

In the general election of 1869, the residents of Newfoundland rejected joining Confederation.[61] They continued to hold their natural resources in high esteem and believed that Confederation with Canada would impair their ability to make decisions for the betterment of their own territory by forcing them to adopt policies that benefited Canada as a whole.

In 1907, Newfoundland became a dominion in the British Empire together with Canada, Australia, and New Zealand. As a self-governing state, it could now stand on its own two feet without always running to Britain for help.[62] This did not mean that it had full independence, however. It had its own government but was still part of the British Empire, and many strings were pulled from Britain. At the same time, it remained economically dependent on the fisheries, with 60 percent of its workforce employed as fishers and much of the remaining 40 percent otherwise involved in the fishing industry.[63]

At the outbreak of the First World War, Newfoundland provided its own regiment, the Royal Newfoundland Regiment, a sign that the colony was maturing. The regiment was assigned some of the deadliest tasks, such as being the first line of offence in the Battle of the Somme in 1916, when most men did not make it back to the British front line alive.[64] Newfoundland's 29th Regiment suffered 710 casualties, with only 68 survivors.[65]

In 1929, during the Great Depression, Newfoundland once again began to weigh the pros and cons of becoming an independent state – without the financial security of being part of Canada – or remaining a colony of Britain.[66] By the time Conservative leader Frederick Alderdice became prime minister in 1932, the dominion's public debt had risen to £100 million. The government desperately needed money in order to avoid mass starvation, yet the effects of the Depression were still being felt around the world and no one had anything to spare. Both Canada and Britain felt that a temporary bailout was necessary, for if Newfoundland defaulted on its loans, the Canadian government's credit would be adversely affected. If Britain intervened in Newfoundland's affairs, the status of "responsible government" that Newfoundland had enjoyed since 1855 would disappear; nevertheless, the British Parliament recommended the appointment of an administration consisting of equal numbers of Newfoundland and British civil servants led by the Newfoundland governor. On February 16, 1934, a Commission of Government was inaugurated and Newfoundland lost its responsible government status.[67]

Figure 1-6: This advertisement was published in the St. John's pro-Confederation newspaper, *The Confederate*, in the 1940s. As can be seen, the debate over Confederation was fierce.

(Image: http://www.fishermansroad.blogspot.ca)

This "temporary measure" was prolonged by the financial ruin of the Western world throughout the 1930s and the outbreak of the Second World War, which suspended all non-emergency-related government issues.[68] During the war, the price of fish rose substantially, significantly strengthening the Newfoundland economy.[69] Clement Attlee, leader of the Labour Party in Britain and later prime minister, visited Newfoundland in September

1943 and commented that without "some great discovery of minerals, the island is unlikely to afford anything but a modest standard of living to its inhabitants."[70] He did not feel that Newfoundland was in any position to consider reverting back to responsible government, and believed that, since becoming a British dominion, it had regressed in its capability for self-government.[71]

In July 1943, Canadian prime minister William Lyon Mackenzie King stated that "if the people of Newfoundland should ever decide that they wish to enter the Canadian Federation and should make that decision clear beyond all possibility of misunderstanding, Canada would give most sympathetic consideration to the proposal."[71] Some in Newfoundland continued to favour returning to responsible government, believing that closer ties with the United States was the key to financial stability.[73] Eventually, with the financial assistance of Britain and Canada, the pro-Confederation side won in the second referendum campaign held on July 22, 1948, with 52.3 percent of the vote (see Figure 1-6).[74] Newfoundland – "New found Isle lands" to the British – together with Labrador became the tenth province of Canada, officially on March 31, 1949.

CHAPTER 2

· ·

A Snapshot of Newfoundland in 1865

Beginning in 1865, the Royal Mint commenced striking new coinage exclusively for Newfoundland, including coins produced in gold. The colony decided to adopt a decimal system for this coinage, aligning itself with Canada, whose first release of coins in 1858 was on the decimal system, and with the United States, whose decimal coinage stretched back to 1792. The state of the colony that year – its population, racial mix, average individual's salary, and other demographic facts – are of interest in assessing whether it was reasonable to produce the magnificent coinage.

A unique source of historical information for any British colony is the Official Blue Book. It contains handwritten reports made by the appropriate colonial authorities with extensive statistics covering virtually every subject imaginable. A perusal of the Blue Book for Newfoundland provides a unique view of the colony at this time, which helps place Newfoundland's distinct coinage in context.

POPULATION

According to the Blue Book, the total population of Newfoundland in 1865 was 122,631. The population of St. John's (Figure 2-1), divided into St. John's East and West, was 30,456; the east end had 8,737 males and 8,595 females, while the west end had 6,701 males and 6,423 females. The census of 1891 lists a total population of 25,738, indicating that the population of St. John's actually declined during this period, unless some of these numbers are incorrect or the latter census covered different areas of the city.

The French Shore, situated along the north coast from Cape Bonavista around to Point Riche, had the smallest population, with 1,778 males and 1,536 females. The Treaty of Utrecht (1713) permitted the French to fish in season along this coast. Every region in Newfoundland is listed with an excess of males over females, typically about 1.1 males for each female. This is somewhat surprising given the dangers encountered by men working in the sealing and fishing industry.

There are columns in the Blue Book for "Coloured Population," but no entries were made in 1865, possibly because the population was 100 percent white at the time. During the early 1860s, the US Civil War was raging and the Underground

Figure 2-1: St. John's, looking down Water Street, before the Great Fire destroyed the city in 1892.

(Image: Library and Archives Canada: MIKAN 3191528 ca. 1886)

Railroad was transporting tens of thousands of fugitive black slaves northward into Canada, where slavery was prohibited. The existing data suggest that most former slaves settled in Ontario, and it appears from the Blue Book that virtually none found their way to Newfoundland. Interestingly, the vast majority of Newfoundlanders, based on 2006 statistics, is still Caucasian, listed as 98.9 percent of the population.[1]

A total of 98,500 $2 gold coins were struck between 1865 and 1888; given the total population of 122,631 at the time, there were about 0.8 such coins for each man, woman, and child in the colony. By contrast, between 1912 and 1914 Canada struck a total of 364,059 $10 gold coins and 295,634 $5 gold coins. With a Canadian population of 7.6 million

in 1913, this amounted to 0.09 gold coins per person, a ratio almost ten times smaller than those struck for Newfoundland. While this comparison has to be tempered by the different periods and values of the gold coins, it does roughly indicate that Newfoundland should not have suffered from a deficiency of gold coinage. One can imagine, however, that these coins were not distributed uniformly throughout the populace, given the poverty of the fishermen and sealers. No doubt most of the gold coins circulated close to St. John's.

SALARIES

Newfoundland salaries in 1865 covered about the same range that we see today. A skilled worker in the current economy will make approximately $60,000 per year, while a highly paid CEO can earn over a hundred times more. In 1865, the governor's yearly salary was $9,600, while a constable in one of the outports made $55.38. In the more populous outports, the salary for the same job was $92.31, while in St. John's it was much higher at $253.85. It mattered a lot where you lived and worked in the Newfoundland of the 1860s. By contrast, the salary for constables in the Royal Newfoundland Constabulary today ranges from $49,000 to $91,000.[2]

The Blue Book does not list salaries for fishers or sealers, since much of their compensation came through the barter system. We can assume, however, that it was less than the $55.38 paid to a constable in one of the fishing outports. The concern that Premier Hugh Hoyles expressed in 1864 about the small size of a putative $1 gold coin for Newfoundland (see Chapter 3) makes sense in light of these numbers. In an outport, a week's salary for a constable was about $1 (and certainly less for a sealer or fisher). If Newfoundland had chosen to mint such small coins, which could have easily gotten lost, their high value relative to salaries meant that the loss would have been keenly felt.

COINAGE

The 1865 Blue Book maintains that it is difficult to estimate the value of coinage in circulation, but it provides an estimate of £80,000 to £100,000. Since this was before any newly minted coins arrived in the colony, the ones circulating at that time were mainly British, French, American, Spanish, and South American coins. The entry in the Blue Book goes on to state that the greater part of the colony's trade was carried out by barter, so any estimate of this sort is likely to be a wildly inaccurate measure of the total value of the economy.

We can, however, monitor the evolution of the Blue Book entries by searching for later entries, knowing that significant new coinage had by then arrived in the colony. The main source of uncertainty with this approach is our ignorance of the amount of foreign coinage retired from circulation, a common occurrence, as they were largely debased because of the high intrinsic metallic value of the Newfoundland coins. Table 1 provides these numbers from a few Blue Books of this era.

Clearly, there is little change in these entries even though $54,400 (equivalent to £11,300) had been introduced into the Newfoundland economy by the coinage of 1865. By the end of 1881, a total of $363,400 (equivalent to £75,708) had been introduced through new coinage, but the total in the Blue Book was still only £120,000. This suggests that the estimates recorded were very rough or that retirement of debased currency was widespread.

In 2013, Canada minted a total of $166,979,000 worth of coins. With a population of 35 million, this amounts to about $4.77 for each person in Canada. The equivalent ratio for Newfoundland in 1865 (the first issue of coinage produced for the colony) was $0.44. Given the state of the economies of the two regions – Canada's GDP in 2013 was about 2.6 million times larger than Newfoundland's in 1865 – the coinage production

Table 1. Coins in circulation in Newfoundland in various years.

YEAR	VALUE OF COINS IN CIRCULATION
1865	£80,000-£100,000
1869	£100,000
1870	£80,000-£100,000
1879	£120,000
1882	£120,000

Source: Newfoundland Colonial Blue Books, Memorial University of Newfoundland.

for Newfoundland seems remarkably high. This observation needs to be tempered, of course, by the many other alternatives for payment available today (e.g., cheques and credit and debit cards). Nevertheless, it appears that Newfoundland was adequately served by this new coinage, since its value per person amounted to a few days' salary for an average worker.

DUTIES, REVENUES, AND EXPENDITURES

In the 1865 calendar year, the colony collected £95,684 in duties from all sources. Most of this came from duties on rum (£13,762), molasses (£8,399), tea (£8,223), and tobacco (£5,262). Total revenue amounted to £130,447, up from £125,158 the previous year.

In the area of government department expenditures, by far the largest amount was for relief of the poor (£28,170), followed by the legislature (£15,010), education (£13,379), interest on loans (£10,777), and roads and bridges (£10,094). The expenditure for relief of the poor had almost doubled from 1864, reflecting the decline of the fishing and sealing industries, while most other costs exhibited only minor fluctuations. Total expenditures climbed to £156,454, from £125,159 the previous year.

NEWSPAPERS

One of the main objectives in writing this book was to uncover the effects of the spectacular coinage on the population of Newfoundland. Did it increase commerce (it should have had an important effect by reducing the need to convert from one currency to another), or did introducing a new system of currency cause more confusion? Did it instill a sense of pride in Newfoundlanders, or did the dire economic conditions prevailing in the colony during this era dampen such emotions? This period saw a decline in the seal hunt, a collapse of the cod and herring fisheries, and an increase in the number of Newfoundlanders on government assistance. Did the Confederation discussion overshadow almost any other news stories, or were the headlines dominated by the US Civil War and the assassination of President Abraham Lincoln in April 1865?

To answer these questions, a search through the Newfoundland newspapers being published at the time was initiated in order to gauge public sentiment regarding the introduction of the new coins. After all, when the Canadian government decided to eliminate the 1¢ coin in 2013, stories about the impending withdrawal filled the press for months on end.

In the mid-1860s, there were about ten or twelve newspapers operating in Newfoundland, with a decided concentration in St. John's. Among these were the *Royal Gazette*, Newfoundland's first newspaper, which was published every Tuesday, as well as two dailies, several weekly and semi-weekly journals, including the *Temperance Journal*, published on the first and fifteenth of each month, and even a triweekly paper. In Harbour Grace, there was a weekly, the Standard, with a somewhat limited circulation.

In order to search the newspapers, which are currently not indexed, it proved necessary to view several miles of microfilm. The search spanned the years from 1864 to 1888, and there were only a few independent stories that related directly to the new coinage. Newspapers between 1864 and 1866 carried long stories about the introduction of the coinage, but these were mainly reports on the debates in the House of Assembly, largely extolling or denigrating the virtues of the upcoming decimal system compared with the British system of pounds, shillings, and pence. This coverage also provided a forum for acquainting the populace with the new system, which was formally introduced on January 1, 1865.

Strong support for the new currency was expressed by an article in the January 3, 1865, issue of the *Royal Gazette*: *There is a simplicity about the system which will render it generally acceptable, once our people become familiar with it.* Further support was expressed in the *St. John's Daily News* two days later:

Under the old system we were tricked and imposed upon day after day, with a heterogeneous mass of copper belonging to no recognized system of coinage in the world; and so intolerable was the nuisance that any change was then, upon all sides, deemed but a change for the better. Well, the change has come at last; and the old currency has been replaced by as handsome and convenient a coin as could be desired.

Most of the stories amounted to complaints about converting currencies or expressed a desire to revert back to the British system. On March 29, 1865, the St. John's Daily News reported on a discussion in the House of Assembly between Frederick J. Wyatt, the Conservative representative from Trinity Bay, and Daniel Woodley Prowse representing Burgeo-La Poile – basically pitting a St. John's businessman against a South Shore representative from a fishing outport on the coast of the Grand Banks. Surprisingly, the South Shore member expressed more progressive views:

Mr. Wyatt – All the commercial people wanted was a Bill that would make the Pound Sterling or British sterling equivalent 24 shillings. There was certainly a

very general feeling against the decimal currency; the feeling was that whilst the government could keep their accounts in any way they pleased. There were those here who were strongly in favor of the adoption of the British sterling currency; and he (Mr. W) was himself very much in favor of such a course. But the decimal system he was quite opposed to – it would create much difficulty in the pricing of goods, and was in other respects decidedly objectionably [sic].

Mr. Prowse was sorry to see the hon. Member for Bonavista so opposed to the spirit of progress, and every facility in the way of trade and business. And so desirous of going back to the old complicated and worn out style of currency.

In its October 9, 1865, edition, the *Morning Chronicle* published a letter to the editor from a reader identifying himself or herself only as CASHIER. This person expressed a serious issue with the introduction of the coinage.

Sir – As you are generally forward in giving place to the various grievances of the Public in the Morning Chronicle, I would solicit you to publish what I consider a great injustice, and also to ask advice with respect thereto. I refer to the copper currency just now in circulation throughout the island. 'Tis true it is not of such various forms as it used to be, but, what is of great and paramount importance, it is of various value, when paying and receiving in most business houses in town. I must send to the Bank once or twice a week for coppers, which I receive in a bag containing Ten Shillings worth (twenty to the shilling), and these I must pay away twenty-four to the shilling, thereby losing twenty pence on every ten shillings worth because parties who do business in a small way will only take them as half-pence, which they keep for a week or so and then pass off in the larger houses at Bank rate, thereby gaining two-

pence on every shillings ... said it was the poor people that lost by introduction of Dollars and Cents; but I think that is not the case, as the poor people get them in Water street for half-pence and pass them to gain by them, and the larger business houses are the losers. I scarcely think I would be wrong in saying that there are parties in town who have Pounds worth saved up, taken as half-pence, which they will pass when dollars and cents become more general.

It is not obvious how to interpret this correspondence. If the bank was providing only the new 1¢ pieces to CASHIER, then the problem, it would seem, stemmed from the banks. In the initial purchase of the new 1¢ coins, CASHIER bought ten shillings worth of coppers. This should have been the equivalent of 240 of these new coins, but the bank gave only 200 – a loss of 40¢ per transaction as CASHIER had to pay them out at the official rate of 24 to the shilling. CASHIER seemed to blame the poorer people and the businesses for their ills, but under this scenario the finger should have pointed directly at the banks. It seems remarkable that the government would have allowed this to transpire with its new coinage.

On the other hand, the 10s. bag could have contained a portion of British 1d. coins, which were then accepted by small dealers as ½d. only. The dealers later returned these to the bank for 1d., making a profit on the transaction. Although a more subtle argument that also removed blame from the banks, this latter interpretation does seem more in line with the sentiments expressed in CASHIER's correspondence.

The Harbour Grace Standard complained about the availability of the coins in its November 1, 1865, edition: *The new coins have, we believe, been circulating very generally in St. John's, but we are sorry to observe that but a very small quantity has reached Harbour Grace as yet, causing a considerable annoyance to the trade generally.*

The value of the decimal system was often discussed in the newspapers of 1865 and later. As late as March 1, 1866, *The Newfoundlander* reported that Mr. Ambrose Shea, Colonial Secretary, was objecting to keeping the public accounts in dollars and cents. It was felt that the proposal might lead to *"capricious disturbances on the part of the Government, and that until some more clear and definite course might seem necessary it was better not to move at all."*

On March 19, *The Newfoundlander* relayed a discussion between Ambrose Shea and George Hogsett (opposition member representing Harbour Main), which concluded with Mr. Hogsett's assertion that if the decimal system was to be accepted, *"it was the duty of the government to render it imperative upon the public teachers to teach the decimal system in their schools."*

Continuing this discussion in the same issue, *The Newfoundlander* reported that Mr. Henry Renouf (opposition member for St. John's West) commented that

the present system has been in existence some three years and was yet quite inoperative. And why? Because the public never sought for the change. There had been no petitions presented, and surely it would be time enough for the Government to introduce changes when the public wished for them ... There was no shop keeper in town who kept his accounts in dollars and cents, but all kept them in the old style of pounds, shillings and pence ... The cents now passed for a halfpenny. The five-cent piece for three pence, the ten cent piece for six pence , and the twenty cent piece for one shilling currency. The other colonies, Nova Scotia, Canada, and New

Brunswick, had adopted the decimal system; but look at the different position which we occupied. Those colonies had a large trade with the United States, and the people understood the system. But let a man from Twillingate or Fogo come here and ask the price of Fish, and how would he look if he were told it was $1.75.

This correspondence brings up an important issue regarding colonial coinage in general and the valuation of foreign monies in local currencies. All the colonies had their own currencies before they joined Confederation. Although pounds, shillings, and pence were used for bookkeeping purposes, each colony assigned to them values in the local currencies that were generally overrated with respect to sterling and that differed from colony to colony. For example, the original valuation of the Spanish American dollar was 4s. 6d. Nevertheless, in Halifax it was valued at 5s., in New England at 6s., and in New York as much as 8s. The higher valuations in the various colonies represented an effort by them to retain gold and silver coins and alleviate their scarcity in circulation.[3]

A final footnote to all the discussion related to the introduction of the decimal system can be found in the *Twillingate Sun* of May 21, 1887 (this paper did not begin publication until 1880), where the efficacy of the decimal system was finally fully appreciated:

When the existing law was enacted, the people were not so accustomed to the principle of computation by dollars and cents as they have become since ... As regards the decimal system itself, it is now admitted on all hands, that as applied to coinage and weights and measures, it has special advantages over every other system of computation ... so great is its superiority and facility of being worked, as compared with others, that the decimal mode will come into vogue in most enlightened countries within the next thirty or forty years.

While the *Twillingate Sun* was certainly prescient in this editorial, its timeline was somewhat incorrect. Britain itself waited until February 15, 1971, another eight-four years, before adopting a decimal system for its own currency. Many of the countries in the British Empire also used the British system at some time during their history (e.g., Australia, Barbados, British West Africa, Jamaica, New Zealand, and South Africa), but over time all of them also adopted a decimal system.

CHAPTER 3

· ·

An Act for the Regulation of the Currency

On March 25, 1863, the Legislative Council of Newfoundland passed "An Act for the Regulation of the Currency" (reprinted in its entirety in Appendix 1), along with others of somewhat lesser importance: "An Act to Encourage the Killing of Wolves in This Colony," "An Act to Provide for the Sewerage of the Town of St. John's," and "An Act for the Establishment of a Fire Brigade." According to the Act for the Regulation of the Currency, effective January 1, 1865, the currency of the colony was to be decimalized in dollars and cents, in contrast to the British system in use at the time. The act mandated that all public accounts be kept in the new currency.

Because of the close association between Newfoundland and Britain, the Newfoundland currency was to be tied to the British pound. Newfoundland was the closest colony to Britain in terms of distance, as well as its oldest, and it was rather isolated from what eventually became Canada in 1867. When the Maritime colonies met in Charlottetown in 1864 to consider union, Newfoundland was not even represented. That October it was invited to and did attend the

Quebec conference that laid the foundation for the eventual formation of Canada, but its delegates were instructed simply to observe and not commit to any of the proposals made. Given their close association, it is not surprising that Newfoundland aligned its new currency more closely with Britain than with the United States or the nascent Canadian provinces. Note, however, that it did denominate the new currency in dollars and cents, not pounds, shillings, and pence.

The British pound had a value equal to $4.80 in the new Newfoundland currency. Before the British established their own decimal system in 1971, 1 pound contained 20 shillings and there were 12 pence per shilling. Thus a pound was composed of 240 pence, equal to 4.80 Newfoundland dollars. One dollar in Newfoundland currency was thus 240/4.8 = 50 pence, making 2 Newfoundland dollars 100 pence. This was of some consequence for the coinage design that was struck two years later, as we shall see below.

US gold and silver coins would also be accepted in the colony. The US gold eagle ($10) minted after 1834 had not changed in fineness or weight since that time. It was to have a legal tender value of 9.85 Newfoundland dollars. All multiples and parts of the US gold eagle would be valued accordingly. The act also included valuations of other foreign gold coins, such as the doubloon (containing 362 grains of pure gold and valued at $15.35) and the dollars of the Americas (United States, Peru, Mexico, and Colombia) containing no less than 373 grains of pure silver. These were to pass as 100 cents each in Newfoundland.

The act also laid out the penalties for counterfeiting. A person found guilty of such an offence would be liable to "Transportation beyond Seas for life, or for any term not less than Seven Years; or to be imprisoned with hard labour for any term not exceeding Four Years." Such offences were obviously taken extremely seriously in the colony.

In the early 1860s, the Newfoundland legislature did its homework carefully and laid the groundwork for the special and highly successful coinage. What it did not do in this initial act was declare what denominations of coins were to be struck and in what quantities. That it had not yet decided on these details can be inferred from the wording of the beginning of clause 8 of the act: "Such Gold and Silver Coins, representing Dollars or multiples or divisions of the Dollar Currency, as Her Majesty shall see fit to direct to be struck for that purpose …" It is clear, however, that even at this early stage the legislature had already considered minting gold coins.

There does not appear to be any detailed literature on the question of why Newfoundland requested its own coinage, particularly those coins struck in gold. No other British North American colony had such a gold coinage. What is known is that by 1850 Newfoundland's economy was much more robust than at the beginning of the century. It

Figure 3-1: Photograph of Thomas Graham, first published in *Photographic Portraits of Living Celebrities* in December 1856.

(Image in the public domain)

was still dangerously dependent on sealing and the cod fishery, both of which suffered steep declines beginning around 1860, but the future of the colony, with a population exceeding 122,000, seemed much more promising than fifty years earlier. It was therefore not surprising that Newfoundland desired its own coinage. For many decades, it had been plagued with insufficient coinage in circulation, a reliance on the truck credit system, and, even when available, a variety of coinage often of uncertain value. There was pressure to expand the economy, and what better way to accomplish this than with a unique colonial coinage?

In a dispatch dated December 18, 1863, the Secretary of State for the Colonies, Henry Pelham-Clinton, the 5th Duke of Newcastle, informed

Newfoundland governor Sir Alexander Bannerman that he had advised Her Majesty Queen Victoria to give Royal Assent to the Newfoundland Currency Act, and that he would let Bannerman know when the Queen had done so. In the meantime, he sent Bannerman a copy of a letter from the Master of the Royal Mint, Thomas Graham, who commented briefly on some of the provisions of the act.

Graham was Master of the Royal Mint from 1855 to 1869 (Figure 3-1). He was an accomplished scientist, a Fellow of the Royal Society (1836) and winner of its Copley Medal (1862), the first president of the Chemical Society of London (1841), and winner of the Prix Jecker of the Paris Academy of Sciences (1862). His main scientific accomplishment was the famous Graham's Law of Diffusion, which states that the rate of passage of a gas through a small hole in a container is inversely proportional to the square root of the mass of its particles. A gas composed of more massive particles would thus pass through more slowly. In recent times, this law provided a basis for separating isotopes of the same gas through diffusion, which was a critical requirement in the development of the atomic bomb – clearly a use of this law not envisioned by Graham.

It was not unusual for the Master of the Royal Mint to be a person of such scientific eminence. Sir Isaac Newton, perhaps the greatest scientist of all time, was Master for over a quarter-century, from 1700 until his death in 1727. The Master just before Graham was Sir John Herschel, a Fellow and former secretary of the Royal Society. Like his father, he was primarily an astronomer but also made significant contributions to the theory of light.

In his short dispatch, Graham called the creation of new coins of gold and silver "very

proper." He suggested one minor change to clause 8 of the act, which stated:

… the standard of fineness of such Coins, (new dollar, &c added) being the same as that now adopted for Coins of the United Kingdom, and their intrinsic value bearing the same proportion to their current value as British Coins respectively bear to their current value under this Act.

He commented that since the Newfoundland currency was to be a decimal one, it might be natural to consider a fineness of exactly nine-tenths for the gold and silver coins, instead of the fineness of 0.917 used in the gold pieces in the United Kingdom. He felt that the colony should not introduce any clause that would *preclude* a fineness of nine-tenths for Newfoundland's own coinage. He suggested that this clause be removed if it was not too late. Perhaps what he had in mind was that in the future Newfoundland might find itself more closely aligned with the United States; if so, having coins of similar fineness (the US standard for gold and silver coins was 0.900) might be beneficial to the colony. In any case, he felt that Newfoundland ought not to preclude such a system.

Graham also noted that a new gold dollar of 50 pence [sic] in value and of 0.9 standard would form "a beautiful crowning ornament to the Newfoundland system." Indeed, it would, except that eventually a gold coin of 100 pence ($2 in the new currency, with a fineness matched to the British system of 0.917) was struck, not the smaller-denominated one. When did this change occur? Graham's dispatch was dated December 18, 1863. In the ten months between December 1863 and October 1864, the denominations of the Newfoundland coins were decided upon

Figure 3-2: Bronze statue of a Newfoundland dog in Harbourside Park in St. John's. The park is located opposite the National War Memorial on Water Street. Other suggestions for the reverse design on the coinage were a codfish or seal, both staples of the Newfoundland economy in 1865.

(Photograph by the author)

and the original suggestion of a $1 gold coin was changed to a $2 coin. The key document relating to this, as well as the denominations and quantities of coins to be struck initially, is probably the letter dated February 8, 1864, written by Newfoundland premier Hugh W. Hoyles (1861-65), to Governor Bannerman. By this time, there was a desperate need for coinage in the colony. The urgency is clearly seen in Hoyles's letter (UK National Archives, MINT 13/75, C5988400, pages 7-8):

I beg leave to enclose an address from the Executive Council praying that Her Majesty will be pleased to direct that under the provisions of the Currency Act recently confirmed, bronze cent pieces, silver five, -ten cent and twenty cent pieces, and gold two dollar pieces may be struck at the Mint for the use of the Colony.

The quantity required of each coin will be of one

cent pieces 240,000, of silver five cent pieces 80,000, of silver ten cent pieces 80,000, of silver twenty cent pieces 100,000 and of gold two dollar pieces 10,000.

... We should be very glad if as little delay as possible might be permitted to occur in the manufacture of these coins as some of them are urgently required and in the hope that they will be ready by that time we have thought that the first of July should be the latest date at which the act should be put into operation.

The numbers requested here are exactly the quantities of each coin that were eventually struck in 1865, but the colony would wait almost a year before the first coins arrived.

Hoyles went on to make a number of suggestions for the designs of the coins, few of which were actually adopted:

The device for these coins would be, I presume,

Figure 3-3
Left: A close-up view of a pitcher plant.

(Image: Courtesy of Steve Campbell)

Right: The pitcher plant on the reverse of an 1865 Newfoundland 1¢ coin.

(Image: Courtesy of Heritage Coins)

on one side the Queen's Head [sic] with the words Victoria Regina 1864 and on the other the words Newfoundland one cent or (as it may be) with either a wreath round the latter words or the figure of a crown or a Newfoundland dog over them as the Master of the Mint may consider most appropriate.

The suggestion of a dog on the reverse did not go unnoticed in London as Horace Morehen, a well-known British designer in the mid to late nineteenth century, who provided early drawings for these coins, actually visited the International Dog Show (date not given by Morehen). He provided sketches (for which he was paid by the mint) of a Newfoundland dog (Figure 3-2) incorporated in the coinage. Unfortunately, no record seems to exist of these sketches.

Morehen also visited the Botanical Gardens to sketch the carnivorous pitcher plant (*Sarracenia purpurea*), currently the provincial flower of Newfoundland and Labrador. It appeared on the first striking of bronze cents in 1865 even though its status did not become official until 1954. Its rendition on the 1865 1¢ coin is not entirely satisfactory. Comparing a photograph of a real plant with the image seen on the reverse of the coin shows that the design on the coin was distorted to make the plant fit around the periphery (Figure 3-3). This resulting dissatisfaction in Newfoundland was not resolved until a new 1¢ coin design appeared in 1938 (Figure 3-4).

Figure 3-4: A pitcher plant on the reverse of a 1938 Newfoundland 1¢ coin. The plant is far more realistic in this rendition than on the 1865 1¢ coin.

(Image: Courtesy of Heritage Coins)

Hoyles did not just request this coinage; he also provided a letter of credit drawn on the Union Bank of London to pay for it. The bank was also charged with receiving the coins and shipping them to the colony. Hoyles was overly optimistic in his suggested timing, however. He hoped that they could be delivered by the first of July 1864, but ended up having to wait for more than a year beyond this date for the gold and silver coins, while the first bronze pieces arrived in October 1864.

Hoyles's last major point in this important letter was a request:

[I]nstead of a gold dollar, a piece to represent two dollars is desired for immediate use the larger coin being for the present preferred in consequence of its having been found in the United States that a gold dollar is rather small for common use and amongst our people rough fisherman accustomed to handle only large coins, a strong objection to one as small, when of so large a value would be found to exist.

This is apparently why Newfoundland ended up with $2 and not $1 gold coins.

In a long letter dated October 11, 1864, Graham commented in detail on the Newfoundland legislature's plan for its coinage and confirmed mintages of the various denominations. He referred specifically to a $2 gold coin when discussing mintages. Interestingly, he also stated that it should be of standard British gold, which suggests that the fineness issue had been settled by this time. He also lamented that the North American colonies would now have three different values for one dollar: the New Brunswick and Canadian dollars, which were tied to the US dollar; the Nova Scotia dollar, which was tied to the British pound but with a value different from the planned Newfoundland dollar;

and now the Newfoundland dollar.

Remarkably, the issue of gold coins for Newfoundland was unique among the British colonies in North America. The British never minted gold coins for New Brunswick, Prince Edward Island, Nova Scotia, or Canada even though they were far wealthier than Newfoundland, whose economy was dominated by fishing and sealing. Gold coins were produced in Australia by its own mints, but the average salary there was several times Newfoundland's average, and, in any case, the gold mintage was largely a response to the gold rush that began in 1851. There was extensive gold coinage for India, of course, but India's political status was quite different from that of Newfoundland. India was governed directly from London whereas Newfoundland made its own laws in both civil and commercial matters. So why did Newfoundland request – and Britain agree to – a gold coinage? The answer can be gleaned from a careful reading of Graham's letter of October 1864.

Graham noted that this would be the first occasion of gold coins being minted on the dollar system in a British colony. He recognized that paper money was prevalent in Canada, and this likely reduced any direct need for gold coinage as there were larger-denomination species available for commerce. He noted that the $2 coins might be somewhat confused with the half-sovereign, but if the $2 coin were slightly smaller, and with a unique design, this issue could easily be avoided. Graham commented that the existence of such a gold coin could give "fixity" to Newfoundland's system of currency, which was lacking in the other colonies. The dollar of the other provinces was merely money of account and not directly associated with any gold coinage. In this sense, the coinage, other than the gold coins, was considered to be subsidiary token coinage, with the bronze cents not legal tender beyond 25¢ and the silver coinage not legal tender beyond $10. No such restrictions were placed on the gold coinage. From a more practical perspective, Graham commented that it was difficult to preserve British gold coins in Newfoundland – they were continually being drawn away in fishing vessels of foreign countries. It was therefore felt that a special colonial gold piece for Newfoundland would remain in the colony for local circulation. This is likely one of the main reasons that Britain did not object to the minting of gold coins for Newfoundland.

Graham made an odd mistake in this letter. He commented that the amount requested in these gold coins was modest at just $10,000. Near the end, he constantly referred to a 50-pence dollar, while on the last page he listed a mintage of 10,000 of the $2 gold pieces. He went on to say that the coinage should be on a trial basis, but generally he spoke in very favourable terms about the new coinage and the request from the Newfoundland legislature. He asserted that the preparation of the first year of coinage should proceed, with expenses to be borne by the colony. The quantities requested that eventually got minted, and that Graham gave his stamp of approval to, were as follows (note the absence of 50¢ pieces – this coin did not appear until the coinage of 1870):

240,000 1¢ pieces in bronze
80,000 5¢ pieces in silver
80,000 10¢ pieces in silver
100,000 20¢ pieces in silver
10,000 $2 pieces in gold

By November 1864, no coinage, other than the bronze 1¢ pieces, had been delivered to the colony.

In fact, Morehen was even at this late date still working on sketches for the gold and silver coins. In the Mint Archives, there is an invoice from Morehen to the Master of the Royal Mint dated January 10, 1865, for numerous coinage designs for Newfoundland. A letter dated November 1, 1864, from Nicholas Stabb, a member of the Newfoundland Legislative Council, to Thomas Graham clearly expresses the desperation of the colony in its need for coinage. Stabb seems to have formed the (incorrect) opinion that London's slow response to Newfoundland's coinage request was due to "our Gold Coinage." He suggested dropping the gold for now and getting on with the "Silver and Bronze," which he hoped had been dispatched (the bronze pieces had by this time) before the current letter was even received. We should be thankful that Graham ignored this suggestion!

Anthony Musgrave (knighted in 1875) replaced Bannerman as governor of the colony in 1864. Remarkably, he was born in St. John's (Antigua, not Newfoundland). Addressing the Legislative Council of Newfoundland on January 27, 1865, at the opening of the fifth session of the eighth general assembly, he commented on the 1863 Act for the Regulation of the Currency, calling it a "useful measure" and noting that it was "put into force by Proclamation, from the beginning of this year [1865]." He confirmed that the requested copper coinage had arrived:

A sufficient quantity of Copper Coinage has been imported to give effect to the intention of the Legislature, by superseding the debased Copper Currency hitherto in circulation; and gold and silver coins are in preparation at the Royal Mint for more fully carrying out the design of the enactment.

He expressed the hope that the colony would call in the silver coins that contained a value of silver less than their nominal worth still circulating in the colony. By late January, the copper coins had been received and distributed to the population, but the gold and silver coins were a different matter. When the Currency Act came into effect on January 1, 1865, the Royal Mint had not yet sent these coins to Newfoundland. A search of Governor Musgrave's addresses to the Legislative Council in 1866 and 1867 yielded absolutely no reference to coinage whatsoever.

Contemporary newspapers provided more detailed information concerning the arrival of the copper coins in the colony. The *St. John's Daily News* of October 4, 1864, reported that

[a] box of our new decimal copper currency, variously estimated as from $40 to $100 worth, tumbled into the drink at Halifax, whilst being conveyed from the English boat to the Merlin.

The article did not mention whether the coins were ever recovered. The box represented somewhere between 1.7 percent and 4.2 percent of the entire mintage of 1865-dated copper coins (depending on whether it was valued at $40 or $100), so it was an important fraction of the entire mintage. If the box is still at the bottom of the Halifax Harbour, it may be worth salvaging today if the coins are not too seriously corroded by the sea water.

A follow-up story appeared in the *Harbour Grace Standard* the next day. Harbour Grace is about one hundred kilometres west of St. John's, around the northern tip of the Avalon Peninsula. The *Standard* reported that

the Mail Steamer Merlin arrived at St. John's from Halifax on Monday night last ... Anthony Musgrave, Esq., our new governor came in the Merlin ... The Merlin also brought a quantity of copper coin to be circulated under the new currency act.

So by early October 1864, the copper 1¢ coins were being delivered to the colony in accordance with the plan to have the new decimal coinage as legal tender by January 1, 1865. What about the gold and silver coins? A similar notice appeared in the October 4, 1864, issue of the *Newfoundland Express* but pointed out that the gold and silver coins were not yet available:

The Merlin has brought a quantity of copper coin for circulation under the new currency Act. The gold and silver coins from the mint cannot, we understand, be furnished for some time. The Act cannot now come into operation before the 1st January.

The complete correspondence between the Royal Mint and the Newfoundland government related to the new coinage covering the years between 1863 and 1888 (the period over which the gold coins were being designed and minted) has been secured from the UK National Archives. Much of the material in this and subsequent chapters is based on this written record. There is extensive communication from 1863 to early 1865 concerning the coinage: its cost, design, payment by the colony for the coins, and so on. The correspondence ceases in early 1865, not to resume again until 1869, during the planning of the second release of coins, to be dated 1870. After mid-1865, for about another year, what correspondence can be located between the Royal Mint and the colony seems to reside in the archives at The Rooms in Newfoundland. The Rooms, located in St. John's, houses the Provincial Archives of Newfoundland and Labrador as well as its Provincial Museum. One particularly important document is the statement of December 18, 1865, of the complete costs of the 1865 coinage provided by the Union Bank of Newfoundland, which we analyze in some detail in the following chapter.

The archives of the Union Bank of London, the colony's financial agent in London at this time and the institution tasked with paying for and shipping the coins back to Newfoundland, are very spotty for this period. A diligent search for specific records conducted by Sophie Volker, the archivist at the Royal Bank of Scotland (which has taken over the records of the Union Bank of London), uncovered no new documents there.

CHAPTER 4

. . . .

Circulation Strike Newfoundland $2 Gold Coins

Originally, the plan was to mint $1 gold coins for Newfoundland. The coin would have been about the same size as a US $1 gold piece, which was only 12.7 millimetres in diameter, later expanded to 14.3 millimetres and made thinner. These US coins weighed only 1.672 grams and contained 90 percent gold (0.04837 troy ounces of gold) and 10 percent copper. Such a small coin for Newfoundland would not have served its consumers (largely fisherfolk) very well, as they would have been easily lost or misplaced. In addition, $1 was a lot of money for some in those days – typically more than a week's wages for a fisher – and $2 per week was about the salary of a constable in one of the average-sized outports. For this reason, Newfoundland decided to mint a larger, more robust coin in gold, and eventually settled on a $2 coin.

The physical specifications for these coins are as follows:

- They are the same composition as British sovereigns, namely, 0.91666 gold and 0.08333 copper.

- The weight of the coin was to be 3.328 grams (0.107 troy ounces).
- The diameter was 17.983 millimetres.
- The edge was to be milled, unlike the 1865 specimen coins, which have plain edges (see Chapter 6 for more on this).
- The axes of the dies on the obverse and reverse are opposite.
- The fine gold content was to be 0.0981 troy ounces.

With the price of gold fixed near US$20.67 per troy ounce during this period, the pure gold content of a Newfoundland $2 gold coin was worth $2.0277 in US dollars or $1.9973 in Newfoundland dollars. A US eagle ($10) contained 0.48375 troy ounces of pure gold, giving it a value of US$9.9991 in gold. Thus, the US eagle had virtually 100 percent of its face value in gold, as did the Newfoundland $2 gold coin. The gold content of the Newfoundland coins was very much in line with that of US gold coins and British sovereigns, and was almost exactly its face value. We will see, however, later in this chapter, that these coins were

Figure 4-1

Top: An 1862 New Brunswick 10¢ coin. This was the model obverse from which the Newfoundland $2 gold coin was derived. The 1864 pattern Newfoundland $2 coin also used the reverse of this piece, with the denomination removed, "2 DOLLARS" added, and the dated changed to 1864 (see Chapter 6, Figure 6-14).

Middle: An 1865 Newfoundland 10¢ piece.

Bottom: An 1865 Newfoundland $2 gold coin that was struck for circulation. Note that the obverses of the three coins are identical, except for "NEW BRUNSWICK" instead of "NEWFOUNDLAND" in the first coin, thus saving the cost of preparing a new design.

(Images: Courtesy of PCGS and Heritage Coins)

actually produced at a loss when the totality of costs is included.

The Newfoundland $2 gold coins were struck for circulation irregularly between 1865 and 1888 in eight different years – 1865, 1870, 1872, 1880, 1881, 1882, 1885, and 1888 – with mintages ranging from a low of 2,500 coins (1880) to a maximum of 25,000 (1882 and 1888). These coins apparently circulated widely, not only in Newfoundland but

also in Canada. R.W. McLachlan highlights this in his book *Canadian Numismatics*.[1] McLachlan lived in Montreal from 1845 to 1926, during the era when these coins actually circulated, so he was in a wonderful position to have observed, in person, their use as a medium of exchange. Their wide circulation is the main reason why they are now so scarce in uncirculated condition – they performed their function, as units of commerce in the colony.

On the other hand, one rarely encounters a Newfoundland $2 gold coin that is very heavily worn, which would be an indication of extensive circulation. Thus, it appears that the coins circulated widely but perhaps not for a very long period of time.

The obverses of these coins are the same as those struck for New Brunswick between 1862 and 1864, except that the name "NEWFOUNDLAND" appears instead of "NEW BRUNSWICK" (Figure 4-1). This obverse is also the same as that used for the Newfoundland 10¢ pieces of Queen Victoria. This was a matter of convenience and expediency since no new obverse dies needed to be prepared. "NEW BRUNSWICK" could just be ground off and "NEWFOUNDLAND" added. The directive for this can be traced back to a memorandum of May 14, 1864, in the Master of the Royal Mint's Orders and Instructions.[2]

The reverse of the Newfoundland $2 gold coin is entirely different from that of the New Brunswick 10¢ coins, and possesses the unique feature of having the denomination expressed in three different ways, as 2 dollars, 200 cents, and 100 pence. According to the Currency Act passed by the legislature on March 25, 1863, the currency of the colony was to be in dollars and cents, and all public accounts were to be kept in this currency. The British pound would still be legal tender, however, and pass for an amount equal to $4.80. The 1865 $2 coin illustrated in Figure 4-1 is a normal business strike coin meant for circulation. Note that it lacks the high definition of the specimen illustrated on the cover of this book, which was struck twice on a highly polished coin blank or planchet.

Although the effigy of Queen Victoria appears on all Newfoundland coins, the monarch never visited the island. Indeed, she never visited any location in what was to become Canada and restricted her trips to Scotland, Ireland, and a few European countries such as Italy and Germany. The first official visit of royalty to the colony was that of her son, the Prince of Wales and later King Edward VII, who visited in July 1860. According to a plaque in Harbourside Park in St. John's, almost the entire populace turned out to witness his departure (Figure 4-2).

There are only a few major die varieties among

Figure 4-2: The departure of the Prince of Wales from St. John's in July 1860.

(Image: The Rooms, Provincial Archives, St. John's)

Figure 4-3

Obverse 1: On the top is an 1870 Newfoundland $2 gold coin with a dot after the last "D" in "NEWFOUNDLAND." Note the youthful portrait of Queen Victoria, particularly around the lips.

Obverse 2: In the middle is an 1872 coin, also with a youthful portrait but no dot after the "D."

Obverse 3: On the bottom is an 1888 Newfoundland $2 gold coin with a dot after the last "D" in "NEWFOUNDLAND." Note the more aged portrait, particularly around the lips, compared with the other two. Also on this coin, the dot is closer to the "D" than in obverse 1.

(Images: Courtesy of PCGS)

the Newfoundland gold pieces, and only three stand out at all (Figure 4-3). There are two distinct portraits of Queen Victoria. One has a younger-looking engraving exhibiting a more pronounced lower lip and an extension of the upper lip down her cheek (Figure 4-4, left). This type can have a dot after "NEWFOUNDLAND" (obverse 1 in Figure 4-3) or not (obverse 2). Obverse 1 was used in 1865 and 1870. Obverse 2 is seen on some 1870-dated coins as well as some dated 1872, 1880, 1881, and 1885. A more mature portrait is seen on the coins of 1882 and 1888 (Figure 4-4, right).

With the exception of the coins struck in 1882, all the Newfoundland $2 coins were struck at the Royal Mint on Tower Hill in London. Those dated 1882 were struck at the Heaton Mint in Birmingham, as the Royal Mint was busy striking coins for all the other colonies as well as

Figure 4-4
Expanded view of the obverse of the two major portraits of Queen Victoria. On the left is the youthful portrait, on the right a more mature portrait. The main differences are around the lips, eyes, and chin.

(Images: Courtesy of PCGS)

for domestic purposes. From time to time, the Royal Mint used Heaton as a subcontractor when it became too busy to handle all its orders. This was, however, only the second time that Heaton was called upon by the Royal Mint to strike gold coins; the previous commission was a small issue of 837 £1 coins dated 1874 for President Burgers of South Africa.[3] The Newfoundland $2 gold coins executed at the Heaton Mint are distinguished by

the presence of a large "H" under the date on the reverse, as shown in Figure 4-5.

There has been some controversy recently over whether there exists an 1888 coin with obverse 2 (a young portrait of the Queen and no dot to the right of the "D" in "NEWFOUNDLAND") (see Figure 4-6 for a hypothetical likeness). One professional grading service had one such coin in its 2012 population report. It disappeared in the

Figure 4-5
An 1882 Newfoundland $2 gold coin. Note the "H" under the date on the reverse, signifying that the coin was struck at the Heaton Mint in Birmingham.

(Image: Courtesy of PCGS)

Figure 4-6: This is what the excessively rare variety of an 1888 $2 coin would look like if it existed. Note the young obverse portrait of the Queen and the absence of a dot after "NEWFOUNDLAND." Shown here is not a real coin but simply the obverse of an 1885 coin coupled with an 1888 reverse.

2014 compilation, so presumably it was a mistake. Another report continues to list a single example. All the dealers that have been canvassed report that they have never seen one. One should remain skeptical of this claim until a real physical example is seen.

In a sense, the process of obtaining coinage from the Royal Mint on the part of a colony was remarkably easy; all that was required was that the colony, such as Newfoundland, submit a request for the amount of coinage needed to the Secretary of State for the Colonies, who would then transmit the request to the Lords Commissioners of the Treasury. This was an extremely high-level committee – sometimes including sitting or future prime ministers and chancellors of the exchequer – that made most of the major financial decisions for the United Kingdom. For example, in the period from about 1870 to the late 1880s, two prime ministers, Benjamin Disraeli and William Gladstone, were commissioners.

These requests for new coinage were generally approved rather rapidly, and after Newfoundland arranged for the appropriate funds to be transferred to the Royal Mint, the coins were struck and delivered to the colony. The entire process generally took less than a year. The financial agent acting for the colony in these matters was the Union Bank of

London in collaboration with its Newfoundland counterpart, the Union Bank of Newfoundland. The latter played a pivotal role in the colony's coinage requests and acquisitions, as detailed below for the coinage request of 1870.

The following sections provide some highlights of the processes for obtaining coinage and the interaction between the colony of Newfoundland and the Royal Mint in the years when gold coins were struck. Files from the Royal Mint Archives are not available for every year, which accounts for the selective nature of these narratives.

THE COINAGE OF 1865

This first release of Newfoundland gold coins displays Queen Victoria with a youthful portrait. Ten thousand coins were issued, in accordance with the colony's request in a letter dated February 8, 1864, from the attorney general's office to the governor of Newfoundland, Sir Alexander Bannerman.

The only die records from the Royal Mint that are available for Newfoundland gold coins of any date are those for 1865. Before discussing these records, it is important to appreciate how coins were actually produced at the Royal Mint in the mid-nineteenth century.[4] The aim here was mass production of dies that were used to strike the coins, together with a simple procedure to change the date in succeeding years.

The process began with the production of a master matrix from the artist's rendering. This would initially have only the portrait, with lettering added while the metal was still soft. The matrix was incuse, or a negative mirror image of the final way the coin would appear. Everything in the minting process rested on the quality of the master matrix; hence the Royal Mint expended considerable effort, often taking many weeks to perfect it.[5]

The master matrix was then hardened and, in a series of steps, used to manufacture a master punch (not incuse), a working matrix (incuse), and working punches (not incuse) from which working dies (incuse) were produced. These dies were eventually used to strike the coins. Dies were not used long enough for details to become obliterated by the coining process. The usual way a die failed was through the development of cracks due to the stresses of coining, after which the die was retired. These would appear as raised lines on the actual coin and are often useful diagnostic signs in tracing coins that were struck from the same die. We will explore such signs on Newfoundland $2 gold coins in Chapter 6.

The foregoing process applied to the obverse of the coin. The reverse was much simpler and its master matrices could be engraved directly. In the striking process, one of the dies was the "hammer" die – usually the upper die in the coining press. It moved up and down and hit the planchet with great force (typically one hundred tons per square inch) to produce the coin, while the other die remained stationary. The hammer die generally failed more often than the stationary die in the minting process.

The entire process was very efficient. The Royal Mint was not manufacturing collector coins in the nineteenth century, even though we view them as such today. The mint was in the business of mass production for Britain and her colonies. Because of this, the reverse working punches generally contained only the first three numerals of a given date. The fourth number was inserted by hand into the working die. This tended to result in some variations in the positioning of the digits in the dates on coins struck from different dies. Again, some examples of this will be mentioned in Chapter 6.

Figure 4-7 shows the die record for the 1865 $2 gold coin. The only one available for any date of Newfoundland gold coins, this record was kindly made available by Rob Turner, who found it in his

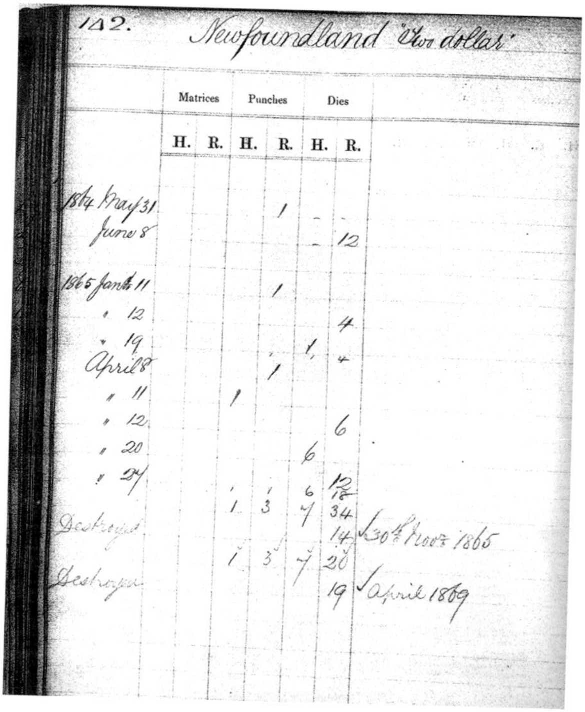

Figure 4-7: The die record for the 1865 Newfoundland $2 gold coin.

(Image: Royal Mint Archive 14/15)

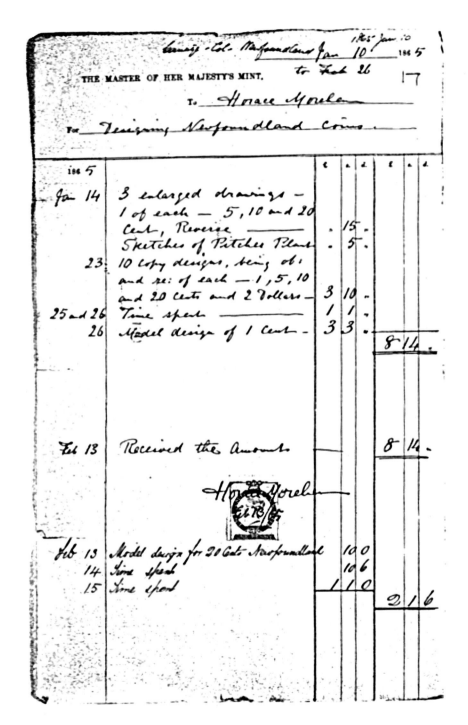

Figure 4-8: An invoice and receipt from Horace Morehen to the Royal Mint for designs of various Newfoundland coins, including the $2 gold pieces.

(Image: Royal Mint Archive, MINT 13/75, C598400, page 17)

search of the UK National Archives in Kew, Surrey. In this compilation, "H" refers to the obverse and "R" to the reverse of the coin. Note that no matrices are listed here. This is a bit odd as the Royal Mint Collection has three matrices for the gold coins: two for patterns and one for the business strike coins. The lack of a matrix for the obverse here probably means that the mint used a 10¢ matrix to produce the single obverse punch on April 11, 1865. Since the reverse of this coin was a new design, it is reasonable to assume that the three reverse punches were made from a hand-engraved matrix. Also, note that thirty-four reverse and only seven obverse dies were sunk. This almost certainly implies that the reverse die was the hammer die, which was the general practice of the Royal Mint in the 1860s. By April 1869, the mint still had all of the punches it had produced earlier – all of the seven obverse dies but only a single reverse die.

The mint produced a number of pattern pieces in addition to the $2 coins meant for circulation (see detailed discussion in Chapter 6). These patterns had either the adopted reverse lettering or lettering in block type. In addition, there were two distinct obverse types. On May 31, 1864, the mint produced a single reverse punch and sunk from it twelve reverse dies. The design here is unknown; it could have been either the circulation strike reverse or the pattern one in block type. Producing so many dies for a pattern was uncommon unless the final design had not yet been decided on. A further reverse punch was made on January 11, 1865, and four dies were produced from it; again, we do not know the design. On January 19, a single obverse die was produced, but, remarkably, no obverse punch appears in the record. The likely explanation for this is that it was raised from a dime punch. In April 1865, both an obverse and a reverse punch

were raised, but again we do not know for which design. Since this was the only obverse punch raised, it may well have been for the pattern obverse, which was different from the adopted design.

What can we conclude (or speculate) based on this die record? It is likely that the six reverse and obverse dies produced on April 12 and 20 were the production dies that struck the ten thousand coins in that year. This is consistent with an invoice (shown in Figure 4-8) from Horace Morehen dated January 26, 1865, listing further work done by him, including a copy design of the obverse and reverse of the $2 coin. If these were the production dies, then the coins were struck no earlier than April 20, 1865. The colony had been waiting for the coins since July 1864.

Two points of interest emerge from a study of the complete ledger for the 1865 coinage. The total coinage for this year in all denominations amounted to $54,400 (£11,333) in Newfoundland dollars. The expenses for the cost of the coinage amounted to £10,506 3s. 8d., yielding a profit (seigniorage) of £1,160, before shipping and handling costs were included. In subsequent years, the gold bullion would be ordered from Johnson Matthey, but for this initial year of production the supplier was Mocatta and Goldsmid. There are two entries (July 6 and 25, 1865) for the cost of the gold bullion (£4,000 and then £167). These two amounts together were equivalent to $20,001.60 in Newfoundland dollars – almost exactly the dollar amount minted.

In the archives at The Rooms in St. John's, there are several documents whose numbers do not quite agree with these with respect to the cost of the initial coinage and that also reveal a number of odd charges by the bank. These documents are exchanges of correspondence largely between the

Union Bank of Newfoundland (whose sister bank, the Union Bank of London, acted in that city for the colony) and the government of Newfoundland. In a note with its letterhead dated December 18, 1865, the Union Bank of Newfoundland provided a statement of expenses (Figure 4-9) for the gold, silver, and bronze coins for the government of Newfoundland for the current year. These amounted to a total of £10,436 11s. 10d. (not very different from that quoted by the Royal Mint), to which the bank added an "exchange" of 20 percent, yielding costs well in excess of the coinage produced. Although termed an "exchange," this was probably just a commission for the services provided by the bank to secure the coinage. The effect of such an "exchange" was to make the coinage unprofitable to the colony.

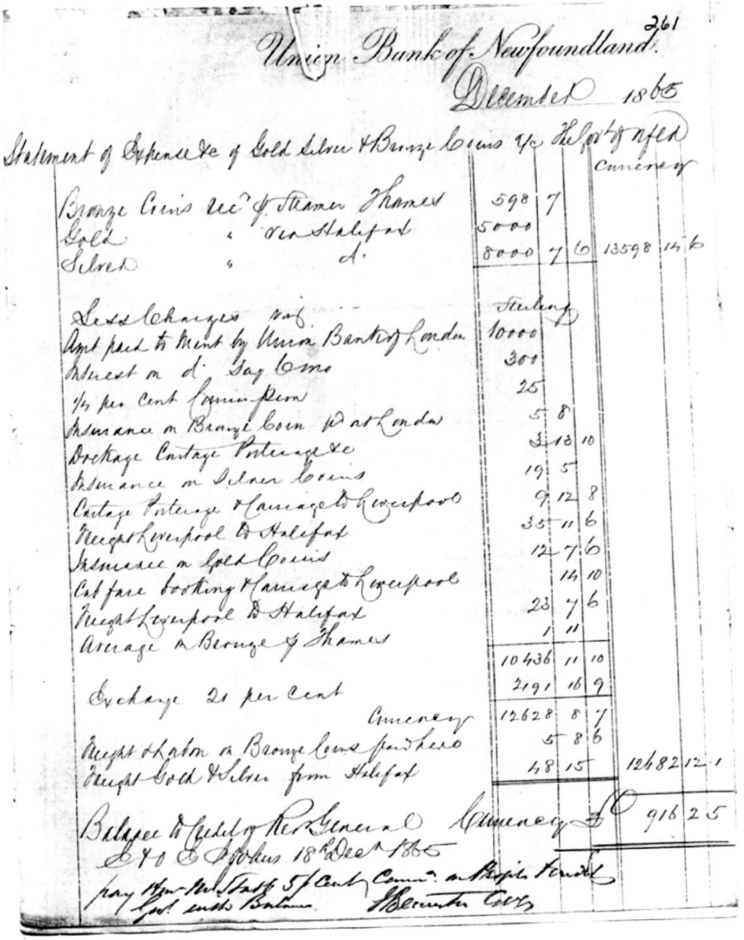

Newfoundland was not unique in paying such a large commission to a representative in London during this era. When Prince Edward Island ordered 1¢ coins in 1871, it had a strict limit of £1,500 for the minting costs, but the final bill presented to the government by its agent was for £2,722 5s. 9d., almost double the budget.[6] The Province of Canada, on the other hand, in its coinage issues of 1858 and 1859, appears to have avoided the worst of these problems. While it also had financial agents in London (two of them, in

Figure 4-9: A statement of expenses from the Union Bank of Newfoundland for the Newfoundland coinage of 1865.

(Image: The Rooms, Provincial Archives, St. John's)

fact: Baring Brothers and Company, and Glyn Mills and Company), existing correspondence suggests that the Province paid funds directly to the Royal Mint, thus avoiding exorbitant commission charges. The Province also appears to have kept all the profits on the coinage.[7]

As an aside, the note dated December 18, 1865, shown in Figure 4-9 indicates that only 5,000 of the 10,000 gold $2 coins minted for 1865 were

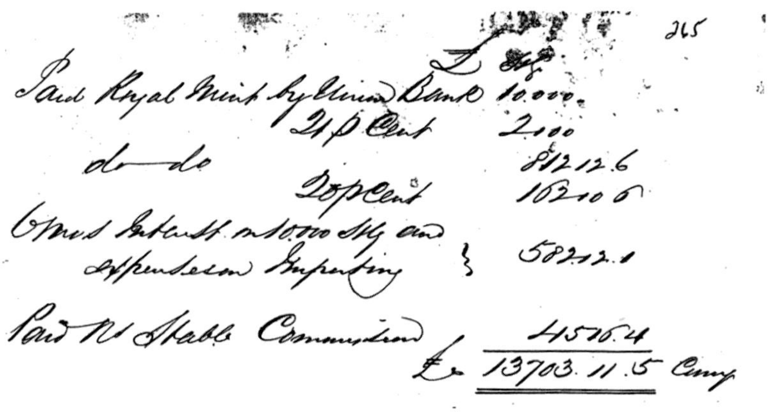

Figure 4-10: Part of a government document dated December 1865 regarding payment for the Newfoundland coinage. Note the payment to Nicholas Stabb on the second to last line.

(Image: The Rooms, Provincial Archives, St. John's)

actually shipped and received by that date. This is also the only document found that summarizes the complete charges for the coinage, including all the shipping costs. The coins had been sent by cart from London to Liverpool (£9 12s. 8d.) and then freighted from Liverpool to Halifax at a cost of £23 7s. 6d.; the gold coins were insured at a cost of £12 7s. 6d.

In addition, and most curiously, there is an amount of £45 16s. 4d. by way of a commission to Nicholas Stabb, member of the Newfoundland legislature and a local director of the International Life Assurance Society (Figure 4-10). The commission was requested over the signature of the Honourable John Bemister, member of the House of Assembly from Bay de Verde and Receiver General in the Hoyles government. It is not at all clear why a member of the legislature was being paid a commission for work that one would have thought was part of his normal job.

A later document in The Rooms archive that is perhaps related to the confusion over the cost of the coinage is a letter dated July 31, 1866, from the Master of the Royal Mint, Thomas Graham, in response to a query from John Bemister. Bemister's letter was not found in the archives

but its content is clear from Graham's response: he was obviously requesting clarification of the cost of the coinage, feeling that the profits were not large enough. Graham detailed the costs (Figure 4-11), and his accounting yielded a profit of £520 14s. 2d. He felt that this was sufficient given that the coinage contained only a small proportion of bronze, which always yields the largest proportion of profit. But, of course, Graham was probably unaware of the extras that were being tacked on by the bank, nor did he include any shipping costs.

THE COINAGE OF 1870

Sir Stephen John Hill become governor of Newfoundland in July 1869 (Figure 4-12). Early in this role, he became embroiled in the question of Confederation with Canada. There was a strong anti-Confederation vote in the 1869 election, which ran counter to his personal views and prompted him to comment that

the mass of voters in this colony are an ignorant, lawless, prejudiced body, the Majority of whom living as they do in outports in almost a primitive state of existence are unfit subjects for educated and intellectual men to attempt to reason with on the advantages of Confederation. I therefore consider that it was a fatal error to have submitted to such a population the decision of such an important question.[8]

He went on to argue that those in favour of joining Canada, even though a minority, were "with respect to intelligence, wealth, position and honesty of purpose, in a large Majority."[9]

Hill actually believed that Britain should force Newfoundland into Confederation to realize its aim of uniting all of British North America. He went so far as to suggest to London that Newfoundland be threatened with the cession of Labrador to Canada or with turning the colony into a Canadian dependency. That he could make such suggestions illustrates his deep lack of understanding of the nature of responsible government and the role of the governor in that system. He had previously been associated with the British Crown colonies Gold Coast (Ghana) and Sierra Leone, where the governors were all-powerful. It does appear, however, that he soon adapted both to his new position and to the political realities of Newfoundland. Although he made no secret of where his sympathies lay, Hill accepted that the results of the 1869 election had effectively ended any possibility of Confederation for the foreseeable future.[10]

Despite this somewhat inauspicious start, Hill

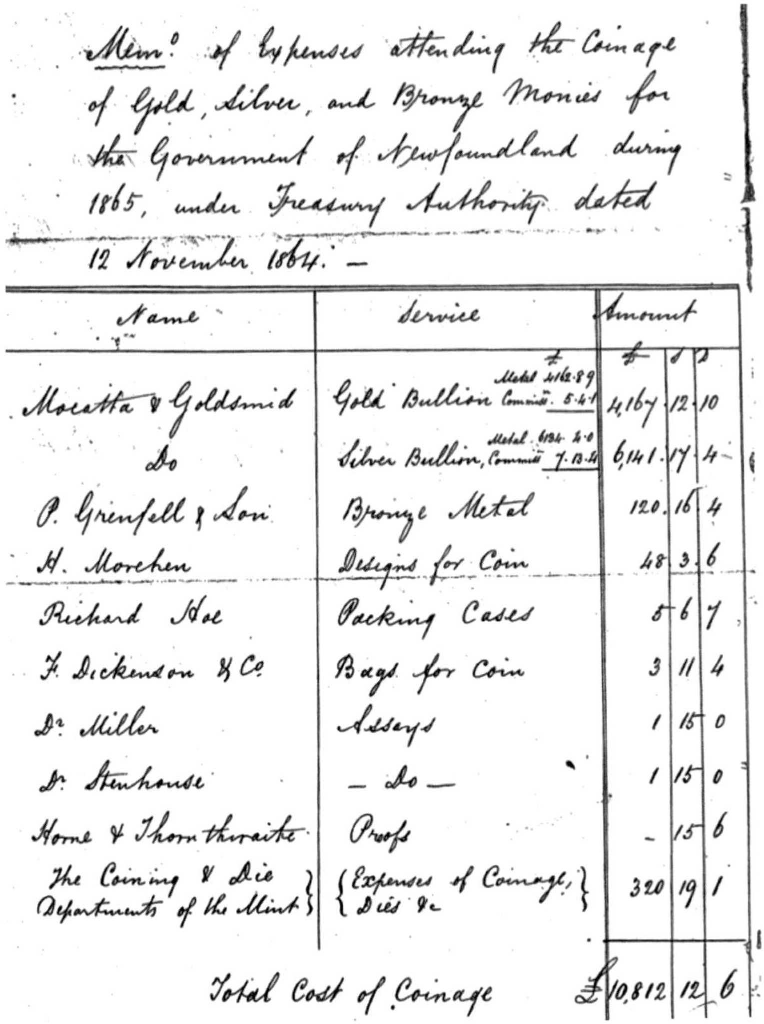

Memo. of Expenses attending the Coinage of Gold, Silver, and Bronze Monies for the Government of Newfoundland during 1865, under Treasury Authority dated 12 November 1864. –

Name	Service	Amount £	s	d
Mocatta & Goldsmid	Gold Bullion (Metal £4162.8.9, Commission 5.4.1)	4,167	12	10
Do	Silver Bullion (Metal 6134.4.0, Commission 7.13.4)	6,141	17	4
P. Grenfell & Son	Bronze Metal	120	16	4
H. Morchen	Designs for Coin	48	3	6
Richard Hoe	Packing Cases	5	6	7
F. Dickenson & Co	Bags for Coin	3	11	4
Dr Miller	Assays	1	15	0
Dr Stenhouse	— Do —	1	15	0
Horne & Thornthwaite	Proofs	-	15	6
The Coining & Die Departments of the Mint	Expenses of Coinage, Dies &c	320	19	1
Total Cost of Coinage		£10,812	12	6

Figure 4-11: Part of a letter dated July 31, 1865, from Master of the Royal Mint Thomas Graham to Newfoundland Receiver General John Bemister, detailing the cost of the coinage of 1865. Note that shipping costs are not included.

(Image: The Rooms, Provincial Archives, St. John's.)

became a well-respected governor. By January 1870, according to him, the colony was experiencing "great inconvenience" regarding its trade "in consequence of the small supply of silver coins" available. Note that once again gold coins are not mentioned. These apprehensions were expressed in a letter of January 19, 1870, from Hill to Earl Granville, Secretary of State for the Colonies, requesting that

the British Government direct the Master of the Mint to pursue for this colony the following supply of gold and silver coins, namely

$2 Gold pieces $20,000
50-cent Silver pieces $25,000
20-cent Silver pieces $10,000
10-cent Silver pieces $3,000
5-cent Silver pieces $2,000

This is the first time the colony asked for 50¢ pieces; remarkably, no 1¢ coins were requested. Since the latter were the most desired coins from the original mintage of 1865, this seems unusual.

In his letter, Hill continued that his secretary would convey to Granville the necessary instructions for the supply of the gold and silver coins. He noted that the Union Bank of London was once again engaged to provide the needed funds. The Newfoundland government, in its coinage dealings, was being advised by the Union Bank of Newfoundland, specifically by its manager, John W. Smith. The 1865 and subsequent coinage were deposited in the bank, and when coinage was requested by a client, in exchange for either existing paper money or other legal coinage (British, American, Mexican, and so on), the Newfoundland bronze, silver, or gold pieces were provided. In

Figure 4-12: Sir Stephen John Hill, governor of Newfoundland from 1869 to 1876. This photograph was taken by famed photographer William Notman (1826-1891) around 1870. Hill probably sat for it either in Montreal or Halifax.

(Image: Courtesy of McCord Museum, Montreal)

this way, the new coinage slowly diffused into the public domain. Smith was thus in a unique position to know when additional coinage was required. It appears that the coinage requests from the colony to the Royal Mint were initiated through his reports to the governor until 1877, when ill health caused him to retire. As we shall see below, the coinage request of 1880 was the first one after

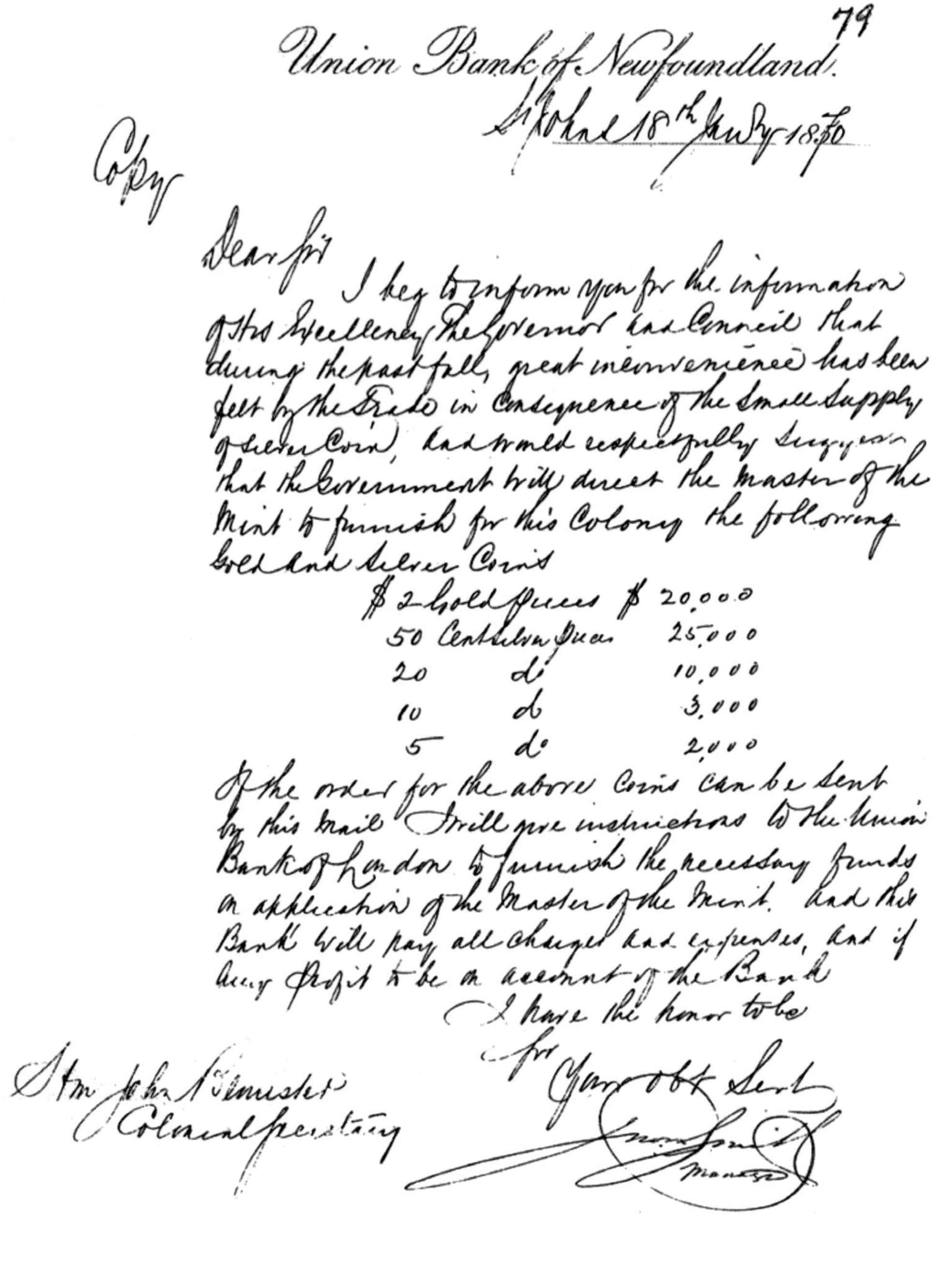

Union Bank of Newfoundland.

St John 18th Jany 1870

Copy

Dear Sir

I beg to inform you for the information of His Excellency the Governor and Council that during the past fall, great inconvenience has been felt by the Trade in consequence of the small supply of silver coin, and would respectfully suggest that the Government will direct the Master of the Mint to furnish for this Colony the following Gold and Silver Coins

$2 Gold Pieces	$	20,000
50 Centibin Pieces		25,000
20	do	10,000
10	do	3,000
5	do	2,000

If the order for the above Coins can be sent by this mail I will give instructions to the Union Bank of London to furnish the necessary funds on application of the Master of the Mint. And this Bank will pay all charges and expenses, and if any profit to be on account of the Bank

I have the honor to be

for Your obt Servt

Manager

To John Bemister
Colonial Secretary

Figure 4-13: A letter to John Bemister, Colonial Secretary, from John Smith, manager of the Union Bank of Newfoundland, suggesting an amount of coinage for the year 1870.

(Image: The Rooms, Provincial Archives, St. John's)

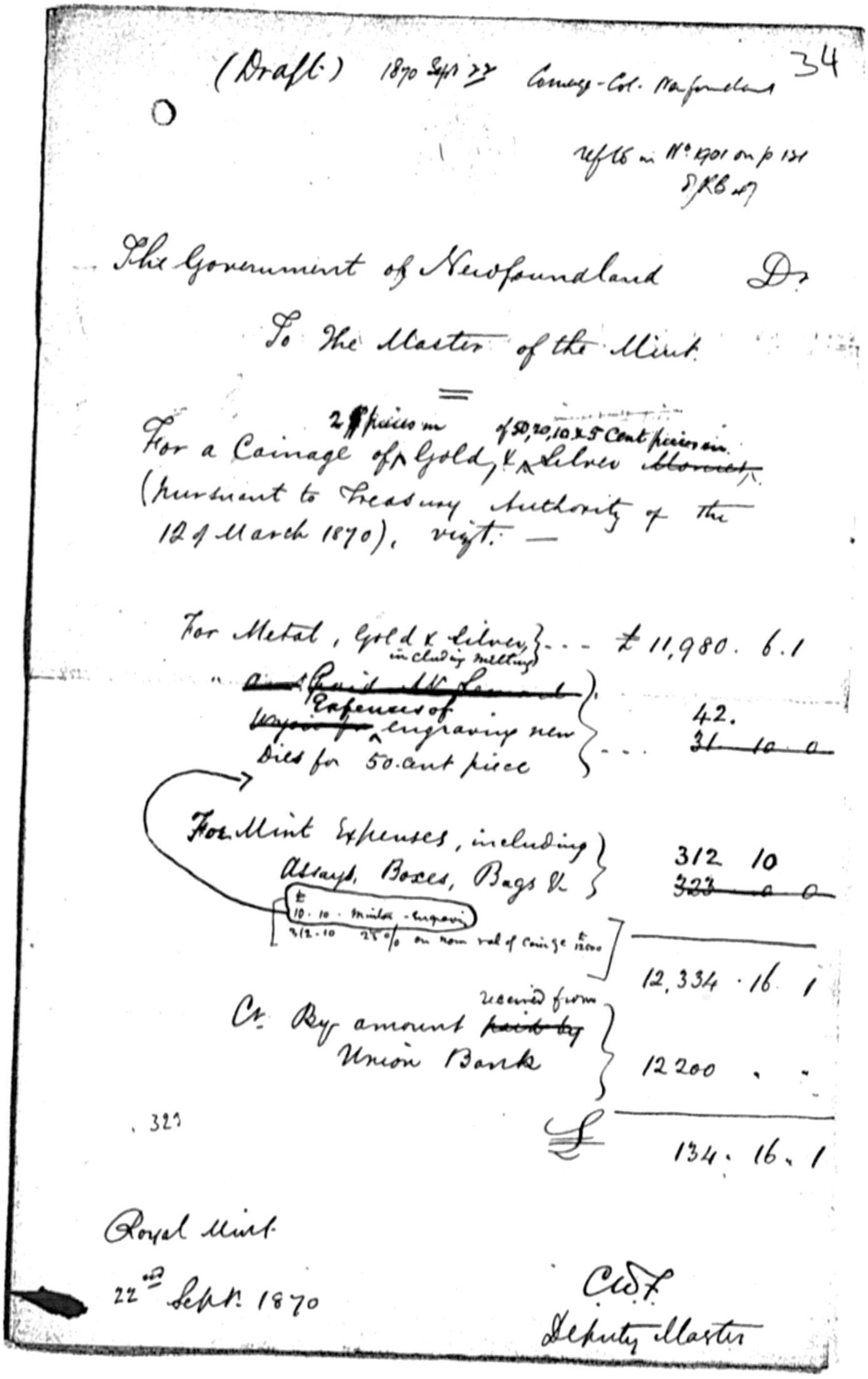

(Draft) 1870 Sept 22 Coinage - Col. Newfoundland 34

The Government of Newfoundland Dr

To The Master of the Mint

For a Coinage of 2$ pieces in Gold, & of 50, 20, 10 & 5 Cent pieces in Silver Moneys
(pursuant to Treasury Authority of the 12 of March 1870), viz. —

For Metal, Gold & Silver including melting ...	£ 11,980. 6.1
" Expenses of engraving new Dies for 50 cent piece ...	42. ~~31 10 0~~
For Mint Expenses, including Assays, Boxes, Bags &c	312 10 ~~323 0 0~~
	12,334 . 16 . 1
Cr. By amount received from ~~paid by~~ Union Bank	12 200 . -
£	134 . 16 . 1

Royal Mint
22nd Sept. 1870

C.W.F.
Deputy Master

Figure 4-14: Costs for the production of Newfoundland coins in gold and silver for the year 1870.

(Image: UK National Archives, MINT 13/75, C598400, page 34)

Smith's retirement, and it did not go well.

The request by Hill was almost certainly initiated by correspondence between Smith and John Bemister (by then Colonial Secretary) the previous day (Figure 4-13). Smith bemoaned the small supply of silver coins currently available to the colony and requested the quantity of coinage listed above. The relationship between the Newfoundland government and the Union Bank of Newfoundland was somewhat unusual. In this letter, dated July 18, 1870, the bank, apparently on behalf of the governor, made a request for a new issue of coinage. The letter ended with the words "and if being profit to be on account of the Bank." Rowe and colleagues interpret this to mean that the bank would keep all the profits.[11] It could also simply mean that the profits were in an account at the bank that was being held for the colony, but this seems unlikely, as Smith might have said so explicitly if that was the situation. Several economists and historians with whom I discussed this letter all agreed that the bank was indeed keeping the profits for itself. There is thus at least the appearance here of potential for misconduct. Clearly, the more coinage that was produced for the colony, the larger were the expected profits on this coinage. If the Union Bank was in fact keeping the profits, does this then explain the almost inexplicably large coinage request for 1882?

An interesting letter dated April 12, 1870 (again from Hill to Granville), stated that the colonial government was of the opinion that the design of the new 50¢ coin should be similar to that of the present coins except that the diameter and weight should be commensurate with its value. But of course this did not happen. The 50¢ obverse portrait of the Queen was entirely new.

The total cost of the 1870 coinage amounted to

Figure 4-15: Charles Fremantle, Deputy Master of the Royal Mint from 1868 until 1894. It is largely due to him that a number of spectacular proofs of Newfoundland $2 gold coins exist.

(Image: Royal Mint Museum.)

£12,334 16s. 1d. The bulk of this was for the metal, amounting to £11,980 6s. 1d. The cost of engraving new dies for the 50¢ coins was £42. This was all tabulated in an invoice dated September 22, 1870, from the Royal Mint with Deputy Master Charles Fremantle's signature (Figure 4-14).

The mint had a standing order to annually transfer examples of the new coinage to the British Museum. The document for the transfer of the 1870-dated coins is dated March 14, 1871. Similar documents exist for most years of coinage, and

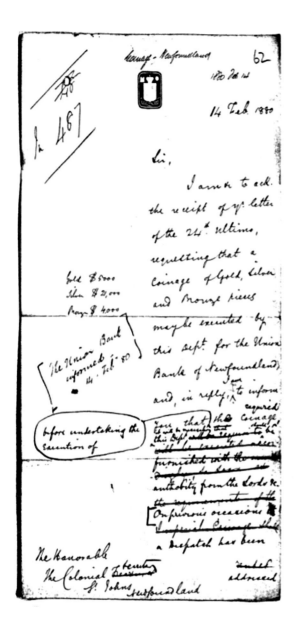

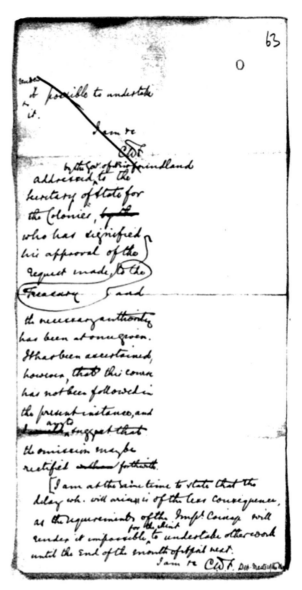

Figure 4-16: Letter from Charles Fremantle to the Colonial Secretary commenting on the colony's request for coinage in 1880. The colony did not follow protocol and he chastises it for this breach; however, he sounds much more conciliatory towards the end of the letter.

(Image: UK National Archives, MINT 13/75, C598400, pages 62 and 63)

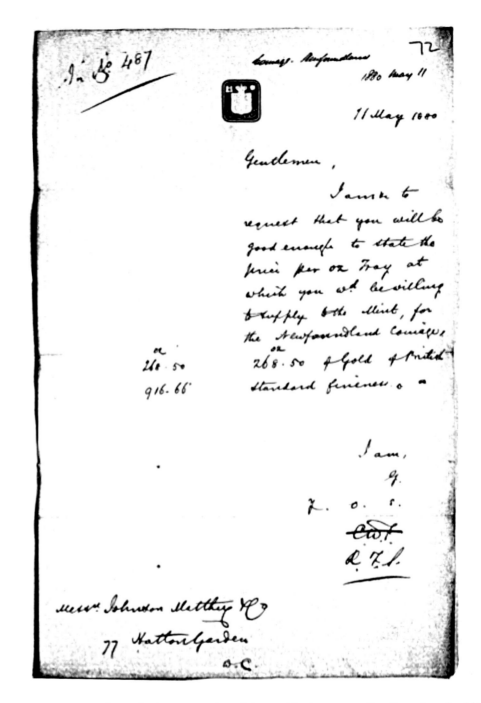

Figure 4-17: Letter from Charles Fremantle to Johnson Matthey requesting the price of gold in standard British fineness for the Newfoundland coinage of 1880. Note that Fremantle's initials are crossed out and replaced with "R.F.S."

(Image: UK National Archives, MINT 13/75, C98400, page 72)

these transfers are why the British Museum has such a superb collection today – the visionaries, especially Charles Fremantle, made sure that the coinage legacy of the country was preserved (Figure 4-15). Transfer occurred for both British and colonial coins. Each Newfoundland coin minted that year had an entry and a cost, including the gold coin. Its cost was 8s. 4d., as expected, as this is its face value.

THE COINAGE OF 1873

There are no existing documents related to the 1872 mintage of the gold coins. Beginning on January 16, 1873, there is, however, extensive correspondence between Governor Hill, the Union Bank of Newfoundland, Charles Fremantle, and the Secretary of the Treasury in the United Kingdom over the coinage requested for that year. The first document provides a list of the coins requested:

Bronze cents	$2,000
5-cent Silver pieces	$2,000
10-cent Silver pieces	$2,000
20-cent Silver pieces	$8,000
50-cent Silver pieces	$16,000

Haxby's Guide Book of Canadian Coins reports 200,025 cents (compared with 200,000 requested) and 37,675 50¢ coins produced (compared with 32,000 requested).[12] It is likely that the small excess reported by Haxby was melted. Beginning with the first exchange of letters in mid-January, absolutely no mention is made of gold coins. No reason for this is given, but we can reasonably surmise that the supply from the previous year (1872) was not yet exhausted. No more gold coins would be struck until 1880.

Having earlier praised the British for their far-sighted approach to preserving their numismatic heritage, I should mention a strange letter dated March 13, 1875, from the Trustees of the British Museum to Deputy Master of the Royal Mint Charles Fremantle. The trustees wish "to sell certain Gold Coins which are false, and are desirous of ascertaining what may be their real value." They ask Fremantle if he would assay the coins so that they can set a value for them. The number of coins they are considering selling is 148. The curious nature of this request revolves around the word "false." Are these counterfeits or are they underweight? I obtained clarification from Thomas Hockenhull, curator at the British Museum. Originally I was optimistic that they were thinking of selling something far more interesting. Like most mints, the Royal Mint produced patterns to test new designs and perhaps also minted some off-metal coins. For example, they might have been testing a new design for a gold coin by using a cheaper metal such as copper. Both the patterns and off-metal strikes are generally extremely rare and greatly sought after by collectors. Is this what the trustees were contemplating? Is this how the Newfoundland $2 pattern gold coins of 1865 (see Chapter 6) got into the public domain? Hockenhull provided a complete explanation of the events related to this request. The 148 coins, consisting of 28 Greek, 93 Roman, 1 Oriental, and 26 Gothic pieces, were all modern forgeries, and the plan was to melt them and sell the resulting metal as bullion. The estimated value of this sale was put at about £100. The reason for the sale was that the museum's Coin Department was raising funds to purchase a large collection from the French dealers Rollin and Feuardent. The rest of the money needed for the purchase was raised through the sale of duplicate coins from the collection.

THE COINAGE OF 1880

The process for the acquisition of coinage for the colony seemed to unravel in 1880. Four years had elapsed without a request for coins from the Royal Mint, so perhaps the procedures had been forgotten or the retirement of John Smith had had an effect. In any event, on January 24, Charles Fremantle, now Master of the Royal Mint, received a coinage request directly from Newfoundland's Colonial Secretary. This was the first time since 1872 that gold coinage was included in the solicitation. The request was for $5,000 in $2 gold coins, a mere 2,500 coins, thus giving rise to the major rarity in the Newfoundland gold series. In a reply dated February 14, 1880, Fremantle chastised the colony, informing it that it was required to follow procedure and make the initial request to the Secretary of State for the Colonies, after which that body would contact the Lords Commissioners of the Treasury. Fremantle also indicated that no serious delay would actually occur since the Royal Mint was heavily involved with imperial coinage at the time, and that no other work would be undertaken before the end of April 1880. His umbrage with the colony shows through clearly in his letter, reproduced in Figure 4-16, showing numerous additions and corrections.

By early April, Fremantle had requested quotes for the cost of the silver (25,000 ounces) for the coinage of that year, and on May 11 he asked for a quote from Ralph Heaton and Sons for two tons of bronze bars of the same composition as that used for imperial coinage. In a separate letter written on the same date, he also solicited a quote from Johnson Matthey and Company for 268.50 troy ounces of gold of standard British fineness (Figure 4-17). The reply from Johnson Matthey arrived the next day, and the quote was 78s. 3d. per ounce for the gold (Figure 4-18). The Royal Mint approved the quote the following day. (Business appears to have been transacted extremely efficiently at the Royal Mint in those days.)

With the cost of the gold per ounce (of fineness 0.9166) at 78.250s., and a weight of 0.107 troy ounces per coin, the cost of metal alone per coin was 8.373s. This amounted to £0.41865, and since each Newfoundland $2 gold coin was £0.416667, the cost of metal per coin exceeded its face value by £.00198, or 0.04s, excluding both minting and shipping costs.

The amount of metal ordered for the 1880 gold coinage would have been sufficient for minting only 2,509 coins (the mintage for 1880 was 2,500 coins). This seems like an almost impossibly tight tolerance, particularly when we view the gold request for the 1881 mintage. In the 1881 case, twice the required amount of gold nominally needed was ordered, whereas for 1880 the excess was only about 0.4 percent. Did the mint learn from the experience in 1880 that wastage for this small coin would be higher than expected? We can speculate that, with so little excess gold on hand, perhaps the mint may have run out of gold and produced somewhat fewer coins than requested by the colony. Several documents from the mint indicate, however, that the mintage was indeed 2,500 coins for 1880 (see the section on the mysterious 1890 $2 gold coin later in this chapter), so we must assume that this mintage is correct. Provisions were also made for the return of unused metal, the first time this is seen in the correspondence between the Royal Mint and Johnson Matthey. In a letter dated May 14, 1880, Fremantle noted that the gold had already been received at the mint, and he requested a payment for the entire cost of the gold in the amount of

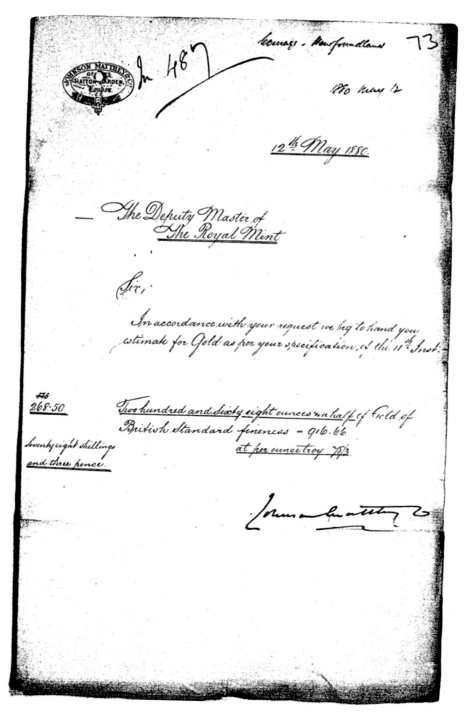

Coinage - Newfoundland

Jr 487

1880 May 12

12th May 1880.

— The Deputy Master of
The Royal Mint

Sir,

In accordance with your request we beg to hand you
estimate for Gold as per your specification, of the 11th Inst.

£8
268·50

Two hundred and sixty eight ounces & a half of Gold of
British Standard fineness – 916.66
at per ounce troy 78/3

Twenty eight shillings
and three pence.

Johnson Matthey & Co

Figure 4-18: Johnson Matthey's response to Fremantle's request for a quote for the gold to mint the
Newfoundland $2 gold coins for the year 1880.

(Image: UK National Archives, MINT 13/75, C598400, page 73)

Figure 4-19: Sir John Hawley Glover, governor of Newfoundland (1876-81), and Lady Glover in front of Government House in St. John's. The governor and his wife are in the front seat.

(Image: Library and Archives Canada: MIKAN 3192340 ca. 1877–85)

£1,050 10s. 2d. This is the correct amount for 268.50 troy ounces at 78s. 3d. per ounce.

Seigniorage is the difference between the value of a coin and the cost to produce it. It can be either positive or negative. If positive, a government makes an economic profit on the production of its coins; if negative, it suffers an economic loss. It is possible to calculate the seigniorage of the 1880 production of the $2 gold coins from the information available in the mint documents. As we saw earlier, there was effectively a negative seigniorage of 0.040s. for the metal cost for each coin, excluding minting and shipping costs. According to a letter from the Union Bank of London (which was representing the colony in these financial matters) to the Master of the Royal Mint, dated May 27, 1880, the costs associated with the manufacture of the coins, shipping boxes, bags, and so on, amounted to £26 0s. 10d. This was for the entire mintage, so only a small fraction of this could be attributed to the gold coins. In addition, this amount does not include the cost associated with shipping the coins to the colony. Thus the seigniorage in minting the gold coins was negative, probably amounting to about 1 percent of their face valu in production). As mentioned by Rowe and colleagues, the seigniorage for the full release of coinage for 1880 was large and positive, amounting to $6,069.42.[13] Excluding the issue

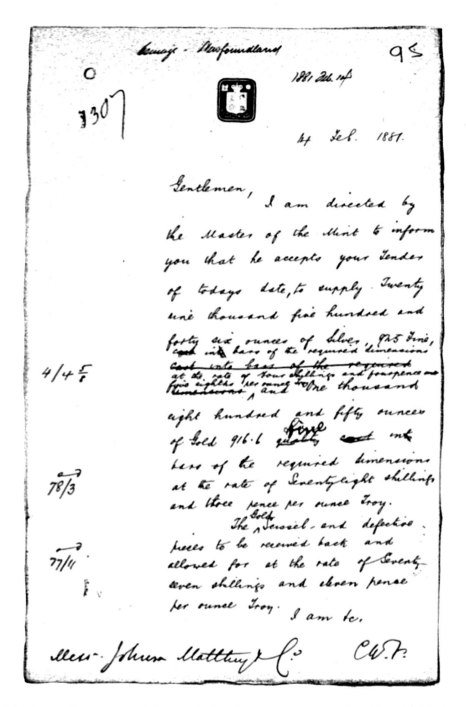

Figure 4-20: Royal Mint request to Johnson Matthey for a quote, among other things, for 1,850 ounces of gold of standard British fineness (916.67 parts pure gold per thousand ounces) to mint the 1881 Newfoundland $2 gold coins.

(Image: UK National Archives, MINT 13/75, C598400, page 95)

of gold coins, it was clearly in the interests of the Union Bank to order as large a coinage as possible since this increased the profits, which the bank kept for itself.

THE COINAGE OF 1881

The colony did things by the book for the 1881 coinage, perhaps chastened by its experience the previous year. On January 18, Governor John Hawley Glover (Figure 4-19) wrote to the Earl of Kimberley, the Secretary of State for the Colonies, transmitting a copy of a letter from the Colonial Secretary requesting a new coinage for Newfoundland. The governor requested a total coinage of $59,000, including $20,000 in $2 gold pieces. On February 11, Fremantle wrote to Johnson Matthey requesting, among other things, a quote for 1,850 troy ounces of gold of "millesimal fineness 916.66" (Figure 4-20). Here, for the first time in his correspondence involving Newfoundland, Fremantle used the term "millesimal" instead of British standard. The quote from Johnson Matthey, which arrived just three days later, was the same as the previous year's, namely, 78s. 3d. per troy ounce.

THE COINAGE OF 1882

The coinage for this year seems to have been initiated by a letter from Sir John Bramston (Figure 4-21), then Under Secretary of State in the Colonial Office, who had received a dispatch from the Officer Administering the Government of Newfoundland. The dispatch, dated March 13, 1882, relayed the request for a supply of gold and silver coins to the value of $129,350 for use by the colony (Figure 4-22). Ten days later, the amount was adjusted to $125,000 with the dollar amounts requested indicated below.

Figure 4-21: Photograph of Sir John Bramston, probably from the mid-1870s. His main areas of responsibility were in general legal business as well as postal and telegraphic affairs, all connected with the North American colonies, Australia, and South Africa.

(Image in the public domain)

$2 Gold pieces	$50,000
50-cent Silver pieces	$50,000
20-cent Silver pieces	$20,000
10-cent Silver pieces	$2,000
5-cent Silver pieces	$3,000

This letter is one of the few original documents that I was actually able to hold in my hand. Most of the documents discussed and reproduced in this

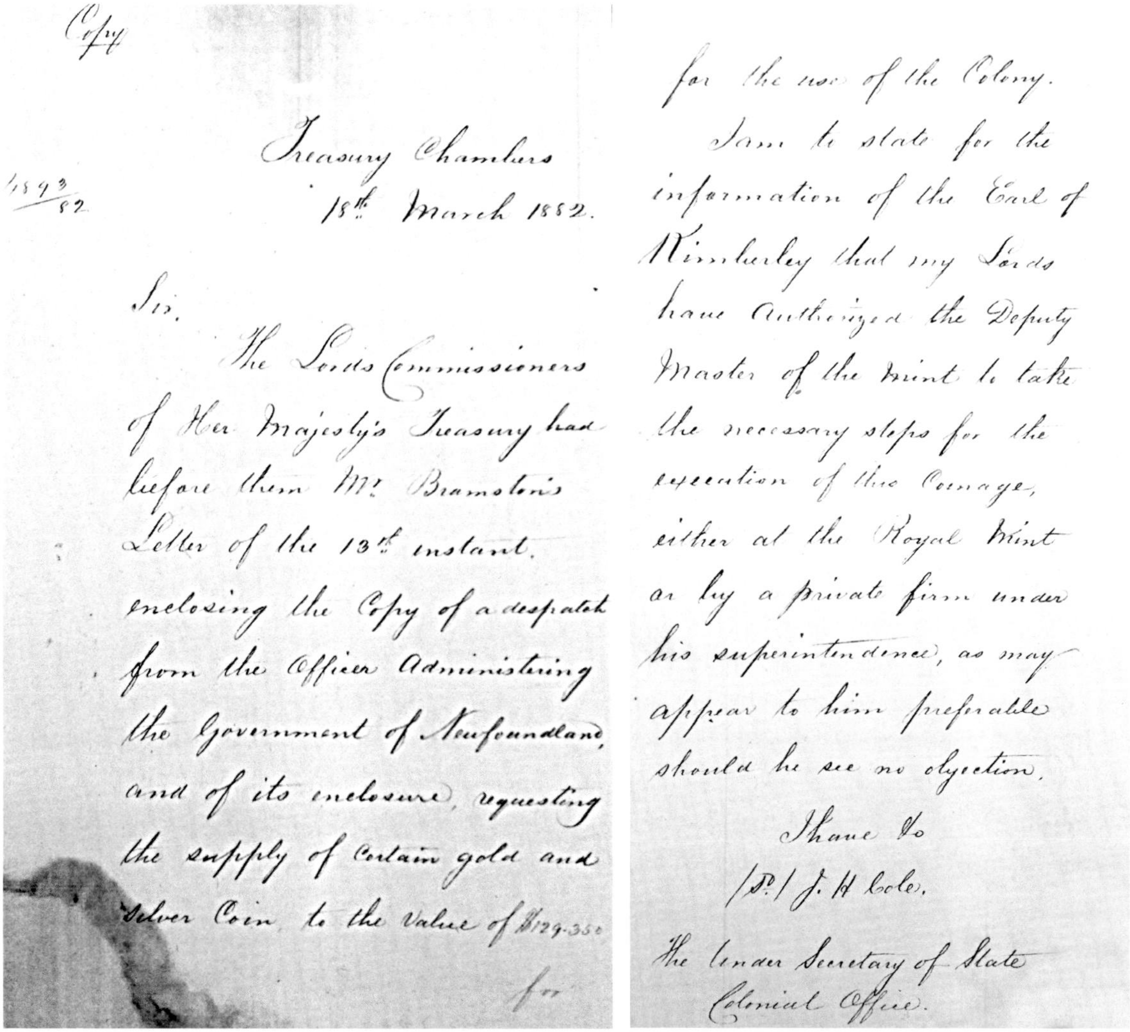

Copy

1893/82

Treasury Chambers
18th March 1882.

Sir,

The Lords Commissioners of Her Majesty's Treasury have before them Mr Bramston's Letter of the 13th instant, enclosing the Copy of a despatch from the Officer Administering the Government of Newfoundland and of its enclosure, requesting the supply of certain gold and silver Coin to the value of $129.350 for the use of the Colony.

I am to state for the information of the Earl of Kimberley that my Lords have authorized the Deputy Master of the Mint to take the necessary steps for the execution of this Coinage, either at the Royal Mint or by a private firm under his superintendence, as may appear to him preferable should he see no objection.

I have &c

(Sd) J. H. Cole.

The Under Secretary of State
Colonial Office.

Figure 4-22: Letter from the Treasury of Newfoundland to the Colonial Office initiating the 1882 coinage request for the colony. Note that the total requested here was $129,350. This was later amended to $125,000. The colony in this letter was also anticipating that the coins might have to be struck at some location other than the Royal Mint.

(Original document: The Rooms, Provincial Archives, St. John's)

book were from prints made by staff at the UK National Archives. The letter reproduced in Figure 4-22 is held at The Rooms, the Newfoundland Provincial Archives in St. John's. I was able to locate it and take a photograph. It was thrilling to hold and see an original slice of history relating to the Newfoundland gold coins.

The 1882 requ est for coinage is remarkably large given that the entry in the Blue Book of Newfoundland (see Chapter 2) for the total amount of coinage in circulation in 1882 was only £120,000 (576,000 Newfoundland dollars). While this estimate is probably low, it does highlight how large the 1882 coinage request was – in fact, the largest coinage request ever made by the colony. We might speculate as to the reasons for such a large request. One might be that the Union Banks of Newfoundland and London retained all the profits from the coinage. For the year 1880 alone (a modest output of new coins), the profit amounted to about $6,000 on a total mintage of only $30,000; most of this came from the mintage of the bronze cents, with a small loss from minting the gold coins. The total request of $125,000 in new coinage for 1882 would have resulted in a profit of $25,000 if the same percentage excess was repeated. This is a very large sum considering that the total revenue for Newfoundland in 1882 was just over $1 million and that the public debt amounted to just over $7 per capita. In addition, recall that the Newfoundland government, in the original legislation for the decimal currency passed in 1863, mandated that all government accounts be kept in the new system starting in 1865. This mandate was not enforced as the coinage arrived late in the colony. In 1877, however, a new law was passed (amended in 1887) requiring that all government accounts be kept in dollars and cents. This law might have necessitated a larger than normal influx of new coins, which might help explain the large request in 1882.

The main issue for this year of production was that the Royal Mint was so occupied with domestic coinage, and with coinage for other parts of the empire, that it was forced to contract the production out to Heaton's. This resulted in a large "H" on the reverse of the gold coin of this date, the only date in the gold series that bears a mint mark. The Heaton Mint had been involved since 1872 in

Figure 4-23: Frederick Arthur Stanley, 16th Earl of Derby, who served as Secretary of State for the Colonies from 1885 to 1886. He was also the sixth Governor General of Canada, serving from 1888 to 1893. Canadian hockey fans will recognize his name as this was the same Stanley who donated the Stanley Cup, which symbolized, at the time, the best hockey team in the dominion. Teams in the National Hockey League still compete for the Stanley Cup today.

(Image: Wikimedia Commons, image in the public domain)

striking Newfoundland coins in bronze and silver, but this was the first and only time it struck the gold coins for the colony.

THE COINAGE OF 1885

The coinage of 1885 was initiated on March 2 that

year, in a letter from Colonial Secretary Edward Dalton Shea to Governor Glover. Just two days later, Glover wrote to the Earl of Derby (Lord Stanley after 1886; Figure 4-23), the Secretary of State for the Colonies, requesting that he provide the "necessary instructions for the preparation by the Royal Mint of a quantity of Newfoundland coinage amounting to the total of $50,000." Glover's letter also expressed a desire for ten thousand $2 pieces, the actual number eventually minted.

As with accepted procedure, the Colonial Office (then located in a massive building also housing the Foreign, India, and Home Offices in London) communicated this request to the Lords Commissioners of the Treasury in April 1885 (no date provided on the letter, which was signed by Assistant Under Secretary of State for the Colonies Sir John Bramston). The Lords Commissioners replied in the affirmative in a letter dated April 9 addressed to the Deputy Master of the Royal Mint. It is remarkable how quickly such requests moved forward in those days. Today one imagines that committees, broader consultations, focus groups, and extended discussions would be undertaken. Coinage for the colony was generally able to move through the required agencies in just a week or two.

Fremantle gives us another opportunity to determine the seigniorage involved in the Newfoundland coinage, although only for the entire mintage. In a letter dated April 17, 1885, he estimated the total cost of the coinage, including bullion and mint charges, at £10,700. The mint charges by themselves amounted to £300 10s. A British pound was 4.80 Newfoundland dollars, so here we see that the colony ends up with a negative seigniorage of $1,360 for the entire mintage of 1885. The cause of this may be traced

to the mintage of 1¢ coins in this year. It was miniscule; at only forty thousand coins, it was the smallest number ever minted for Newfoundland in its entire colonial history. The seigniorage for 1¢ coins was always the largest, so this tiny mintage is likely to have severely curtailed the amount of seigniorage for that entire year's coinage. On April 21, the Union Bank of London confirmed that the Union Bank of Newfoundland had approved the payment and that the exchange rate was $4.80 per pound.

The quote for the gold metal to mint the $2 coins is again affirmed to be 78s. 3d. per troy ounce, and Fremantle requested 1,070.083 troy ounces. This seems absolutely remarkable since the mintage was to be the same as in 1881 (i.e., ten thousand coins) but Fremantle had requested 1,850 troy ounces in 1881. The 1,070 troy ounces requested was sufficient to mint exactly ten thousand coins. It is odd indeed that almost twice as much gold had been ordered in 1881 to mint exactly the same number of coins. No documentation exists to indicate that the excess gold ordered in 1881 was returned to Johnson Matthey – yet another mystery surrounding these coins.

THE CURRENCY ACT OF 1887: POSSIBLE FURTHER EVIDENCE OF BANK FRAUD

On May 18, 1887, the Newfoundland legislature passed an amendment to the Currency Act that had originally come into law in 1863. An earlier amendment had been passed in 1877. The amendment act of 1887 is reproduced in Appendix 2. The main aim of the new law was to reassert that the accounts of the colony should be kept in dollars and cents. A minor alteration to the existing law removed the legal tender status of Spanish and Latin American dollars. There apparently was an error in the printing of the statement of the text of the 1887 act. This can be verified by comparing the statements in section X in the 1863 act (see Appendix 1) with those in section IX of the 1887 act. In section IX, "Weight of Gold Coins, &c.," the new law stated that British gold coins were to be accepted by weight at the rate of $16.69 per troy ounce, while US coins were valued at $18.31 per troy ounce, whereas section X, "Gold coins tender by tale, &c.," stated that "British Gold Coins by weight, at the rate of Eighteen Dollars and Sixty-nine and a half Cents per ounce Troy, and the said Gold Coins of the United States, by weight, at the rate of Eighteen Dollars Thirty-two and nine-sixteenths of a Cent per ounce Troy." Perhaps of some relevance is that two of the Newfoundland banks (Union and Commercial) failed a few years later. The directors were accused of fraud in these failures but none of the cases actually came to trial, and in the end the charges were dropped. How does this relate to the 1887 act?

On January 17, 1889, W.L. Hertslet, an accountant with the German Reichsbank, wrote to Charles Fremantle, Master of the Royal Mint, inquiring about the exchange rates for British sovereigns and US $10 gold coins in Newfoundland currency. Hertslet was apparently tabulating these rates for the German Stock Exchange. He pointed out a discrepancy – essentially that the British sovereign was being valued at $16.69 per troy ounce of gold, while the US eagle was taken at $18.31 per troy ounce. Since the fineness of the sovereign was slightly higher than that of the eagle (0.9167 compared with 0.9000), the sovereign should have had a somewhat higher value, namely, $18.69. Hertslet asked what new law was used to make these changes, as they appeared in the original 1863 act with the (apparently correct) values, $18.33 and $18.69 for the US and British coins, respectively.

There is further correspondence between Germany and London; the final document pertaining to this issue is a letter from the Union Bank of London (which was acting for the Union Bank of Newfoundland during this period) to Charles Fremantle signed by an "R. Slater." I inquired with the archivist at the Royal Bank of Scotland (where the archives of the Union Bank of London are currently being held) as to the nature of Mr. Slater's appointment, but no records on this were available. This suggested to the archivist that Slater was not a branch manager, and that he probably worked in head office. However, his name and signature appeared again on an April 21, 1885, letter to Charles Fremantle on the letterhead of the Union Bank of London. The letter confirmed that the Union Bank of London had received funds from its sister bank in Newfoundland as payment for the 1885 coinage.

Mr. Slater claimed that an error had been made in copying the Newfoundland Currency Act of 1887. Examination of the portion of the document reproduced in Appendices 1 and 2 and abstracted above confirms this. Mr. Slater went on to state that the error was discovered only a few months previously, and that he was told that the colonial government would be introducing a short bill returning the value of the sovereign to $18.69 per troy ounce of gold instead of the current $16.69.

This is all quite odd. Why did it take an accountant in Berlin to bring this discrepancy to light? Did the banks in Newfoundland and London ever realize that there was a problem? The incorrect law had been in effect for over a year. The banks were the ones most likely to have benefited from this state of affairs, as they were the intermediaries through which most of these exchanges would have been made. Furthermore, Mr. Slater's letter makes no mention of any restitution to customers who, for the past year or more, had received $2 less than they deserved for a troy ounce of gold in sovereigns.

THE MYSTERIOUS 1890 NEWFOUNDLAND $2 GOLD COIN

A Canadian book on coins by P.N. Breton published in 1894 lists a Newfoundland $2 gold coin dated 1890 for which there is no credible report either at auction or by private sale.[14] Assistant Curator Chris Barker at the Royal Mint Museum, with whom I corresponded, could find no reference for such coinage issued by either the Royal Mint or any of its subcontractors, nor is any mention made of the coin in the Royal Mint's annual report for 1890. Mr. Barker also inspected the Royal Mint Museum's collection and confirmed that it does not have an 1890 Newfoundland $2 coin, whether struck by the Royal Mint or the Heaton Mint in Birmingham. All Canadian coinage for that year was struck in Birmingham, while the Newfoundland coinage was struck at the Royal Mint.

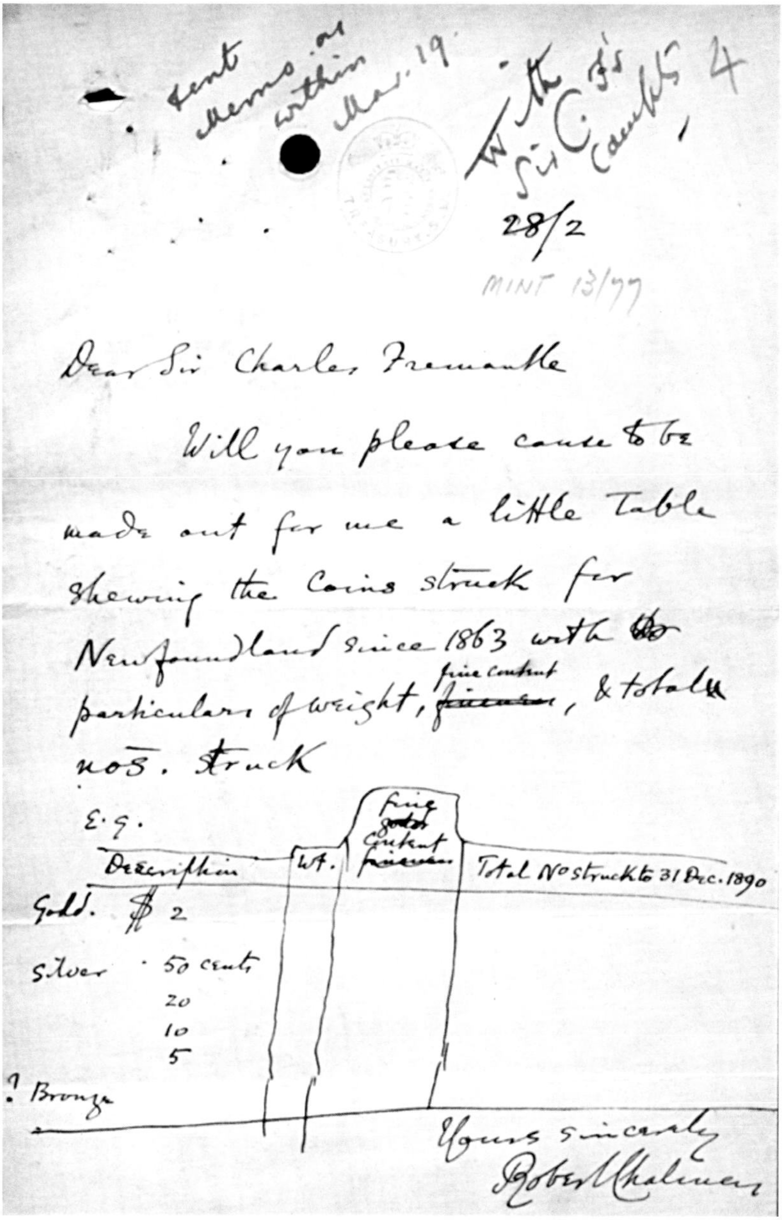
sent memo within Mar. 19

With Sir C. F's compts, 4

28/2

MINT 13/77

Dear Sir Charles Fremantle

Will you please cause to be made out for me a little Table shewing the Coins struck for Newfoundland since 1863 with the particulars of weight, ~~fineness~~ fine content, & total nos. struck

E.g.

	Description	Wt.	Fine content	Total No struck to 31 Dec. 1890
Gold.	$2			
Silver	50 cents			
	20			
	10			
	5			
? Bronze				

Yours sincerely
Robert Chalmers

Figure 4-24: Letter from Robert Chalmers to Sir Charles Fremantle dated February 28, 1891.

(Image: UK National Archives, MINT 13/77-002)

Interestingly, the UK National Archives contain inquiries and responses (Documents MINT-13-77-001 to 007) dated between late February and

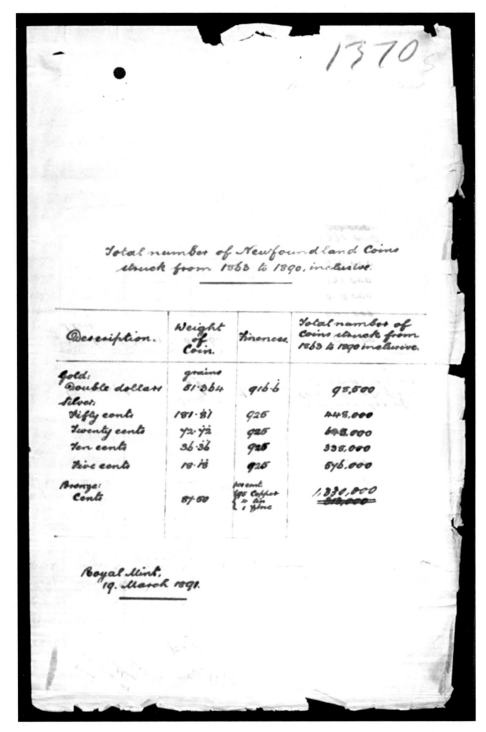

Figure 4-25: Total number of coins of all denominations struck for Newfoundland as of March 19, 1891.

(Image: UK National Archives, MINT 13/77-004)

mid-March 1891 that are relevant to this issue. On February 28, 1891 (people worked on Saturdays then!), Robert Chalmers, who was employed in the Treasury Department, wrote Sir Charles Fremantle (Deputy Master of the Royal Mint; he had succeeded Sir Thomas Graham in 1868) requesting an accounting of the number of coins struck for Newfoundland since 1863 (see Figure 4-24). Such inquiry was probably related to a book that Chalmers was researching and that appeared in 1893, titled *A History of Currency in the British Colonies*.[15]

There are several responses. The first (MINT-13-77-004), dated March 19, 1891, is from the Royal Mint and indicates that a total of 98,500 $2 gold pieces were struck between 1863 and 1890 (inclusive) (see Figure 4-25). This number tallies exactly with the known business strike mintages, including those from the Heaton Mint. Note that the specimens and patterns (see Chapter 6) are not included in this total.

The subsequent document (MINT-13-77-006) breaks this down by year, but since it originated from the Royal Mint, it does not include 1882 coins, which were struck at the Heaton Mint in Birmingham (see Figure 4-26).

The next reply (MINT-13-77-007) shows that 25,000 gold pieces were struck for Newfoundland in 1882 at Birmingham; it also includes the totals from all years for all the denominations of Newfoundland coinage up to and including 1890 (see Figure 4-27).

Curiously, however, even with all this information, Chalmers's book contained the table shown in Figure 4-28. Note that the indication here is that 98,550 $2 gold pieces were minted instead of the total of 98,500 listed in the various tables above. Whether this has any relevance to the question of the 1890 $2 gold piece, whether it is simply a typographical error, or whether it includes specimens and patterns (see Chapter 6) is unknown, but it seems to be an interesting entry given the information available to Chalmers.

Based on these documents (excluding the table from Chalmers's book) and correspondence with Assistant Curator Barker, one can assert with a fair degree of confidence that no 1890 $2 gold coins were ever struck. Why it got listed in Breton's 1894 catalogue remains a mystery. The coin was still listed in some catalogues as late as 1960, when reference was made to it in the *Canada Coin Catalogue* compiled by Neil Carmichael.[16] Carmichael concluded that "this coin was probably prepared but never issued";[17] nevertheless, he assigned to it a value of $1,500! At that time this was an enormous sum – about thirty times greater than the average Newfoundland 50¢ piece in uncirculated condition in this catalogue; about a third of the most expensive Canadian coins listed (the 1921 50¢ piece, with a value of $5,000); and at about the same price level as the ultra-rare and expensive 1936 dot coins, whose recent auction realizations are at the $400,000 level.

There are even more egregious errors regarding Newfoundland $2 gold coins in at least two catalogues besides Breton's. The 1889 edition of *Coins and Tokens of the Possessions and Colonies of the British Empire* by James Atkins listed Newfoundland $2 gold coins for the years 1865, 1870, 1872, 1873, 1874, 1876, 1880, 1881, 1882(H), and 1885.[18] Atkins may not have had access to the 1888 coin given the date of publication of his book, but where did he get the idea that there were coins dated 1873, 1874, and 1876? He also claimed that specimens of all dates exist, but there is no record of any specimen dated 1881 (see the discussion

Newfoundland.

Year	Gold. 2-dollar	Silver. 50 cents	Silver. 20 cents	Silver. 10 cents	Silver. 5 cents	Bronze. Cents.
1870	20,000	25,000	10,000	3,000	2,000	—
1871	—	—	—	—	—	—
1872	12,800	—	—	—	—	—
1873	—	16,000	8,000	2,000	2,000	2,000
1874	—	40,000	—	—	—	—
1875	—	—	—	—	—	—
1876	—	—	—	—	—	—
1877	—	—	—	—	—	—
1878	—	—	—	—	—	—
1879	—	—	—	—	—	—
1880	5,000	12,000 / 24,000	6,000	1,000	2,000	4,000
1881	20,000	25,000	12,000	—	2,000	—
1882	—	—	—	—	—	—
1883	—	—	—	—	—	—
1884	—	—	—	—	—	—
1885	20,000	20,000	8,000	800	800	400
1886	—	—	—	—	—	—
1887	—	—	—	—	—	—
1888	50,000 / 10,000	10,000	15,000	3,000	2,000	500
1889	—	—	—	—	—	—
1890.	—	—	22,000	10,000	8,000	2,000
Total:	124,000 √	148,000 √	79,000 √	19,500 / 21,000	18,800 / 16,000	9,900 √
1864	20,000 √		10,000 √	8,000 √	4,000 √	2,400 √
Total:	144,000 √	148,000 √	89,000 √	27,500 / 35,000	22,800 / 30,000	11,300 √
Pieces:	73,500 √	296,000 √	445,000 √	360,000 / 278,000	600,000 / 456,000	113,000 0

Figure 4-26: Document from the UK National Archives (MINT 13/77-006) listing mintages of Newfoundland coins by date from 1870 through to 1890 (inclusive) struck at the Royal Mint. The last line of the first column indicates that a total of 73,500 gold pieces were struck. Adding to this the 25,000 coins minted in 1882 by Heaton yields 98,500, exactly the number known to have been minted. Note the lack of an entry for $2 gold coins for the year 1890.

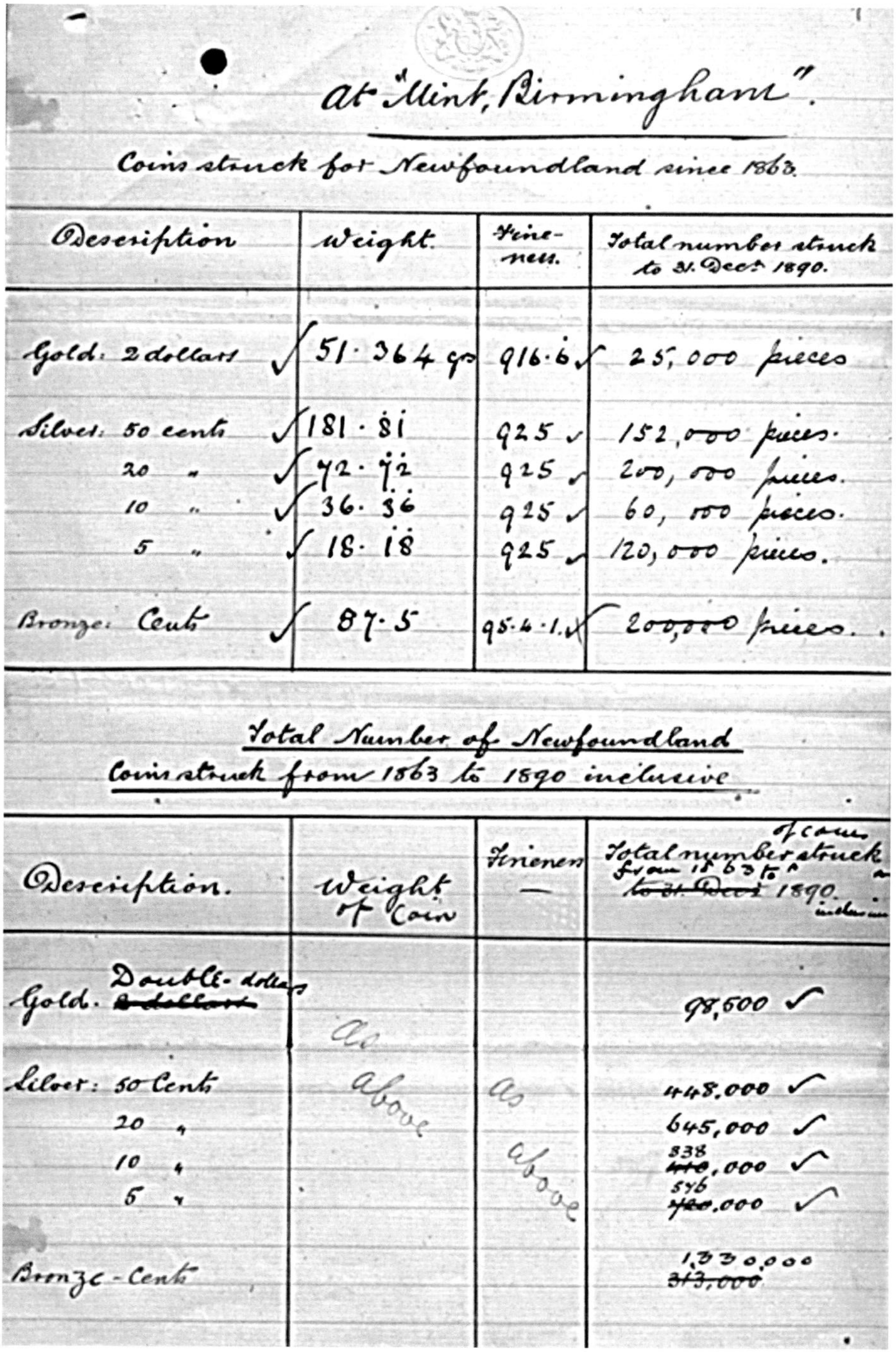

At "Mint, Birmingham".

Coins struck for Newfoundland since 1863.

Description	Weight.	Fine-ness.	Total number struck to 31. Dec.ʳ 1890.
Gold. 2 dollars	51·364 grs	916·6	25,000 pieces
Silver: 50 cents	181·81	925	152,000 pieces.
20 "	72·72	925	200,000 pieces.
10 "	36·36	925	60,000 pieces.
5 "	18·18	925	120,000 pieces.
Bronze: Cents	87·5	95·4·1.	200,000 pieces.

Total Number of Newfoundland
Coins struck from 1863 to 1890 inclusive

Description.	Weight of Coin	Fineness —	Total number struck of coins from 1863 to to 31 Dec.ʳ 1890. inclusive
Gold. Double dollars	as		98,500
Silver: 50 Cents	above	as	448,000
20 "			645,000
10 "		above	338 ~~440~~,000
5 "			576 ~~420~~,000
Bronze - Cents			1,330,000 ~~313,000~~

Figure 4-27: Document from the UK National Archives (MINT 13/77-007) indicating mintages of Newfoundland coins of all denominations struck from 1863 to 1890 (inclusive), both at Birmingham and the Royal Mint. The total for the "Double Dollars" is 98,500.

Description.	Weight of Coin.	Fineness.	Nominal Value of Coins struck from 1865 to 1891, inclusive.
Gold :	Grains.	Per mille.	$
$2 piece - - -	51.364	916·6	197,100
Silver :			
50 cents - - -	181.81	925	236,000
20 cents - - -	72.72	925	147,000
10 cents · -	36.36	925	34,800
5 cents - - ·	18.18	925	28,800
Bronze : Cents - - ·	87.50	per cent. { 95 copper 4 tin 1 zinc }	15,300
Total Nominal Value - - $			659,000

Figure 4-28: Table from Robert Chalmers's book listing the dollar value of all coins struck for Newfoundland between 1865 and 1891.

in Chapter 6) and certainly none for 1873, 1874, and 1876. Joseph Leroux, in his book *Numismatic Atlas of Canada*, lists all the same dates as Atkins, including the nonexistent 1873, 1874, and 1876 coins.[19] Since Leroux's book was published earlier, in 1883, he may have been the source of Atkins's errors.

THE EFFECT OF THE BANK FAILURES OF 1894 ON THE GOLD COINS

On December 10, 1894, both the Union Bank and the Commercial Bank of Newfoundland failed. The paper money from these banks was severely discounted – originally the Union Bank's currency by 20 percent and the Commercial

Figure 4-29: An 1888 $10 note from the Commercial Bank of Newfoundland that has been stamped with its value (TWO DOLLARS) after the bank failed in 1894. The Newfoundland government guaranteed this amount. Note that the bill has been cancelled with a large punched hole in the upper left, a smaller punch in the lower right, and the word "cancelled" (abbreviated) spelled out at the top in smaller punched holes.

(Image: Courtesy of Geoff Bell Auctions)

Figure 4-30: At left, the reverse of an 1888 Newfoundland $2 gold coin, the last date to be struck in this series. At right: If any Newfoundland $2 gold coins had been minted after the bank failures of 1894, the reverse would have had to appear as shown on the "fantasy" 1895 coin pictured here. Note in particular the change in equivalent value in pence between the two coins.

Bank's by a whopping 80 percent. The government of Newfoundland guaranteed these values and eventually the reasonably well managed Union Bank's currency was accepted at 97.5 percent of its stated value and that of the Commercial Bank at 22 percent (see Figure 4-29).[20]

The Canadian banks arrived shortly after the bank failures to fill the banking void. The result was that the Canadian dollar now became the unit of currency. This dollar was different from the Newfoundland dollar and required that the British pound now be valued at $4.8667 per Newfoundland dollar instead of $4.80, a devaluation of the existing currency of about 1.4 percent. There had been no gold coinage for Newfoundland since 1888 and none could be minted after the devaluation of the currency because the reverse of the coin would no longer make sense. Two dollars was no longer equal to 100 pence; instead it was to be valued at 98.6 pence. So the reverse of the coin would have had to look like the one fancifully shown in Figure 4-30 if it had been minted in 1895, after the bank failures the previous year. This is why no Newfoundland $2 gold coins were produced after 1888.

CHAPTER 5

. . . .

Extant Populations of Newfoundland Gold Coins

An examination of the number of Newfoundland gold coins of different dates in various states of preservation offers insight into how extensively these coins circulated in the colony and in which years they were most important to Newfoundland's economy. For example, if the 1865-dated coins are rarely available in mint state, one could surmise that when the coins finally arrived, they were rapidly disseminated into the channels of commerce and hence circulated widely. Or if they were hoarded in a particular year, perhaps because the colony lost confidence in paper currency, we might see a relatively large number of coins that never circulated. Hence populations of coins that never circulated provide a unique insight into the economic activity of Newfoundland in the years 1865 to 1888 and beyond.

Before we delve into existing populations of various high-grade Newfoundland $2 gold coins, it is useful to present examples of these coins in various grades. Coins are generally graded on a 70-point system, 1 being the lowest grade (a coin that is barely recognizable as being of a particular type) and 70 being a perfect coin with no distractions whatsoever. A coin grading AU59 (AU = almost uncirculated) is one that shows just the tiniest amount of wear; hence, it circulated just a very small amount. An MS60 coin (MS = mint state) is the lowest-grade coin that did not circulate (these coins are also termed "uncirculated"). Such a coin will exhibit no wear whatsoever, but it will possess numerous abrasions and disturbances from being mishandled, either at the mint at the time of striking or subsequently. Coins were generally shipped loose in canvas bags, with nothing to prevent them from scraping against each other, resulting in disturbances to their surfaces. This is particularly true for coins struck in gold, which is a rather soft metal. Among the coins grading from MS60 to MS70, the amount of nicks, scratches, and general distractions decreases, so that by MS70 the coin is as it appeared just after being struck, except that it may possibly possess some natural toning acquired over time. Only modern coins reach grades of MS70; no Newfoundland coin of any denomination is graded that high. The highest-graded Newfoundland coins of any denomination

1872 AU55

1870 two dots AU58

1870 three dots MS61

Figure 5-1a

1870 three dots
MS62

1870 two dots
MS63

1888 MS64

Figure 5-1b

1885 MS64+

1882H MS65

1881 MS66

Figure 5-1c

are graded MS68 (fewer than ten coins in the entire Newfoundland series), and no gold coin struck for circulation is graded higher than MS66.

Figure 5-1 shows a grouping of Newfoundland $2 coins in grades from almost uncirculated (AU) to one of the three coins graded MS66 (an 1881 coin). Of the other two coins graded MS66, one is also dated 1881 and the other is an absolutely spectacular 1885 coin – probably the best business strike Newfoundland coin known. Both of the latter two pieces reside in the Perth Collection located in Toronto (not Perth). On the AU coins, the tiniest amount of wear can be seen on the high points of the design (the Queen's eyebrow and the braid around her ear); the uncirculated coins have no wear, and the amount of abrasions and distractions decreases with higher numerical grades. Note that the 1885 coin is graded with a "+"; such grades are assigned if a given coin is better than a given grade but not quite up to the next highest grade. As the reader might surmise, there is an element of subjectivity in all this. This is controlled to some extent by professional grading companies that hire experts to grade the coins. The grades assigned for the coins shown in Figure 5-1 are all from the Professional Coin Grading Service

Figure 5-2: An 1882-H Newfoundland $2 gold coin in the hard plastic holder (commonly termed a "slab") of the PCGS grading company. The H after the date indicates that the coin was struck at the Heaton Mint in Birmingham. A coin struck at the Royal Mint would bear no such mintmark. Note the assigned grade of the coin, MS61.

(Image: Courtesy of PCGS and Heritage Coins)

Figure 5-1a, b, and c: A grading set of Newfoundland $2 gold coins. There is no business strike coin graded by any of the major grading services higher than MS66. Note the decrease in surface abrasions on the coins from the lower grades of uncirculated up to the MS66 coin, and the general increase in attractiveness illustrated by a coin's overall lustre and undisturbed fields.

(Images: Courtesy Heritage Coins and PCGS)

(PCGS), which professionally authenticates, grades, and encapsulates coins in hard plastic to keep them safe from further degradation (see Figure 5-2). As expected, the commercial value of a coin of a given date increases with its MS grade.

Numerous sources have mentioned that the coins of Newfoundland circulated widely, not just in Newfoundland but also in Canada.[1] From

Table 2. Newfoundland $2 gold circulation strike populations graded by Professional Coin Grading Service (PCGS).

DATE	MS60	MS61	MS62	MS63	MS64	MS65	MS66
1865	...	2	9	1	...	1	1
1870(2)	...	1	5	5	1	...	...
1870(3)	...	4	3	1	...	...	...
1872	...	...	10	3	2	1	...
1880	2	11	8	4	1	...	...
1881	4	8	15	3	1	...	2
1882H	6	24	40	27	5	1	...
1885	5	20	24	34	3	...	1
1888	4	40	57	29	9	...	...

Source: Data used with permission from PCGS.

Notes: Coins with a "+" grade are included with those without (e.g., MS64+ is lumped with those in MS64). The numbers in parentheses beside the 1870 date refer to the number of dots on the obverse of the coin between the last "D" in Newfoundland and "Reg:". See Figure 5-1 for examples of both types of coins.

a collector's point of view, this means that truly uncirculated pieces will be rare. This is borne out for all of the Newfoundland coin series, but especially for the gold coins; extremely few have survived in high grade mainly because the $2 coins were the only circulating gold coins specifically minted for any North American colony in the nineteenth century in all of the region that later became the Dominion of Canada. Tables 2, 4, and 5 contain listings of the current (late 2015) surviving populations of Newfoundland $2 gold coins from the three major grading services. Although there may be examples that have lain quietly in dresser drawers, beautifully wrapped in tissue paper since they were minted, the numbers graded by the various services should comprise most of the extant high-grade population. In addition, there is likely to be some overlap between coins graded by different services. Sometimes an owner may prefer a particular service to an existing one for a given coin, so the coin is sent in to a different service and hence gets double-counted in the overall census of these coins. To avoid this, if a coin is graded by a second service, the owner should send this information, including the grading slip, to the original service so that it can be removed from the original service's population of graded coins. Unfortunately, this is not always done.

Two points are immediately obvious from Table 2. First, the last three dates in the series are by far the most often sent in for grading; presumably this results in these coins being the most generally available in higher grades. The 1882 and 1888 dates also have the largest mintages, at 25,000 each. Second, the populations fall to very small numbers with grades of MS64 or higher. If one were willing to accept only coins with a grade of MS65 or better (as some collectors are), then only five of the eight dates would be available. One variety of the 1870 date is not available with a grade higher than MS63. In general, these gold coins are extremely rare in lofty grades, again indicating that they really did circulate widely and that there was little hoarding, at least in the early years of production. This seems contrary to the scenario discussed in Chapter 8, where we will see that the Newfoundland coins were valued more highly than their nominal face values originally set out in the 1863 Act for the Regulation of the Currency. According to economic theory, this should have resulted in hoarding of the more valuable coins. Of course, it is not possible to tell from the small fraction of coins that have been graded by the various grading services whether we can account for most of the mintage. While 98,500 $2 gold coins were minted between 1865 and 1888, less than 1 percent of this number has been graded as uncirculated (MS60 or higher) by all the grading services combined. Does this mean that the most widely circulated coins are now worn, or are there secret caches of pristine pieces lying about in old Newfoundland homes?

To gain some insight into this, we can look at the surviving populations of US $2.50 gold coins. These are of similar face value but circulated in a very different environment. The United States was of course much richer, and by the 1870s had already developed a modest collector community. Hence some coins might have been put away as collector items, an unlikely scenario in Newfoundland given their enormous value compared with average salaries. Table 3 shows a selection of US $2.50 coins with similar mintages (the smallest number of $2 coins produced for Newfoundland was 2,500, in 1880; the largest was 25,000, in 1882 and 1888) and of the same era as the Newfoundland $2 coins. One should not make too much of this comparison, but it is interesting nevertheless. The coins are listed by increasing mintage for easy comparison. Clearly the survival numbers for the US coins in various grades

Table 3. US $2.50 gold circulation strike populations graded by PCGS

DATE	MINTAGE	MS61	MS62	MS63	MS64	MS65	MS66
1883	2,002	13	6	1	1	...	...
1884	2,023	7	8	7	7	2	...
1880	2,996	8	8	8	8	5	...
1868	3,625	2	6	...	1	...	...
1871	5,350	7	5	6	6	2	...
1875S	11,600	1	5	4	...	1	...
1873S	27,000	3	4	2	3	...	...

Source: Data used with permission from PCGS.

Note: An "S" after the date means that the coins were minted in San Francisco; otherwise, they were minted in Philadelphia.

Table 4. $2 gold circulation strike populations graded by Numismatic Guaranty Corporation (NGC)

DATE	MS60	MS61	MS62	MS63	MS64	MS65	MS66
1865	...	2	2	...	...	1	...
1870*	1	4	1	...	...	...	...
1872	...	1	...	...	...	...	...
1880	...	4	3	...	...	...	...
1881	1	2	5	1	...	...	...
1882H	1	25	19	10	2	1	...
1885	...	12	8	3	2	...	...
1888	1	34	34	8	1	...	...

Source: Data used with permission from NGC.

*NGC does not distinguish between two dot and three dot. The population indicated here is the combined total for both varieties.

of mint state are not enormously different from those for the Newfoundland $2 coins. There seem to be more Newfoundland coins in the lower grades of uncirculated, and somewhat more US pieces in the higher grades, but the surviving uncirculated populations in both cases are very small.

The Numismatic Guaranty Corporation is another large US company involved in grading and authenticating coins. While NGC has graded far fewer Newfoundland $2 gold coins than PCGS, the story remains the same: few high-grade coins, with the latest three dates being by far the most common (Table 4).

The final grading service we consider is the International Coin Certification Service (ICCS), a Canadian company that specializes in Canadian coins, although it also grades world coins. The same trends seen with the major US services are seen with ICCS: few high-grade coins of any date, with the last three dates in the series being the most common (Table 5).

A unique perspective (albeit of only a rather tenuous nature) on the Newfoundland economy during this era can be obtained from analyzing these tables. From the tiny size of the existing high-grade population, the coins seem to have circulated extensively. We would expect to see many more pristine examples if they had simply been stored away by wealthy families or the banks. Of note is that the mintages of the 1865, 1870, 1881, and 1885 coins are identical at 10,000 each. The early years have many fewer high-grade coins surviving than 1885 and 1888, implying that when the coins first appeared, they rapidly entered the commercial stream, but then one of two things happened: either the supply became saturated and more coins were put away, or Gresham's law (undervalued money disappears from circulation, leaving overvalued money behind) set in when the economy deteriorated and the coins were hoarded.

Table 5. $2 gold circulation strike populations graded by International Coin Certification Service (ICCS)

DATE	MS60	MS61	MS62	MS63	MS64	MS65	MS66
1865	8	...	4	3	...	...	...
1870(2)	6	...	2	1	...	...	...
1870(3)	2	...	3	3	1	...	...
1872	4	...	2	2	1	...	...
1880	6	...	3	2	...	...	...
1881	10	...	7	1	...	...	...
1882H	24	...	27	17	7	3	...
1885	23	...	19	13	1	2	...
1888	63	...	49	26	4	1	...

Source: Data used with permission from ICCS.

Note: The numbers in parentheses beside the 1870 date refer to the number of dots on the obverse of the coin between the last "D" in Newfoundland and "Reg:".

The mintage in 1882 was 25,000 pieces, and it may not have been easy for the economy to absorb such a large number. This may account for the relatively large uncirculated population of 1885 coins even with only 10,000 minted: fewer coins of this date were required for commerce so they were put away either by the banks or by individuals.

From a collector's perspective, based on these population reports, it is clear that trying to form a high-grade Newfoundland $2 gold coin collection can be a frustrating business. It is extremely difficult to find good, high-grade examples of these coins. If an exceptional coin comes along and you are interested in this series, my advice would be to purchase it if you can afford to. In early 2010, I made the mistake of not following my own suggestion. I was offered an 1865 MS65 coin – one of only two graded MS65 or higher. The coin had some copper spots and a few planchet defects on the reverse. However, the obverse, which is the most important part of the coin from an appearance and grading point of view, was quite lovely. The price seemed high at the time, although these days it seems more reasonable. I let the coin get away and have regretted it ever since. It later sold at auction for significantly more than I could have had it for. I have tried off and on to purchase the coin from the buyer, but no luck. The other 1865 high-grade coin is actually graded MS66 and is in the Perth Collection. It is definitely not for sale – so I am stuck with an MS62 example for my own collection, with almost no hope of an upgrade.

CHAPTER 6

· ·

Specimens and Patterns

SPECIMENS

The appearance of a coin and the ability of the mint to strike it properly are often not known until several examples have been struck. A particularly poignant example of this is the high-relief double eagle ($20 gold coin) struck by the United States in 1907. President Theodore Roosevelt had commissioned the highly acclaimed sculptor Augustus Saint-Gaudens to redesign the US coins and give them a more artistic and classical appearance. This was a task Saint-Gaudens never completed because of his ill health. The original design for the $20 piece was in very high relief, and it proved extremely difficult to strike the coin so that all the features in the design would be readily visible: up to eleven strikings of the planchet were required. In addition, the coin did not stack well, making it a difficult piece for banks to handle. The design had to be modified a number of times so that the intended detail could be well defined through a single striking. This work was not carried out by Saint-Gaudens himself, whose health was failing, but by the US Mint's chief engraver, Charles Barber. Eventually he achieved a design that satisfied both

the artistic intent and the practicality of having a coin that could stack and that simultaneously exhibited all the design features with a single strike of the die.

A similar process (albeit much more straightforward) was followed for the Newfoundland $2 gold coins. In 1865, the Royal Mint struck a number of "specimens" of this date with the anticipated design. These were done on highly polished planchets and were struck twice and often more slowly than circulation strike issues in order to bring out the full design. The terms "specimen" and "proof" are used almost interchangeably in Canadian numismatics, particularly for coins struck by the Royal Mint for Canada in the late nineteenth century. However, recent usage classifies them as specimens, terminology that we will adhere to here. Although it has not been possible to locate a definitive document indicating how many of these $2 gold coins were struck, the consensus seems to be that between six and ten such coins were produced that bear the date 1865. The coins served the dual purpose of enabling the designs to be checked and

Figure 6-1: The finest known 1865 specimen $2 gold coin in collectors' hands. Like the coin shown on the cover of this book, this piece has a plain edge. It was originally in the famous Norweb Collection, auctioned in 1996 by Bowers and Merena, and it sold for $7,260. The coin was obtained by the Norwebs from the New Netherlands Coin Company; it is documented in Chapter 7 as having resided earlier in the Virgil Brand Collection. It currently forms part of the Kingston Collection.

(Image: Courtesy of PCGS)

providing samples of the first Newfoundland coins for distribution to dignitaries. The Royal Mint also struck specimens of the other coin denominations in 1865 (1¢, 5¢, 10¢, and 20¢ pieces). All these specimens were manufactured with a plain edge instead of the milled edge normally found on silver and gold coins.

The specimen coins in gold, silver, and bronze dated 1865 come from the double specimen sets issued in this inaugural year of Newfoundland's coinage. The sets contained two specially struck coins of each denomination presented in a velvet-lined case. They were probably produced for dignitaries (with not more than about five such sets ever manufactured). All coins in these sets have plain edges, and the die axes are in the same direction on the obverse and reverse, unlike the

circulation strike pieces but similar to medals. With the exception of 1870, all other dates of $2 proofs have milled edges. The 1¢ pieces in these double proof sets were dated 1864. There are at least two well-documented appearances of a complete 1865 double specimen set at auction. The first was at the Caldecott Sale in 1912 (lot 368; see Chapter 7), purchased by the London coin dealer Baldwin for £7. The second appeared as lot 606 in the W.W.C. Wilson Sale, auctioned by the American coin dealer Wayte Raymond in 1925. The lot was bought by L.A. Renaud, who later became the curator of the Chateau de Ramezay Collection in Montreal. The set was described as follows: "1865 double-proof sets, gold 2 dollars, silver 5, 10, 20, pattern cent 1864. In original case arranged to show obverse and reverse, Very rare."[1] These offerings may be the same

Figure 6-2: Obverses of four different 1865 Newfoundland $2 gold coins.
Top: Two specimen examples. Note the broken stems in the two last N's in "NEWFOUNDLAND," and the large and small dots after "D" in "D : G :." The first pair of dots after "REG" is smaller than the third dot. *Bottom*: Two circulation strike examples. These same die characteristics are present only on the coin on the right. The coin does have a die crack emanating from the "G" in "REG" not seen on the specimens, but this is attributable to later die wear. The circulation strike 1865 coin on the left does not display the same die characteristics.

(Images: Courtesy of Heritage Coins, PCGS, and National Currency Collection of the Bank of Canada)

set; there is no known earlier provenance for the set offered in the Caldecott Sale.

Specimens of these gold coins are stunningly beautiful (see Figure 6-1). Queen Victoria's portrait is youthful, and a classic touch is provided by the laurel crown and the hair bun. The reverse is simple and elegant with the denomination in dollars, the date boldly presented in the centre, and the other two denominations around the periphery – an uncomplicated but wonderful design. Specimen strikings exist of every date in this gold series with the exception of 1881. Such a coin may exist but none has been reported.

Some of these specially prepared specimen coins may have been struck as presentation pieces, which is likely the case at least for those coins now residing in the Melbourne (Victoria) Museum in Australia. The 1872 and 1880 $2 pieces were presented to the government of Australia for the Sydney International Exhibition of 1879-80, and later found their way to the museum. The records of the Melbourne Museum suggest that the Royal Mint provided these two specimens to the Australian Mint for the purposes of the exhibition. The gold coins were part of complete or partially complete (in the case of 1872) specimen or proof sets. Similarly, the 1888 $2 specimen in the Melbourne Museum (from a complete Newfoundland specimen set of that year) formed part of the Melbourne Mint exhibit at the 1888 Melbourne Centennial Exhibition. Interestingly, all these three gold specimen coins in the Melbourne Museum have a milled edge, whereas all 1865 $2 specimens have a plain edge. The Deputy Master of the Royal Mint during this era was Charles Fremantle, who was known to have had a few unusual pieces like these struck off from time to time for such occasions.

Of some interest is whether all the 1865 specimens were struck from the same set of dies. They were supposedly all made for the specimen sets of that year, so we would expect that the same die was used to strike all these coins. This can be investigated through an examination of detailed die characteristics on a number of specimens. An analysis was carried out by the author on five of the coins, and there is absolutely no doubt that all were struck from the same set of dies. In all cases, the second and third "N" in the word "NEWFOUNDLAND" on the obverse have a broken stem on the left of the letter. In addition, the subtle variations in the sizes of the dots seen around the periphery of the obverse are the same on every coin examined. Some of these die characteristics are also seen on business strike 1865 coins, whereas other coins do not have them. The latter coins were clearly struck from a different obverse die. (See Figure 6-2.)

The Melbourne Museum contains other remarkable Canadian coins in its collection, provided by the Royal Mint for exhibitions in 1880 and 1888. Among these are an 1871 specimen Canada 20¢ pattern piece as well as an 1875 5¢ specimen coin with no "H." All the regular issue 1875 coins for Canada were struck at the Heaton Mint in Birmingham and bear the "H" mint mark.

Only three 1870 $2 gold specimens are known. One is in the Kingston Collection of a Canadian collector (and earlier was part of the Norweb Collection until it was auctioned in 1996) (Figure 6-3), another is in the Royal Mint Museum in Wales, and the third, obtained from the Royal Mint in 1972, is in the National Currency Collection of Canada.

Prior to the Norweb auction, the sole piece currently in private hands (now in the Kingston Collection) appeared in only a single public offering

Figure 6-3: An 1870 specimen Newfoundland $2 gold coin. Like the 1865 specimen, this coin possesses a plain edge. It last sold publicly in the Norweb Sale, where it realized $10,340. The Norwebs obtained this piece from Spink and Son's sometime in the 1940s or 1950s (see Chapter 7). It is currently in the Kingston Collection.

(Image: Courtesy of PCGS)

(as far as could be traced): in the January 1894 Spink and Son's circular. Two 1870-dated Newfoundland gold coins were offered in that circular: (1) what appears to be a circulation strike coin (listing number 11803), and (2) a specimen (proof in the Spink listing, 11803^A). The listing does not indicate whether it is plain-edge. The proof is listed as being extremely rare. The price was £6, which was incredibly high for the time. By contrast, the circulation strike 1870 coin was listed for £1 5s., and F.D.C. 50¢ coins of 1881 and 1882H were 5s. each.

There are perhaps six to ten known 1865 specimens (Professional Coin Grading Services [PCGS] has graded and encapsulated a total of eight), and probably a similar number of 1872 pieces (PCGS has encapsulated five). Several of the pieces are in private collections. The Melbourne Museum also has an 1872 example, obtained by Dr. William Howat, a local art and curio collector,

from the Sydney Mint Museum when it closed in 1926 (see Figure 6-4 for an image of an 1872 $2 gold coin in a private collection, not the one in the Melbourne Museum). The coin was transferred from the National Gallery of Victoria to the Melbourne Museum in 1976; as mentioned above, it had formed part of the mint's exhibit at the 1879-80 Sydney International Exhibition. The National Currency Museum in Ottawa does not possess an 1872 Newfoundland $2 gold specimen in its collection.

Perhaps the most interesting of all the Newfoundland specimens is the 1880 coin. Only two of these are known: one currently resides in the Kingston Collection (earlier held by the Norweb Collection) and the other in the Melbourne Museum. The latter formed part of the Melbourne Mint exhibit at the 1880 Melbourne International Exhibition, the eighth officially sanctioned World's Fair and the first one held in the Southern

Figure 6-4: A gem specimen (PCGS SP66) example of the 1872 coin with a milled edge. This date together with the 1865 and 1882H are the most commonly encountered specimens in the Newfoundland gold series (if we can say that a coin is common when it probably has a population of fewer than ten!). A similar coin sold for $11,550 in the Norweb auction in 1996. More recently, a slightly inferior coin was sold at auction for $27,025, and a private offer of $35,000 was recently made for a Specimen 65 coin. The offer was turned down.

(Image: Courtesy of PCGS)

Hemisphere. The 1880 coin was transferred from the Melbourne branch of the Royal Mint to the museum in 1976.

Of all the Newfoundland gold specimens and patterns auctioned in the Norweb Sale, the 1880 was by far the most expensive coin, selling for US$70,400, an enormous sum at the time. Given the exchange rate in 1996 between the Canadian and US dollars, this sale amounted to almost Cdn$95,000. At a paltry 2,500 coins, the 1880 coin has the smallest mintage of any of the circulation strike issues.

One reason for the interest in the two 1880 coins, other than their rarity, is that the reverse die used to strike them is not the same as the one used for the regular issue pieces. This can be seen clearly by comparing Figure 6-5 and Figure 6-6. Compare the ex-Norweb 1880 specimen shown in Figure 6-5 with the reverse on a normal business strike coin shown in Figure 6-6. Note that on the former, the last three letters ("ARS") in "DOLLARS" are set higher than the rest and that the second "8" in the date is punched over a "7." None of these features is seen on the business strike coin. These discrepancies might suggest that the die used for this specimen was the same one used for the 1870 specimen or business strikes; however, this cannot be the case because neither business strike nor specimen 1870 coins exhibit the raised letters "ARS." So this appears to be a new die, perhaps intended for the 1870 coins but not used there – or anywhere else, apparently. The misalignment of the letters appears

Figure 6-5: One of the two known 1880 specimen coins. It has a milled edge and resided in the Norweb Collection until it was sold to a Canadian collector in 1996. This coin is currently in the Kingston Collection.

(Image: Courtesy of PCGS)

to be unique to these two 1880 specimens.

No example specimen is known for the year 1881.

The 1882 Newfoundland specimen gold coins (suspected to have a population of around ten pieces but, based on auction records, probably closer to five) were struck at the Heaton Mint, as indicated by the prominent letter "H" below the date on the reverse. The finest specimen is the Specimen 66 example, shown in Figure 6-7, which apparently came from a museum in India! Again, this coin resides in the same Canadian collection where the ex-Norweb specimens are found, but it does not carry a Norweb provenance itself. Two other 1882H specimens have recently been sold at auction. One resided in the Heaton Mint Collection for many years and was on display in Birmingham. It was acquired by John J. Pittman, the famous collector

Figure 6-6: The reverse of a circulation strike 1880 Newfoundland gold coin.

(Image: Courtesy of Heritage Rare Coins)

Figure 6-7: A gem example (Specimen 66) of the 1882 specimen from the Kingston Collection.
Note the "H" (for Heaton) on the reverse.

(Image: Courtesy of PCGS)

from Rochester, New York. He obtained it from the Kissel and Victoria Collection in September 1989, at a cost of $1,210. This was probably the last major purchase that Pittman ever made. The coin later appeared in the John J. Pittman Collection, Part Three (August 1999), catalogued by David Akers. It was lot 2676 in that auction and went for $3,450. It next appeared in the Belzberg Collection (Heritage) auction in January 2003, but did not sell. In that auction it was in a PCGS holder grading SP60. An SP58 piece from the Bentley Foundation sold recently for $4,700 at a January 2014 Heritage auction.

A real prize at the Norweb auction in 1996 was the 1885 specimen Newfoundland $2 gold piece. It is, by all accounts, the finest of the Newfoundland gold specimen coins that have ever been available at auction or by private sale. A flawless gem graded Specimen 67 by PCGS, it remains together in the same collection with all the other Norweb Newfoundland $2 gold specimens. It sold for

$44,000 in the Norweb Sale and is worth many times as much today.

This 1885 specimen coin, as pointed out to me by dealer Sandy Campbell, has a peculiarity associated with it. The circulation strike 1885 coins were struck with obverse 2 – namely, a young portrait and no dot after the last "D" in "NEWFOUNDLAND" as shown in Figure 6-8. The specimen coin shown in Figure 6-9 has an obverse 3 portrait – namely, the older regal portrait plus a dot, which appeared on the 1882 and 1888 coins. So this coin is likely a mule from an 1882 or 1888 die for the obverse and an 1885 die for the reverse. Examination of the obverses of the three specimens (1882H, 1885, and 1888) indicates that the obverse of the 1885 coin is not identical to that of the 1882H piece. A number of subtle diagnostics (shapes of the dots, for example) are more reminiscent of the 1888 obverse, which suggests that these two were possibly struck from the same die. This may be further evidence that Charles Fremantle used dies that were available at

Figure 6-8: An 1885 business strike. Note the youthful portrait and the lack of a dot after "NEWFOUNDLAND."

(Image: Courtesy of PCGS)

Figure 6-9: The fantastic 1885 specimen Newfoundland $2 gold coin. It currently resides in the Kingston Collection. Note the differences between the obverse of this coin and the business strike in Figure 6-8.

(Image: Courtesy of PCGS)

Figure 6-10: The 1888 specimen Newfoundland $2 gold coin in the National Currency Collection of the Bank of Canada. It has a milled edge and is an absolutely superb coin, probably originally from the Royal Mint Collection in the United Kingdom.

(Image: Courtesy of the National Currency Collection, Currency Museum, Bank of Canada)

the mint to strike coins for special purposes.

The final date in the Newfoundland gold series is 1888 (but see the discussion in Chapter 4 concerning an unlikely coin dated 1890). Two 1888 specimens have been documented: one in the National Currency Collection of the Bank of Canada in Ottawa (Figure 6-10), and one in the Melbourne Museum (Figure 6-11). The National Currency Collection obtained its piece from the Royal Mint in 1970 (as revealed by collection chief curator Paul Berry in June 2015). No record exists of any 1888 specimen being sold at auction or by private sale. In personal conversations, the owner of the Kingston Collection revealed that he had attempted to complete his collection by purchasing the 1888 specimen in the National Currency Collection (only seven specimen dates are known and this was the only one the Kingston Collection lacked). In the end, his efforts proved fruitless. The Bank of Canada treasures its rarities very highly and has no

inclination to part with any of them – at any cost.

It is not obvious from the photographs in Figure 6-11 that the Australian coin is indeed a specimen. The overall appearance of this coin, judging from the images only, is very different from that of the Ottawa coin. The rim on the Ottawa piece is high and broad, and the profile of the lettering is flat across the top, whereas the rim on the Australian piece has no flatness to it and the lettering is rounded. There are also curious differences in the dies for the reverses used to strike the two specimen 1888 coins, as illustrated in the comparison in Figure 6-12.

Note the distinctive die breaks on the Melbourne coin beginning at the "D" in "hundred" at the top of the coin and progressing around to the two dots at the right edge. Imperfections of this sort result from fatigue in the die as it begins to deteriorate after numerous strikings. These are entirely absent from the Ottawa coin but clearly present on the business strike (although more prominent on the Melbourne

Figure 6-11: The 1888 specimen Newfoundland $2 gold coin in the Melbourne Museum, Australia.

(Image: Courtesy of Museums Victoria, Australia)

Figure 6-12: Comparison between reverses of a normal business strike 1888 coin (left), the Melbourne Newfoundland $2 gold coin (middle), and the Ottawa specimen (right).

coin). Note also that the placement of the letters "AR" blend together on the Melbourne piece and the business strike but are well separated on the Ottawa coin. Also, the last 8 in the date is closer to the second 8 in the Melbourne and business strike coins shown in Figure 6-12. All of these diagnostics indicate beyond a doubt that two separate reverse dies were used in striking the various 1888 coins – the Melbourne coin and this particular business strike from one reverse die and the Ottawa specimen from a different die.

What does a larger sample of business strike 1888 coins reveal? From a survey I conducted of about one hundred 1888 Newfoundland $2 coins from the archives of a major auction house, it is clear that more than half the business strike coins have this die break. However, all the coins examined have the "AR" touching – no examples were found with the "AR" well separated, as on the Ottawa specimen. The survey also found no coins that had the last "8" widely separated from the second to last "8" in the date. This suggests that a unique die was used to strike the Ottawa specimen reverse and that either (1) a single die was used for the business strikes, which began degrading about halfway through the act of striking the coins, or (2) two or more dies were used for such strikes, one of which shattered rather early. The Melbourne coin and an important fraction of the circulation strikes were definitely made from the same die. It would have been odd to strike the Melbourne coin in the middle of the run for commercial pieces, but since we know that this coin was probably specially struck by the mint for the 1888 Melbourne International Centennial Exhibition, it gives credence to the idea that Fremantle used dies that were lying around to strike special coins for events of this sort.

My suspicions regarding the specimen nature of the Melbourne 1888 coin caused me to inquire at the museum whether they were convinced of the proof status of the coin. Dr. Richard Gillespie, the head of the Humanities Department at the museum, passed on my queries to John Sharples, the curator emeritus of numismatics, who replied as follows:

Table 6. Census of specimen Newfoundland $2 gold coins

DATE	NUMBER KNOWN	LOCATIONS
1865	~10	Ottawa; Priv
1870	3	Kingston; Ottawa; RMM
1872	~10	Mel; Priv
1880	2	Kingston; Mel
1881	0	
1882H	~5	Kingston; Priv
1885	1	Kingston
1888	2	Mel; Ottawa

Note: Ottawa = National Currency Collection of the Bank of Canada; Mel = Melbourne Museum, Australia; RMM = Royal Mint Museum; Kingston = Kingston Collection; Priv = Private collections, various locations.

I have examined the 1888 Newfoundland $2 proof many times and am happy it is a proof. It was struck on request for the 1888 Melbourne Exhibition by the Royal Mint. It has been seen by many collectors including some from Canada and the USA; none have suggested it is not a proof. At that time I believe the Royal Mint would do special jobs for special events; from memory it came with proof Newfoundland silver of the same date. I do not know where the Ottawa Mint coin came from.

On a recent trip to Brisbane, Australia, I took a day trip to Melbourne to inspect the coin as well as the museum's two other specimens. The museum archivist, Nick Crotty, arranged for me to view the museum's Newfoundland gold holdings. I carefully inspected all the Newfoundland gold coins in my glove-covered hand, and it was possible to verify that the museum's 1888 piece is, without a doubt, a specially struck coin, although the Melbourne 1888 $2 gold coin clearly differs from the Ottawa specimen in both die and striking characteristics. The most likely explanation is that Fremantle used an 1888 die that was available to him, specially polished and prepared a planchet for the Melbourne Exhibition coin, and had it struck off. We cannot call this coin a specimen in the sense that the Ottawa coin is a specimen – its correct designation is a "specially struck coin," containing none of the diagnostics usually encountered on a true Royal Mint specimen.

Table 6 provides a summary of the number and locations of the various dates struck as specimens in the Newfoundland $2 gold series. This listing is probably not complete.

PATTERNS

As is often the case, the designers of a new issue of coins will provide a number of designs; the mint

Figure 6-13: Portrait of Leonard Wyon based on a photograph likely taken just before his death in 1891.

(Image: National Portrait Gallery, UK)

will then select a few, have them engraved, and strike off a small quantity of each to test the design. These are called pattern coins and are highly prized by collectors as they represent designs often quite different from the one adopted. Sometimes they are even struck in unexpected metals, different from that of the coins eventually struck for circulation. They will generally have mintages of only a few pieces. With regard to the Newfoundland $2 gold coins, these mintages may be as small as a single piece, and probably not more than two or three.

There are three different patterns associated with the first issue of these coins: a possibly unique piece dated 1864 and two other designs dated 1865. There is also a further pattern dated 1870. An early listing of patterns can be found in R.W. McLachlan's 1886 treatise on Canadian numismatics, detailed later in

Figure 6-14: This is the first Newfoundland $2 gold (copper!) coin; it is in the National Currency Collection of the Bank of Canada. It may be unique. The author was able to view this coin in the late 1970s on a visit to the Currency Museum in Ottawa.

(Image: Courtesy of the National Currency Collection, Bank of Canada)

this chapter.[2] Leonard Charles Wyon, the eldest son of the previous chief engraver of the Royal Mint, William Wyon, engraved the Newfoundland $2 gold patterns and the regular issue gold coins (Figure 6-13). Wyon was actually born on the grounds of the Royal Mint in 1826, so from his first breath he was completely immersed in the mint and its activities. Although it has been widely reported that Leonard Wyon also designed the Newfoundland coins, documentation (presented below) suggests that it was in fact Horace Morehen who, at the very least, provided early sketches from which Wyon worked.

The first pattern executed (Bowman 32,[3] NF-5[4]) is dated 1864 and was struck only as a copper specimen (Figure 6-14). The obverse is the adopted design, but the reverse is similar to that of the 10¢ pieces of New Brunswick, except that the denomination "TWO DOLLARS" has been inserted instead of "10 CENTS." It is possible

that Wyon struck this in his own workshop rather than at the Royal Mint, because similar copper trial pieces later surfaced from Wyon's private collection.[5] Only a single piece of this pattern has been recorded, and it is in the National Currency Collection of the Bank of Canada in Ottawa, acquired by the bank from John J. Ford Jr. in 1973. The curator of this collection, Paul S. Berry, commented that he was not aware of the existence of any other examples.

The early pedigree of this coin has been documented by Fred Bowman.[6] The coin first appeared in the Montagu Sale of 1892 and later in the Murdoch (1903) and Caldecott (1912) auctions, discussed in Chapter 7. An almost complete provenance is provided in Appendix 4. The coin currently resides in the National Currency Collection of the Bank of Canada. Bowman states that there is one specimen in the British Museum. I believe that this is not correct, at least not today.

Figure 6-15: An example of McLachlan DXXXIII, Bowman 33, NF-14 in the National Currency Collection of the Bank of Canada. This coin was made available to the author for viewing by Hillel Kaslove, curator of the collection in the late 1970s.

(Image: Courtesy of the National Currency Collection, Bank of Canada Museum)

The coin was certainly not in a catalogue of the British Museum's Newfoundland collection made in 1978, and a current listing of the museum's holdings provided by Curator of Modern Coins Thomas Hockenhull did not include this piece.[7] The compilation of Canadian and Newfoundland coins in the British Museum, carried out in 1959 by H.W.A. Linecar, does not mention this coin either.[8]

There are two patterns dated 1865. Both were struck in the metal of intent for the circulation pieces – namely, gold – which suggests that these pieces were struck at the Royal Mint. The one most like the final release is Bowman 33 (NF-14), which has the final adopted obverse. However, the date and denominations on the reverse, although similar to that finally adopted for the circulation strikes, are in block type (see Figure 6-15), whereas the coins later placed into circulation have more stylized characters (called serif style). Two of these are known. Again, one

is in the National Currency Collection of the Bank of Canada and the other is in the British Museum; the latter was catalogued in 1977.[9] These two coins are specially struck specimens with mirror fields.

Note that on the obverse of the piece from the collection in Ottawa there are two distinct die breaks: one beginning where the Queen's hair and cheek meet, extending slightly downward from her ear and progressing towards her lips; and the other below the ear at the bottom of her hair, extending downward towards the letter "F" in "NEWFOUNDLAND" (Figure 6-15). In addition, the last "N" in "NEWFOUNDLAND" has a crack that progresses downward to the rim of the coin.

Identical characteristics are also evident on the British Museum coin shown in Figure 6-16. This coin exhibits somewhat more die wear than the Canadian coin, as more prominent cracking can be observed in the Queen's hair between her eye and

Figure 6-16: Bowman 33, NF-14, in the British Museum.
Note the identical die breaks on this and the Ottawa coin.

(Image: Courtesy of the Trustees of the British Museum)

the laurel garland. The overall appearance of the coin is also generally "mushier," with all the details much less well defined than the Canadian piece.

These die breaks have not been observed on any circulation strike 1865 pieces (perhaps twenty to thirty examined in detail), and neither do they appear on any of the specimens. Thus, the die used for this pattern appears to be from one not used for circulation strike coins, in contrast to the Melbourne 1888 specimen, whose reverse die was clearly used to strike circulation pieces as well.

In the pattern piece shown in Figure 6-17 (McLachlan DXXXIV, Bowman 34,[10] Charlton NF-15), the portrait of Queen Victoria is quite small, as it appears on the 5¢ coins of Newfoundland (or earlier on the 1858 5¢ coins of the Province of Canada or the 1862 and 1864 5¢ coins of New Brunswick), and resides within a beaded circle surrounded by the legend "Victoria D: G: Reg: Newfoundland." Bowman has reported

that the only example he was aware of was a gold specimen that was offered in Spink's Circular of May 1910, No. 76006.[11] The description in the circular was as follows:

Newfoundland Two Dollars. 1865. Small bust within a beaded circle, legends as before (VICTORIA D: G : REG:). The value and date in block letters. An excessively rare pattern. Brilliant F.D.C. [F.D.C. = Fleur de Coin, literally "with the bloom of the die," a coin that appears absolutely new, in perfect mint state]

Spink listed the coin for sale at £10, an enormous price at the time, on page 12,084 of its circular. Other items offered in the same circular included:

- 1882 and 1888 Newfoundland $2 gold coins F.D.C. at 12s. each (face value was 8s. 4d.)
- India 1893 two Annas in gold F.D.C. for 10s.
- Ceylon 1891 half cents F.D.C struck in gold,

Figure 6-17: The most unusual and interesting pattern in the Newfoundland gold series, Bowman 34.

(Image: Courtesy of PCGS)

silver, and copper (the set of three coins for £2 10s.)

- Straits Settlements 1¢ proof in gold F.D.C. for £4 10s.
- Hong Kong dollars, Britannia standing, proof F.D.C. in gold, 1896, 1897, 1901, £7 each
- Canada 1908C sovereign F.D.C. £2 10s.
- Australia 1852 Adelaide sovereign, £1 7s.
- Australia various dates of proof sovereigns 1870-94 F.D.C. averaging about £1 10s.

Oh, to have been a collector in London in those days!

Enquiry with Spink as to the origin and buyer of the pattern coin elicited the response that they protect their clients so no such information could be made available. This may be company policy but other causes were at work here. Spink, at their location at the corner of King Street and Duke Street in St. James (where they had moved in 1927), suffered from an incendiary bomb strike during the Second World War that burned through the building and destroyed all perishables including most of their library and all their files and records. Hence, no pre-World War II records of Spink that were located on their premises, survive.

William Hocking (Figure 6-18) did not include the 1865 Bowman 34 coin in his 1906 listing of the coins in the Royal Mint Museum.[12] It is likely that the coin listed by Spink eventually found its way into the collection of King Farouk of Egypt. When Farouk was deposed in 1952, the government of Egypt seized his massive coin collection and put it up for auction in 1954 in the famous "Palace Collections of Egypt." It is interesting that Farouk's name does not appear anywhere in the auction catalogue, which was prepared by Sotheby and Company in London. In that auction, Bowman 34 was sold as lot 900 on February 27, 1954, and was purchased by Baldwin's for the account of Emery May Norweb.

The coin realized EGP£115, roughly equivalent

to £118 or about US$332. This means that between 1954 and 2014 (when it sold at auction for US$103,000) the coin increased in value by 307 times, for an average rate of return of 9.8 percent – not a bad investment. This rate of return is similar, however, to that from Standard and Poor's 500 index of the New York Stock Exchange, which was 10.7 percent per year over the same period. The Toronto Stock Exchange started an index in 1957, and in the 58 years since then has averaged 9.2 percent per year. Bonds had an average rate of increase of 6.4 percent during this period, while inflation averaged 3.7 percent. So from an investment point of view, the Norwebs could just as well have put their $332 in the stock market – but, oh, what a difference in pleasure coefficient!

While the Norwebs did very well on this Farouk purchase, it was nothing compared with some of John Pittman's achievements from the same sale. As detailed in David Ganz's book *Rare Coin Investing: An Affordable Way to Build Your Portfolio*, a single four-coin lot purchased at the sale and consisting of US$10 gold coins cost Pittman $590 in total.[13] When his collection was sold by David Akers in 1999, his cost was returned almost twelve-hundred-fold when they sold for a total of just under $700,000. Pittman had appreciated that the Farouk sale was an incredible buying opportunity and had taken out a second mortgage on his home, which was not repaid until six years later. Clearly this was an extremely wise financial decision.

After the Farouk sale, the Newfoundland pattern next appeared in the Norweb auction in 1996, where it realized $39,600 in a sale to Dr. John Temple, a well-known collector of Canadian patterns who hailed from Franklin, Michigan. Temple later sold it into the Kingston Collection, where it was held for only six months. In time, it was brokered to

Figure 6-18: William John Hocking, the first curator of the Royal Mint coin collection. In 1906 and 1910, he published his important book *Catalogue of the Coins, Tokens, Medals, Dies, and Seals in the Museum of the Royal Mint*. According to Chris Barker, one of the assistant curators at the museum, a complete inventory was carried out at the time the books were published.

(Image: Royal Mint Museum)

the owner of the Prager Collection of Canadian Specimen Coins. Eventually, the coin was auctioned in April 2014 at the Chicago International Coin Fair, where it realized $102,812.50, a record price for any Newfoundland coin.

The known whereabouts of this coin are patchy, particularly for the first seventy-five years of its existence, but its locations are known for the most recent six or seven decades. It is quite possible that a coin of this stature might have resided in the Virgil Brand Collection at some time between 1910 and 1940, but, as discussed in Chapter 7, there is no evidence that Brand ever owned this coin.

As early as thirty years ago, I had an interest in Bowman 34. Sometime in the late 1970s, I wrote the prominent American coin dealer Abe Kosoff, who had dealt with the Norwebs and was their friend, and inquired whether the Norwebs were ever likely to sell the coin. I was even so bold as to ask Kosoff to act as my agent in trying to acquire it. He politely informed me that he would never presume to ask them about this. However, he did provide Mrs. Norweb's home address and I sent her a note about the coin. She very graciously acknowledged that, yes, indeed, the coin was in her collection and that she expected it would go to her children as part of her estate. Instead, the coin turned up in 1996 in the auction catalogue of the Norweb Collection of Canadian Coins,[14] which noted that a piece also resided in the British Museum. However, a 1978 Canadian Numismatic Association article on Canadian coins in the British Museum stated that the museum possessed an example of Bowman 33;[15] if the museum did own an example of Bowman 34, it was not together with the other coins from Canada and Newfoundland at that time. When I inquired about this in 2014, the museum responded that it did not possess Bowman 34. The most reasonable conclusion seems to be that the entry in the Norweb catalogue is incorrect – that the cataloguer probably confused Bowman 33 with Bowman 34. The National

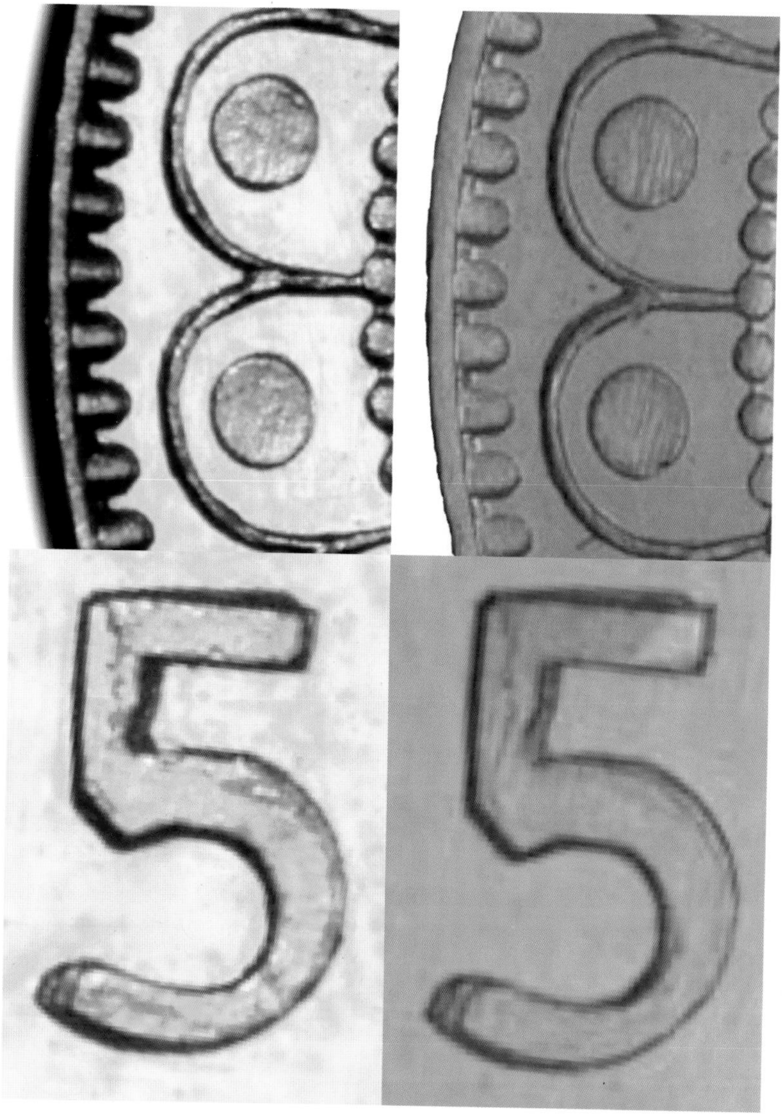

Figure 6-19: On the left are the beads and number 5 in the date from Bowman 34. On the right are the same enlargements from Bowman 33 in the National Currency Collection of the Bank of Canada. Note in particular the striations in the beads on the two coins as well as the lines at the bottom end of the "5."

Currency Collection of the Bank of Canada does not possess an example of Bowman 34, which may be unique.

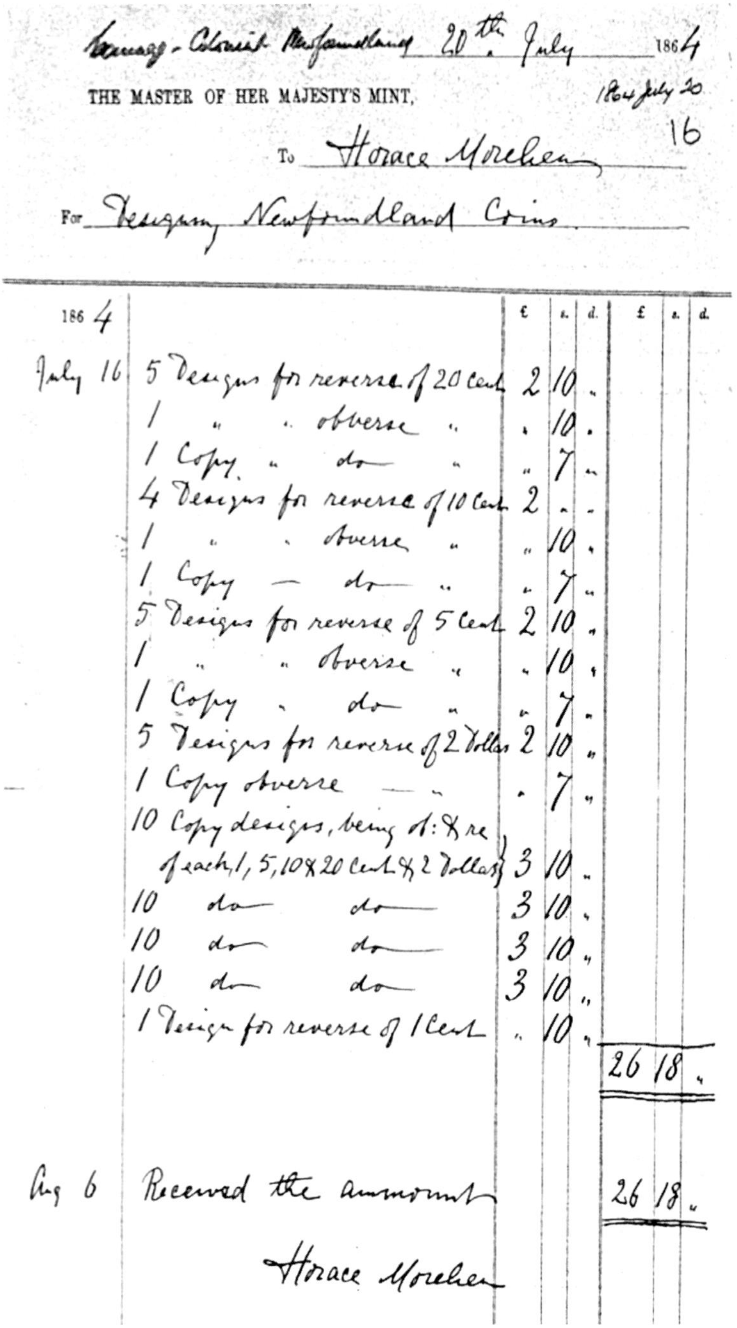

Coinage - Colonial Newfoundland 20th July 1864

THE MASTER OF HER MAJESTY'S MINT, 1864 July 20

16

To Horace Morehen

For Designing Newfoundland Coins

1864		£	s.	d.	£	s.	d.
July 16	5 Designs for reverse of 20 Cent	2	10	"			
	1 " " obverse "	.	10	.			
	1 Copy " do "	"	7	"			
	4 Designs for reverse of 10 Cent	2	-	-			
	1 " " obverse "	"	10	.			
	1 Copy — do "	"	7	"			
	5 Designs for reverse of 5 Cent	2	10	"			
	1 " " obverse "	"	10	"			
	1 Copy " do "	"	7	"			
	5 Designs for reverse of 2 Dollars	2	10	"			
	1 Copy obverse — "	.	7	"			
	10 Copy designs, being ob: & re of each, 1, 5, 10 & 20 Cent & 2 Dollars	3	10	"			
	10 do do	3	10	"			
	10 do do	3	10	"			
	10 do do	3	10	"			
	1 Design for reverse of 1 Cent	"	10	"			
					26	18	"
Aug 6	Received the amount				26	18	"

Horace Morehen

Figure 6-20: An invoice from Horace Morehen to the Master of the Royal Mint for designs executed for various Newfoundland coins, including the $2 gold pieces.

(Image: UK National Archives, MINT 13/75, page 16)

According to William Hocking, the Royal Mint had in its possession a matrix (incuse, negative impression of the coin), punch (raised detail on the coin so that, for example, the date could not be changed except by grinding the metal away), and die (incuse, made from the punch and used for striking the coins) for each of the patterns mentioned above.[16] Aside from regular items used to strike circulation coins, the listing includes a matrix, punch, and die for the obverse of Bowman 34, a similar set for the reverse (which is identical to the reverse of Bowman 33), and a set that was used to strike the reverse of the 1864 copper $2 pattern. At this point, we might ask whether there is evidence that the reverses of Bowman 33 and 34 were struck from the same die. Indeed, it does appear that the two coins have some striking similarities. This can be seen particularly well on the two pellets to the left of the "D" in "DOLLARS" (and on the bottom end of the "5" in the date), where vertical striations are observed on both pieces (Figure 6-19). Since few pieces were struck from this reverse die, it is not surprising that it was used for both patterns.

An interesting document related to the Bowman 34 pattern surfaced in a search through the UK National Archives concerning the Royal Mint's dealings with Newfoundland. Although it is generally believed that Leonard Charles Wyon designed and engraved the Newfoundland coins, evidence seems to suggest that most, if not all, of the coins were actually first sketched by Horace Morehen. Wyon engraved them, but it is likely that Morehen produced at least rough designs. The Royal Mint Archives has documents, one of which is reproduced in Figure 6-20, with invoices from Morehen for payment for these designs.

The invoice to the Master of the Royal Mint shown in Figure 6-20 is dated July 20, 1864, and is for £26 18s. for the design of various Newfoundland coins, including the $2 pieces. The invoice was paid on August 6, 1864. Morehen lists five reverses designed for the gold coin, whereas only two distinct varieties are known: the adopted one and the one with block type (we exclude the bronze 1864 piece here). What were the other three like? No documents or sketches illustrating these other types have surfaced.

A later invoice, initially dated January 10, 1865, and covering the period up to January 26, 1865, lists further work by Morehen, including a copy design of the obverse and reverse of the $2 coin. Apparently, Morehen was quite busy working on the new coins for Newfoundland as late as early 1865. This is well after the Newfoundland government had actually expected to receive the coins (according to a letter from Nicholas Stabb, member of the Newfoundland legislature, to Master of the Mint Thomas Graham, dated November 1864).

An associated document in the archives (also labelled as MINT13/75 by the archivist) contains sketches of both obverses and reverses of the initial Newfoundland coins: 1¢, 5¢, 10¢, 20¢, and $2 coins – with no 50¢ pieces in the original cohort.

Presumably these designs are from Morehen as they appear in the archives together with his invoices. It should be noted, however, that in his book The Wyons, Leonard Forrer, at the end of a listing of all the coins struck for Newfoundland, states: "Obverse and reverse by Leonard Charles Wyon from his own design."[17] These designs, shown in Figure 6-21, all carry the date 1864. What is most interesting about these sketches by Morehen is that the silver and bronze pieces all exhibit more or less their final adopted designs (except for the date and "VICTORIA QUEEN" on the obverse above the portrait instead of "VICTORIA D: G: REG:"), but the $2 coin is very similar to Bowman 34 except, again, that the sketch has "VICTORIA QUEEN" instead of "VICTORIA D: G: REG:" and it carries the date 1864. Figure 6-22 shows a grouping of real coins struck for Newfoundland that mimic Morehen's sketches.

What is the implication here? Was something like Bowman 34 the original choice for the design of the $2 gold coin only to be altered at a later date? No document has surfaced to shed light on this. Was the design rejected because the portrait was deemed too small (but note that it is no smaller than the one on the 5¢ piece)? Or was the eventual choice of design driven simply by expediency – reducing the cost of preparing new dies by reusing those that were already available for the 10¢ pieces? Since all the major varieties present on the Newfoundland 10¢ coins are also present on the $2 gold coins, this is likely to be the correct explanation. In any case, these are interesting subjects for further research. No matter what the eventual answer turns out to be, it increases the importance of the Bowman 34 pattern gold coin.

A final Newfoundland gold pattern is Bowman 35 (McLachlan DXXXV, NF-17), whose obverse is

Figure 6-21: A set of sketches, presumably executed by Horace Morehen, of designs for the original issue of Newfoundland coins. Note that they are all dated 1864.

(Image: UK National Archives)

Figure 6-22: A set of coins mimicking Morehen's sketches for the first issue of Newfoundland coinage. The bronze cent is dated 1864 (a pattern specimen not issued for circulation) and the $2 gold piece is the coin as it appeared in the sketches (but dated 1865). The silver coins are all dated 1865. The sketches all have "VICTORIA QUEEN" on the obverse, while those eventually struck have "VICTORIA D: G: REG:".

(Images: Courtesy of Heritage Coins and PCGS)

Figure 6-23: Bowman 35, milled edge. The coin resides in the Royal Mint Museum in Wales and may be unique. Note the difference between this coin and Bowman 34, discussed earlier. While the obverses are the same, the reverse of this piece is identical to the business strike coins and does not have the block lettering seen on Bowman 34.

(Image: Royal Mint Museum, UK)

identical to Bowman 34 but whose reverse carries the date 1870. The style on the reverse has the adopted design, but the lettering is not in block type. Rowe and colleagues illustrate this coin in their excellent book The Currency and Medals of Newfoundland, as does Haxby in *Guide Book of Canadian Coins*, but the photograph in the former is likely a mule from the obverse of NF-15 (Bowman 34) and the reverse of an 1870 specimen.[18] This suspicion arises from the fact that the obverse images are clearly of the same coin! Both the 1865 and 1870 obverse images have a small dot just above where the chin turns down to Queen Victoria's neck, clearly implying that the obverse images are of the same object. Rowe and colleagues do state that the 1870 coin may be an unofficial concoction or a mint error, but they do not provide a location for this coin.

And then Chris Barker, assistant curator at the Royal Mint Museum at Llantrisant in Wales, provided me with a complete listing of all the museum's Newfoundland $2 gold holdings.[19]

- Two-dollar 1865 – This coin not listed in Hocking.
- Two-dollar 1870 – This coin not listed in Hocking. Plain edge proof is indicated instead.
- Two-dollar 1870 – Obverse bust in beaded circle.
- Two-dollar 1872 – This coin not listed in Hocking.
- Two-dollar 1880.
- Two-dollar 1881 – This coin not listed in Hocking.
- Two-dollar 1882 – This coin not listed in Hocking.

- Two-dollar 1885.
- Two-dollar 1888 ´ 3 pieces – Only a single piece listed in Hocking.
- Two-dollar model obverse.
- Two-dollar 1888 model reverse.

The two-dollar 1870 – obverse bust in beaded circle! – is Bowman 35! Chris Barker kindly provided a photograph of this coin, which is reproduced in Figure 6-23. Thus, this coin, like the 1864 piece in copper and Bowman 34, may be unique.

There are a total of four known specially struck $2 gold coins for 1870; three specimens and one pattern. The pattern is Bowman 35, which has a milled edge, unlike the 1870 specimens. One of the specimens is in a private collection in Canada, another in the National Currency Collection in Ottawa, and a third in the Royal Mint Collection of the United Kingdom. It is of interest to know whether the reverses of the specimen coins and the pattern come from the same die. An obvious die characteristic on three of the coins (a small die crack proceeding to the left of the "A" in "DOLLARS" on the reverse) indicates that, indeed, they do come from a single die. This is shown in Figure 6-24 with an enlargement of this small section of each of the coins. Of similar interest is the question of whether normal business strike coins exhibit the same characteristic. Examination of about twenty 1870 coins on the auction website of a major dealer found no similar die crack – and it did not matter whether the coin was the two- or three-dot variety. Hence, the specimens and pattern appear to have been struck from the same, unique die, unless of course they were produced after the circulation pieces were made and die deterioration occurred late in the run of normal production.

We might also ask whether the obverses of Bowman 34 and 35 are identical – that is, were they struck from the same die? It would be quite surprising if they were not, since perhaps as few as two coins were struck with this design, and it is difficult to imagine engraving separate dies for each coin. Additionally, Hocking indicates that only a single die for this design exists in the Royal Mint Museum. A close examination of these two coins does not reveal any obvious differences, except perhaps for the crossbar in the "A" in "VICTORIA." In the Royal Mint example, the "A" has the appearance of an inverted "V" with a clumsy crossbar added. The other coin does not possess as crude a crossbar. Of more significance, however, is the overall appearance of Queen Victoria. The portrait on the Royal Mint Museum coin appears more mature; the detailing around the lips looks somewhat different on the two coins, and the appearance of the cheek is puffier on the recently auctioned 1865 piece (Bowman 34). This may be due simply to the fact that we are examining images instead of the actual coins, but there may be some subtle variations between the two portraits.

In his listing of Newfoundland coins, R.W. McLachlan includes a number of gold patterns, one of which is somewhat mysterious.[20] He first describes Bowman 32 (DXXXII):

Rev. two hundred cents or one hundred pence. 2 | dollars | 1865 within a dotted circle, a small ornament on either side. Gold. Size 18m. R6. This is a very rare Pattern. The only specimen I have seen is in the collection of the British Museum. Another pattern of the same date is reported to have been struck but I have not been able to locate a specimen.[21]

This description seems to be that of a regular

Figure 6-24

Top: A small section of the 1870 specimen originally from the Norweb Collection.
Middle: Specimen from the National Currency Collection of the Bank of Canada.
Bottom: Bowman 35 from the Royal Mint Museum (UK).

currency strike 1865 gold coin. Unfortunately, McLachlan does not provide any sketches or mention anything about the obverse of the coin. Perhaps he is simply describing a specimen coin of the date, and not a pattern. He then lists what is clearly Bowman 33 (DXXXIII): "Rev. As the last but the letters in dollars and the figures in the date are larger. Gold. Size 18m."[22] Because this clearly seems to be Bowman 33, which has a normal (currency strike) obverse, it makes Bowman 32 (DXXXII) all the more likely to be just a specimen piece. The double specimen sets for 1865, from which the gold specimens of that date presumably emanated, were not so rare (with about five sets supposedly made); a numismatist of McLachlan's stature would almost certainly have seen one, which makes the entry for DXXXII even more curious.

McLachlan goes on to describe Bowman 34 (DXXXIV):

Obv. VICTORIA D: G: REG: NEWFOUNDLAND Two fancy ornaments, one on either side, consisting of three semicircles joined with a dot in the centre of each, separating Newfoundland from the former part of the legend. Coroneted head of Victoria to the left, within an inner circle.[23]

The last pattern he lists is Bowman 35:

Rev. Same as last but dated 1870. Size 18m. R6. This pattern is not in the hands of any collector, and there is only one specimen in the Mint collection, so that it may be classed as unique.[24]

His assertion that this piece is in the Royal Mint

Table 7. Census of Newfoundland $2 gold coin patterns

DATE	PATTERN	NUMBER KNOWN	LOCATIONS
1864 (copper)	Bowman 31	1	Ottawa
1865	Bowman 33	2	Ottawa; BM
1865	Bowman 34	1	Private
1870	Bowman 35	1	RMM

Note: Ottawa = National Currency Collection of the Bank of Canada; BM = British Museum (London); Private = private Canadian collection; RMM = Royal Mint Museum, Wales.

Collection has now been verified. However, he does not mention that the reverse of the 1870 coin is in normal type style, and not block lettering as in Bowman 34.

The surviving and verified Newfoundland gold patterns are among the rarest and most desirable of all the coins in the Canadian series. They are generally unobtainable: due to their minuscule mintages, they appear extremely infrequently at auction or private sale.

In his article "Canada's Ten Rarest Coins" in the *Canadian Numismatic Journal*, Bowman includes those with only one example known: the Newfoundland 1865 $2 coin (Bowman 34) and the Newfoundland 1870 $2 coin (Bowman 35).[25] He is probably correct that both Bowman 34 and 35 are unique. Among the coins in his category with only two known, he includes the pattern 1864 $2 copper coin from Newfoundland, asserting that one specimen is in the British Museum. There is no current record of this coin in the museum, and it is also most likely unique. In the same issue of the *Canadian Numismatic Journal*, John McKay-Clements provided his own listing of Canada's ten rarest coins.[26] He does not include any of the Newfoundland pattern $2 gold coins.

Table 7 lists all the patterns and their locations known to the author as of mid-2015. Although every effort has been made to search out the locations and verify the existence of these pattern coins, this compendium may be incomplete. At the 2014 Royal Canadian Numismatic Convention in Mississauga, Ontario, I came across the Canadian Numismatic Association Convention's sale catalogue for the 1965 sale in Montreal.[27] The auction had some remarkable proofs and patterns in it, and lot 1806 (page 63 in the catalogue) was described as "two Dollar Gold 1865 pattern unmilled proof (Ex-Ferguson)."[28] The coin was estimated at $1,250. It was almost certainly misdescribed (most likely it was a specimen coin), but this shows how relying solely on catalogue descriptions can lead to errors in coin censuses. Apparently, the coin was not sold. The most expensive lot was a Canadian 1870 unmilled pattern and proof set in the original case, also ex-Ferguson, which realized $9,100.

On a visit to the National Currency Collection in Ottawa in the late 1970s, I spent an hour or so with one of the curators, Hillel Kaslove. He was most generous with his time and displayed the treasures of the collection's Newfoundland $2 coins: the 1864 copper pattern coin, the 1865 plain edge, the

1870 (also plain edge), and the absolutely fantastic 1888 milled edge. Notes from the visit suggest that Kaslove stated that the National Currency Collection had obtained some of its coins in an exchange with the Royal Mint in 1970. This is more or less consistent with an article on the history of the National Currency Collection by Graham Esler published in the Canadian Numismatic Journal in 2004.[29] Esler points out that in 1970 the nascent National Currency Collection became aware that the Royal Mint Collection contained a few duplicates of the coins that the mint had struck for Canada and Newfoundland. The mint was apparently prepared to make these duplicates available to the Canadian collection. On May 25, 1970, the available coins were presented by the British High Commissioner to Canada to the Canadian minister of finance, who passed them on to the collection. Only eighteen coins were included in this gift – twelve in copper, four in silver, and two in gold – and most were in specimen condition, with a few patterns among the lot. The two gold coins had to be from Newfoundland as these were the only gold pieces struck by the Royal Mint for what is now Canada. The Canadian sovereigns and the $5 and $10 pieces were all struck in Ottawa. This suggests that the gold coins in the gift, if they were specimens, were the 1870 and 1888 specimens, which is consistent with Paul Berry's information that these two coins were obtained from the Royal Mint in 1972 and 1970, respectively. The other specimens and proofs in the National Currency Collection (1864 copper, 1865 pattern and specimen) were all acquired by the bank from John J. Ford Jr. in 1973.

CHAPTER 7

· ·

Great Auctions and Collections of Newfoundland Gold Coins

Many numismatists are interested in the record of ownership, usually referred to as provenance, of coins in their collection, particularly those that are rare, expensive, or both. Knowing the provenance adds value, history, and general interest to any collectible. Additionally, numismatic tourism is not such a wild fantasy these days. Potentially satisfying both these groups, the collector or historian interested in the gold coinage of Newfoundland would likely appreciate a road map of the museums housing significant collections of this series, or auctions where key coins have appeared. An accounting of major auctions that have featured significant Newfoundland gold pieces should also be of interest, particularly for establishing provenances. To some extent, this repeats aspects covered in previous chapters, but here it is more systematic and comprehensive. There are a few surprises – for example, two of the scarcest Newfoundland $2 gold coins are located in Australia, of all places. The fascinating story of how this came to be is told later in this chapter, and it is an intriguing tale indeed. In addition to museums, there is also a tabulation

of the holdings of a few private collections, done with the permission of the current owners. Of course, the private collections are generally not available for viewing, but they will give the reader a sense of which coins might someday come on the market. Included here are collections that were sold many years ago, as these provide potential early provenances of scarce and rare issues. For these collections, to the extent possible, the listings include the current locations of the coins. The listings in this chapter are alphabetical, and private and museum holdings will be interspersed. One should be under no illusion that this compilation is complete in any sense. It is largely a sample of collections known to the author and auctions that provided provenances for famous pieces.

ASHMOLEAN MUSEUM, OXFORD

The Ashmolean Museum is famous for being the world's first university museum (Figure 7-1). The original buildings were erected between 1678 and 1683 to house a gift of curiosities donated by Elias Ashmole in 1677. Today it contains the world's largest collection of astrolabes, devices used to

Figure 7-1: An engraving of the Ashmolean Museum in Oxford as it appeared around 1909. E. H. New, Ashmolean Museum.

(Image © Ashmolean Museum, University of Oxford; used with permission)

solve problems related to time and the positions of the sun and stars. Additionally, it has an excellent collection of Egypt-related items, including mummies – an impressive display particularly for children. The coins are located in the Heberden Coin Room at the museum, named after Charles Butler Heberden, who left £1,000 to the university around 1920 for any purpose that it saw fit.

If one is solely interested in Newfoundland gold coins, this museum can be overlooked. It was, unfortunately, not until 1892 that the Ashmolean Museum began to regularly acquire Canadian and provincial coins from the Royal Mint. Since the last release of the gold coins was in 1888, the museum has none in its collection. However, it does have an impressive collection of Canadian and Newfoundland coins dated after 1892, many in superb condition as they were obtained directly from the mints (Royal Mint and Ottawa). It

apparently had no working agreement with the Heaton Mint, so none of its superb coins possesses the "H" mint mark.

NATIONAL CURRENCY COLLECTION OF THE BANK OF CANADA

The Newfoundland $2 gold holdings of the National Currency Collection of the Bank of Canada were detailed in Chapter 6. The collection owns three specimens (1865, 1870, 1888) and two patterns (1864 copper, 1865 Bowman 33). Its holdings also include a complete date set of circulation strikes, but with only one variety of the 1870 date.

BELZBERG COLLECTION

The Sid and Alicia Belzberg Collection of Canadian and provincial coins was sold by Heritage Auction Galleries on January 13, 2003.[1] Among the rarities in this wonderful collection was an example of the 1911 Canadian dollar ($695,000) and a 1936 dot 1¢ coin ($230,000). There was also a complete set of the British Columbia $10 and $20 in both silver and gold to be sold as a single lot. Just before the auction, the Belzbergs placed a reserve bid of $875,000 on this set; this was not met, so the set did not sell. The collection sold for about $3 million in total.

The Belzberg Newfoundland $2 gold coin holdings consisted of a complete set of circulation strike coins (1865 MS61, 1870 two-dot MS63, 1870 three-dot MS62, 1872 MS62, 1880 MS62, 1881 MS63, 1882H MS62 [ex-Pittman], 1885 MS62 [ex-Pittman], and 1888 MS63). For many years, this was the best circulation strike collection listed on the Professional Coin Grading Services (PCGS) Registry Set website. Compare the grades here with those in the Perth Collection (below) to appreciate the achievement in assembling the latter collection. In addition to their circulation strike coins, the Belzbergs had in their collection a spectacular 1872 reeded-edge proof, which sold for $27,025.

Figure 7-2: Virgil Brand at around fifty years old. His coin collection was one of the largest ever assembled and contained examples from almost every country in the world.

VIRGIL BRAND COLLECTION

Virgil Brand was a Chicago beer baron who died in 1926 at the age of sixty-four (Figure 7-2). He amassed an enormous coin collection whose face value alone was estimated to be near $1 million. His collecting tastes were eclectic – everything from rare Ancients, to European coins and medals, to coins of Asia and the Americas. He documented his purchases in detailed ledgers that contained the coin's country of origin, its denomination, date, cost, and source.

After Brand's death, efforts were made to sell the collection in its entirety, and it seemed possible that the US government would buy it, but given the depressed economy of the time there were no takers. Virgil never married, and because he left no will, his two brothers, Armin and Horace, inherited his collection. Since their relationship was not always harmonious, they eventually went to court to settle ownership of the collection. Beginning around 1932, an expert evaluation of the collection was undertaken with the aim of dividing it equally between the two brothers. This is extremely fortunate as otherwise it would have been difficult to track down specific coins in the enormous ledgers of the original collection. It was this inventory that revealed Brand's Newfoundland $2 gold holdings. One cannot be absolutely certain that this listing contains his entire holdings of Newfoundland gold coins, but we will take it as a working hypothesis.

The inventory ledger listing the Newfoundland gold coins was completed on April 17, 1935, and it was made available to me by David Hill, the Francis D. Campbell librarian at the American Numismatic Society (ANS), which currently houses all the Virgil Brand ledgers. The well-known American numismatist Q. David Bowers helped have them transferred to the society. The inventory reveals that the Brand holdings of Newfoundland gold coins contained the following (all listed as uncirculated): two 1865 coins; one 1870 coin (variety not indicated, but the two varieties were probably not recognized at the time); two 1881 coins; five 1882 coins ("H" not indicated); and one 1888 coin. This means that Brand did not have a complete set: there were no pieces dated 1872, 1880, or 1885 in the collection. The final listing is for an 1865 brilliant plain-edge proof (what we have called "specimen" here). The appraised value for each circulation strike coin was $2.50 and the proof was entered with a valuation of $25.

The proof coin, entered with its serial number 92779 included in the 1935 evaluation, is thus easy to trace through to the original Brand entries. It was acquired from Theophile Leon and entered into the ledger by Brand on September 20, 1919. The cost was $11.25. This coin was later acquired by the New Netherlands Coin Company and eventually found its way into the Norweb Collection, which was sold in 1996. The coin is a superb gem example and currently resides in the Kingston Collection.

Leon managed the Chicago Coin Company,

which had been started by Brand in 1907 and closed in 1915. Brand seemed to be careful when he listed his coins – that is, he was probably aware whether or not a particular piece was a pattern. For example, he listed a number of Australian pieces, some of which are entered as patterns, on the same page in his ledger where the 1865 Newfoundland proof is entered. We can probably assume that Brand would have recognized a Newfoundland gold pattern had he seen it. In particular, the Bowman 34 pattern has such a distinctly different obverse that Brand would certainly have catalogued it as a pattern. From this we can conclude that Bowman 34 never resided in the Brand Collection and that he had no other Newfoundland gold patterns either. The only specimen that he appeared to have obtained was the 1865.

The 1935 appraisal for court purposes is titled "Canada & Newfoundland Gold." This is the only entry for court purposes that contains the word "Canada." However, no Canadian gold coins are included other than a Toronto Exhibition Medal in Proof (in parentheses in the appraisal it is indicated as a "Beauty"). Its value is entered as $35 with a serial number of 132825 (provided here in case some researcher is interested in pursuing the provenance of this piece). The court cases apparently involved only certain parts of the collection that the Brand brothers fought over, so these court battle inventories were not necessarily exhaustive for a particular country. The Latin American coins, for example, are not much represented in the inventories. Thus we cannot be sure that Brand did not have other Canadian gold coins that the brothers just did not consider controversial. We do know, for example, that the collection contained examples of the 1862 British Columbia $20 and $10 pieces, both in gold and in silver. In the Bowers and Merena Galleries sale of part of the collection on November 7 and 8, 1983, a $10 British Columbia gold piece was auctioned together with both a $10 and $20 coin in silver. The gold piece fetched $88,000 while the silver coins went for $10,450 and $14,300, respectively. The catalogue also noted that Brand had acquired a $20 piece in gold. Brand may have had other Canadian gold coins in addition to these, but there is no evidence for this in the easily accessible inventories.

BRITISH MUSEUM

The holdings of the Canadian and Newfoundland series in the British Museum were catalogued in my 1978 article in the Canadian Numismatic Journal.[2] The museum possesses a single 1865 $2 gold pattern, namely Bowman 33, which has the usual obverse design and the reverse lettering in block type. The museum also has all the rest of the gold set in uncirculated condition, but curiously no 1865 business strike. As noted in my 1978 article, the 1881 coin is particularly superb. As an added bonus for anyone visiting, the museum also holds both the $10 and $20 British Columbia coins in gold.

The museum had a standing order with the Royal Mint for the current coins that the mint was striking for both Britain and her colonies. The order was just for the circulation strike coins, leaving open the question of how the museum acquired the Newfoundland gold pattern. It paid face value for the coins from the mint, so each Newfoundland $2 gold coin cost it 8s. 4d. (the exchange value of a $2 coin in the British system).

When I first visited this museum in late 1977, the procedure for accessing the coin rooms was simple. No reservation was required. You just appeared, and after showing some identification you were admitted and trays of coins were placed in front of you. There was little security, which, unfortunately, resulted in some serious thefts from the coin room – notably, the very rare 1889 Canadian 10¢ coin. Back in the 1970s, the only thing the museum checked was that there was a coin in each hole in the trays. There was a coin where the 1889 10¢ coin was supposed to rest, but it turned out to be a circulated 1858 10¢ piece, placed there by the thief, no doubt.

CALDECOTT COLLECTION

J.B. Caldecott auctioned his collection of coins and tokens of the British colonies through Sotheby on June 11-13, 1912.[3] The front page of the auction catalogue states that Mr. Caldecott "is relinquishing this series," which makes it sound as though he got tired of the coins and was getting rid of them! An interesting preface to the printed catalogue indicates that the collection, at the request of the auction house, was catalogued by the vendor himself. This was apparently done as Mr. Caldecott had discovered, through his own research, new facts about many of his holdings since the publication of James Atkins's book The Coins and Tokens of the Possessions and Colonies of the British Empire.

This auction contained three lots of great interest to the Newfoundland $2 gold coin collector:

(1) Lot 366: *Two Dollars (7 coins), 1865, 1870, 1872, 1881, 1882H, 1885 and 1888, all fine.*

These are all business strikes and there is no easy way to discern the quality of the pieces. We can probably conclude that they were not uncirculated. Note that the set is not complete as it is missing the rarest coin in the series – the 1880. The set sold for £4 17s. 6d., with Baldwin purchasing this lot.

(2) Lot 367: *Pattern Two Dollars, 1864, in bronze. Obv as the current piece; R TWO |DOLLARS | 1864,*

under crown within wreath of maple leaves (Atkins p. 267, McLachlan, 18), very fine and probably unique. From the Montagu (lot 245) and Murdoch (lot 456) sales. The coin realized £7, quite a high price for the time, and was purchased by Spink. This was the identical hammer price as the following lot, an 1865 double proof set. In a period of only twenty years, this pattern coin had been at auction at least three times. This was its last public offering that could be traced. The coin currently resides in the National Currency Collection of the Bank of Canada.

(3) Lot 368: *Proof Two Dollars in gold, Twenty, Ten and Five Cents in Silver, all of 1865, plain edge; and Pattern Cent, 1864, in copper, a double set arranged in original case to show obverse and reverse, brilliant.* This is an example of the rare double proof (specimen) set that the Royal Mint probably struck for dignitaries in 1865. Such sets are thought to be the source of the 1865 plain-edge $2 gold specimens. Five sets are generally assumed to have been struck. The only other documented auction sale of such a set was the W.W.C. Wilson Sale in 1925 (see Chapter 6). The set in the Caldecott Sale was purchased by Baldwin for £7. This was the second-highest price for any Newfoundland lot in this auction, exceeded only by a copper pattern cent of 1864 (McLachlan 23, lot 373) that reached £7 10s. Which lot would you prefer to own?

CARTER COLLECTION

Amon Carter was a Texas oil and newspaper executive and a co-founder of American Airlines. He became interested in numismatics around 1920. Being a Texan, he had the opportunity to visit and deal with B. Max Mehl of Fort Worth, one of the most influential US dealers of all time. At one time, Carter owned the excessively rare and valuable 1822 US $5 gold coin, which is currently valued at $8-10 million.

He shared his collection and enthusiasm with his family, and after his death the collection came to be known as the Amon Carter Jr. Family Collection, after his son. As detailed in Chapter 8, part of this collection was auctioned in 1984 and contained 141 Newfoundland $2 gold coins, not one of which was in uncirculated condition.[4]

ELIASBERG COLLECTION

Louis Eliasberg was born in 1896 and moved to Baltimore when he was around twenty years old. He managed the Finance Company of America for many years, providing excellent returns for its investors. He was a founding director of what eventually became the Maryland National Bank and served on its board for almost forty years. He probably started collecting coins in the early 1920s, began seriously investing in the 1930s, and eventually formed the most impressive collection of US coins ever assembled. He had accomplished the virtually impossible task of obtaining an example of every coin ever issued by the US government, and most of his coins were in superb condition. His collection was so famous that he and it were highlighted in *Life Magazine* in April 1953.

In addition to his US holdings, Eliasberg also amassed an impressive collection of world gold coins.[5] Among these was a complete set of Newfoundland $2 gold coins, mostly in the lower grades of uncirculated. The set was unremarkable, with one exception: an 1882H coin, that graded gem MS65. It had been acquired by Eliasberg for $6.50 in the Stack's 1944 auction of the James W. Flanagan collection. In the Eliasberg sale, it went for $10,925.

ELLIS COLLECTION

Lieutenant-Colonel H. Leslie Ellis sold his valuable collection of coins and tokens of the

British possessions and colonies through Sotheby, Wilkinson and Hodge on June 18-19, 1902.[6] There was only a single lot of interest in the current context – lot 280, an 1865 proof $2 coin listed in brilliant condition and rare. It went for £2 10s. A note in the margin of the auction catalogue indicated that it was bought by Rollin. Rollin and Feuardent was originally a small French company founded by Claude Camille Rollin (1813-83). The partnership opened a branch in Haymarket, London, in 1867. After Rollin's death, the company continued in business until 1953.[7]

FRONTENAC COLLECTION

The Frontenac Sale was presented by Bowers and Merena Inc. on November 20-22, 1991, in New York City.[8] The collection contained a superb grouping of Canadian and provincial coins, including a Canadian double specimen set from 1858, the first year of coinage for Canada. High-grade specimens of the $5 and $10 gold coins of Canada were also auctioned, and a pattern $5 coin in bronze dated 1928 sold for $19,800.

The Newfoundland $2 gold section, by comparison, was disappointing. It contained a total of sixty-one coins, including five examples of the rare 1880 date. While the overall grades of these coins were quite high, not a single coin was listed as uncirculated, further indication that these coins circulated widely.

KINGSTON COLLECTION

The Kingston Collection of Newfoundland gold coins consists solely of specimen coins. It is a remarkable high-grade set composed of only six coins, with an example of every date except for the 1888 and 1881 coins. No 1881 coins are known to exist, and there are only two 1888 examples known,

both of which are locked away in museums.

The coins in the Kingston Collection are graded as follows:

1865 Plain Edge SP65 (SP for "specimen") – finest of about ten known
1870 Plain Edge SP66 – finest of three known (another one is SP61)
1872 Reeded Edge SP66 – finest of five known
1880 Reeded Edge SP65 – finer of two known
1882H Reeded Edge SP66 – finest of six known
1885 Reeded Edge SP67 – only one known

The collection was originally assembled by the Norwebs, and the current owner has added a wonderful 1882H to the set. The current owner did not acquire these coins directly from the Norweb Sale in 1996 but through a serious numismatist from Toronto who was present at the sale.

In a candid discussion with the owner of the Kingston Collection, I inquired as to the perceived value of this collection. Recall that there are only six coins in the set. Several of these are possibly the only ones known outside of museums (1870, 1880, and 1885), and the 1885 may be unique. Additionally, the coins are spectacular, in very high grades, and in all cases the best available for each date. The collection is irreplaceable and could not be duplicated at any cost. The owner placed a value on these treasures of $2.5 million.

MELBOURNE MUSEUM

Australia has come to possess quite a few remarkable coins, not only of Newfoundland but also of Canada. Some of these were acquired from the Royal Mint in 1880 for the Sydney International Exhibition and in 1888, when a series of exhibitions helped mark the country's centennial.

MINT
MELBOURNE

Among the Melbourne Museum's holdings are complete Newfoundland specimen sets of 1880 and 1888 (including the gold coins), and complete and stunningly beautiful specimen sets from Canada, also dated 1880 and 1888. One extreme rarity is a Royal Mint striking of an 1875 5¢ coin. This has no "H" (for Heaton) on it. All circulation strike coins for Canada of this date were struck at the Heaton Mint in Birmingham, so this Royal Mint product is extremely rare. These coins are currently housed in the Melbourne Museum.

The history of these coins and their association with the Melbourne Museum is fascinating.

Figure 7-3: Melbourne Branch of the Royal Mint – William Street – as it appeared around 1888, during the centennial of Australia. At the time, Australia was receiving 1888-dated specimen coins of Newfoundland from the London Branch of the Royal Mint.

(Image: http://www.antiqueprints.com.au)

John Sharples, a recently retired curator of the Melbourne Museum Numismatic Collection, outlines this history in an article in the *Journal of the Numismatic Association of Australia*.[9]

Australia has had a long history of museums,

Figure 7-4: The Royal Exhibition Building in Melbourne as it appeared around 1900, shortly after the exhibitions held in that city in 1880 and 1888 (right), and how it appears today (left). The later photo was taken by the author; the earlier photograph, which was found on a postcard at a fair outside Brisbane in May 2015, is courtesy of Frozen in Time Gallery (http://www.frozentime.com.au). The Melbourne Museum, which currently houses the coin collection, is located just a few hundred metres from the Exhibition Building in the Carlton Gardens.

dating back to the early 1800s, and numismatics has always been integral to their holdings. The Melbourne Museum began as the Museum of Victoria, and the first numismatic curator, Johann Joseph Eugene von Guerard, was appointed in 1871. In 1880, the Melbourne Branch of the British Royal Mint (Figure 7-3) had a display at the Melbourne International Exhibition (Figure 7-4) that included examples of coins from the mint highlighting Britain's various colonies. Deputy Master of the Royal Mint Charles Fremantle agreed to provide two (this is important, as we shall see) specially prepared specimen examples of each coin that the mint was striking in that year (1880) and in some earlier years, from both the United Kingdom itself and each of its colonies. The shipment was enormous, ultimately weighing well over two hundred pounds. Today, however, there remains in the museum collection only one coin of the two 1880 $2 gold coins that were originally sent. Why?

The Deputy Master of the Australian Mint at the time was V. Deles Broughton. He had requested the sample coinage from the Royal Mint; unfortunately, he was an amateur numismatist – and one without particular expertise. He fancied ancient coins and at the end of the 1880 exhibition traded one complete set of the 1880 proof coins to a Herr Wilhemj (Sharples mentions that the name is apparently not clear on the original document[10]) for an assortment of ancient coins and some cash. The ancient coins turned out to have little value.

This accounts for several known features of the 1880 Newfoundland specimen $2 gold coins: only two are known, their die characteristics are identical and differ from any other known examples of this date, and one coin remains in the Melbourne Museum while the other has been traded several times since 1880. Fremantle probably used a rejected die for these two coins (the die characteristics are detailed in Chapter 6). There were problems with the die and no circulation strike

CATALOGUE

OF THE

VERY IMPORTANT & VALUABLE COLLECTION

OF

PATTERNS AND PROOFS,

In Gold, Silver, Bronze, Tin, &c.

FOR THE COINAGES OF

𝕿𝖍𝖊 𝕻𝖔𝖘𝖘𝖊𝖘𝖘𝖎𝖔𝖓𝖘 𝖆𝖓𝖉 𝕮𝖔𝖑𝖔𝖓𝖎𝖊𝖘 𝖔𝖋 𝖙𝖍𝖊 𝕭𝖗𝖎𝖙𝖎𝖘𝖍 𝕰𝖒𝖕𝖎𝖗𝖊,

INCLUDING

A FEW SPECIMENS OF THE CURRENT ISSUES,

AND A SELECTION OF ANGLO-HANOVERIAN,

FORMED BY

H. MONTAGU, ESQ. F.S.A. &c.

Among the more Important Rarities may be mentioned—

The Early Gold Coins of Bombay; the Rupee of Charles II for the same Presidency; the interesting Patterns of the East India Company; Double Mohur of William IV; Gold Proofs of various Silver and Copper Pieces of India and Ceylon; Victoria Proofs in Gold, of Silver and Copper Currency; an unrivalled Series of the PATTERN DOLLARS AND CENTS FOR HONG KONG; New England Shilling; the Coinage of Lord Baltimore for Maryland; the probably unique Pattern in Copper for Newfoundland; a set of the excessively rare SOMMER ISLANDS COINAGE; the Bermuda Penny, coined in Gold; the rare

𝕬𝖚𝖘𝖙𝖗𝖆𝖑𝖎𝖆𝖓 𝕻𝖎𝖊𝖈𝖊𝖘 𝖔𝖋 𝕺𝖓𝖊, 𝕳𝖆𝖑𝖋 𝖆𝖓𝖉 𝕼𝖚𝖆𝖗𝖙𝖊𝖗 𝕺𝖚𝖓𝖈𝖊 𝖔𝖋 𝕲𝖔𝖑𝖉.

&c. &c.

WHICH WILL BE SOLD BY AUCTION

BY MESSRS.

SOTHEBY, WILKINSON & HODGE,

𝕬𝖚𝖈𝖙𝖎𝖔𝖓𝖊𝖊𝖗𝖘 𝖔𝖋 𝕷𝖎𝖙𝖊𝖗𝖆𝖗𝖞 𝕻𝖗𝖔𝖕𝖊𝖗𝖙𝖞 𝖆𝖓𝖉 𝖂𝖔𝖗𝖐𝖘 𝖎𝖑𝖑𝖚𝖘𝖙𝖗𝖆𝖙𝖎𝖛𝖊 𝖔𝖋 𝖙𝖍𝖊 𝕱𝖎𝖓𝖊 𝕬𝖗𝖙𝖘,

AT THEIR HOUSE, No. 13, WELLINGTON STREET, STRAND, W.C.

On TUESDAY, the 3rd day of MAY, 1892, and following Day,

AT ONE O'CLOCK PRECISELY.

May be Viewed Two Days prior.   Catalogues may be had.

Figure 7-5: Cover page of the auction catalogue for the sale of Hyman Montagu's patterns and proofs of the coinages of the possessions and colonies of the British Empire.

coins are known to have been struck from it.

In 1885, George Anderson took over as Deputy Master of the Melbourne Branch of the Royal Mint. In honour of the Australian centennial in 1888, he also planned to produce a display of coinage. Fremantle, still in charge at the Royal Mint, was a bit miffed by the treatment of the 1880 shipment, but agreed to ship specimen strikings of every colonial coin minted by the Royal Mint in 1888. The first shipment included a complete set of the 1888-dated Newfoundland coinage, including the $2 gold coin. The cost to the Melbourne Mint was face value. This set of circumstances explains the origin of the 1888 Newfoundland specimen gold coin in the Melbourne Museum, but it does not account for the other piece in the National Currency Collection of the Bank of Canada. As we saw in Chapter 6, these two coins have very different die characteristics. In addition, the Melbourne coin was not struck to the high standards of the Ottawa piece. Apparently, Fremantle simply used an 1888 die left over from the circulation strikings for that year, produced a highly polished planchet, and struck off the Australian piece. It seems unlikely that it was produced at the same time as the coin now residing in Ottawa.

The Melbourne Museum Collection today contains three Newfoundland gold specimens: 1880, 1888, plus an additional piece from 1872. The coins are just lying open in a small box. They are not in any sort of holder whatsoever. Each one of these treasures has handling marks on it – small nicks and scratches. In the 1970s, when I visited with my good friend Saul Hendler, an outstanding coin dealer from Montreal, no talking was permitted when examining coins for fear that saliva might get on their surface and eventually produce an

ugly spot. When I examined these gold coins in May 2015, I wore latex gloves but there were no restrictions on talking while doing this.

In addition to these three proofs, the museum has two circulation strike coins, 1882H and 1888. These are both classified as About Uncirculated.

MONTAGU COLLECTION

Hyman Montagu (born Hyman Moses) was a prominent lawyer and numismatist in late-nineteenth-century London. He specialized in bankruptcy law, and, in the numismatic aspect of his life, he was both a collector and a scholar.[11] The bulk of his holdings, considered by many to be the finest collection of British and ancient coins ever assembled, was sold in November 1895 and March 1896, but the patterns and proofs of the colonies of the British Empire were auctioned on May 3-4, 1892.[12] In the Canadian Numismatic Research Index (published by the Canadian Numismatic Research Society in 1969), Fred Bowman incorrectly lists the dates of these auctions as March 3-4, 1892. This made the catalogue quite difficult to locate, but a sharp University of British Columbia librarian provided the right reference. The cover page of the auction catalogue is reproduced in Figure 7-5. Note that the unique Newfoundland pattern 1864 $2 coin in copper is highlighted in this sale. As far as is known, this was the first public offering for sale of this coin.

The two lots of interest to a collector of Newfoundland gold coins are:

(1) Lot 244: *Newfoundland Gold Proof 1865 plain edge. Extremely rare.* The coin sold for £4 12s. and was bought by Spink.

(2) Lot 245: *Pattern in Copper of the Two Dollar Piece. 1864 (see Atkins, page 267, describing this piece), probably UNIQUE.* The coin sold for £3 13s.

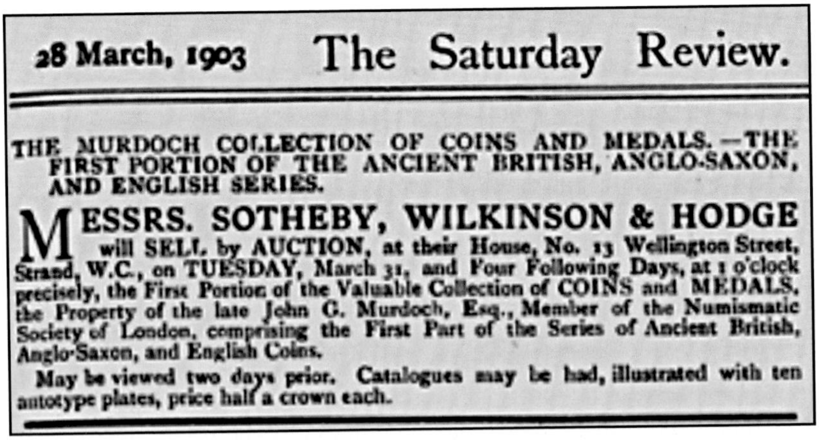

28 March, 1903   The Saturday Review.

THE MURDOCH COLLECTION OF COINS AND MEDALS.—THE FIRST PORTION OF THE ANCIENT BRITISH, ANGLO-SAXON, AND ENGLISH SERIES.

MESSRS. SOTHEBY, WILKINSON & HODGE will SELL by AUCTION, at their House, No. 13 Wellington Street, Strand, W.C., on TUESDAY, March 31, and Four Following Days, at 1 o'clock precisely, the First Portion of the Valuable Collection of COINS and MEDALS, the Property of the late John G. Murdoch, Esq., Member of the Numismatic Society of London, comprising the First Part of the Series of Ancient British, Anglo-Saxon, and English Coins.

May be viewed two days prior. Catalogues may be had, illustrated with ten autotype plates, price half a crown each.

Figure 7-6: Announcement of the first part of the auction of the Murdoch Collection in the March 28, 1903, edition of the *Saturday Review*.

and was bought by a person named Rathbone. Although he bought heavily in this and other sales at the time, it was not possible to locate any further information about him. Inquiry with the British Numismatic Society, which was founded in 1903, turned up no members by this name in the early years of the society. This is also true of a number of other buyers of Newfoundland coins at these early Sotheby sales, such as Chapman, Pinnock, and Watters.

MURDOCH COLLECTION

John Gloag Murdoch (1830-1902) was born at Huntingtower, Perthshire. He was the chairman of John G. Murdoch and Company and a senior partner in both Spencer and Company and Malcolm and Company, which made pianos and organs, respectively. Murdoch appears to have been somewhat reclusive in his collecting. He never published anything on coins and apparently formed his vast collection over a period of less than twenty years, from approximately 1885 until his death in 1902.[13]

The announcement of the first part of the Murdoch auction appeared on March 28, 1903, in the *Saturday Review of Politics, Literature, Science and Arts* (Figure 7-6).[14] The Murdoch Collection was sold by Sotheby, Wilkinson and Hodge in London. The cataloguers called the Murdoch holdings second only to Mr. Montagu's as the most important and valuable coin collection ever formed in England. The coins of British North America appeared in the fourth session, which took place over eight days in July 1903 and comprised 1,233 lots.

The Newfoundland section of the Murdoch Collection was auctioned on July 23, 1903. The coins of interest for our purposes appeared in the fourth part of the auction and were spread out between lots 446 and 456:

(1) Lot 446: *Newfoundland $2 gold 1870, 1872, 1881 very fine and scarce.* These are all business strikes; it is unclear what was meant by "very fine" here. These coins could have been graded anywhere from current-day fine to uncirculated. The lot sold for £1 11s. to a certain Pinnock. Note that face

value for these coins amounts to £1 4s. 4d., so they were bought for very little over face value.

(2) Lot 447: *Other similar coins 1882 (with "H" below the date), 1885 and 1888. All very fine and scarce.* These were sold to Spink for £1 8s.

(3) Lot 448: *1872 not so fine as last.* An assortment of silver coins was included with this lot. It was sold to a certain Watters for £1 1s.

With lot 451 the section on Newfoundland Patterns and Proofs commences:

(4) Lot 451: *1865 proof plain edge and another with "grained" edge. Brilliant and rare. 2 coins.* The cataloguers used the somewhat antiquated term "grained edge," whereas today we would use "reeded edge." The description here is intriguing. This is clearly the section where only proof or pattern coins are listed; thus the description of the latter coin seems to suggest that it is a reeded-edge proof 1865 $2 gold coin – a piece that is not known to exist (but see the listing below for the Norweb Sale). All proofs of this date are believed to have come from the proof sets of that year, and all the coins in these sets are thought to have been struck with plain edges. Is there an exceptional coin out there waiting to be discovered? An absolute bargain at £1 10s., sold to Pinnock.

(5) Lot 452: 1865 and 1880. *Former with plain edge and latter with grained edge. Both brilliant and rare. Second piece is from the Anderson Collection from Melbourne, Australia.* George Anderson was the Deputy Master of the Melbourne Branch of the Royal Mint from March 1885 until April 1895. There is currently one 1880 proof in the Melbourne Museum and another in the Kingston Collection. At one point, two 1880s were sent to Australia for the Melbourne International Exhibition, which ran from October 1, 1880, to April 30, 1881. One remained behind (the Melbourne Museum piece),

while the 1880 coin from the Murdoch auction was eventually acquired by the Norwebs and later by the owner of the Kingston Collection. All this assumes, of course, that this coin was indeed a proof. Further evidence in favour of this hypothesis can be found earlier in this chapter, in the discussion of the Melbourne Museum collection. This lot was sold to the French firm Rollin and Feuardent for £1 14s.

(6) Lot 453: *Another 1865 plain edge proof and proofs also of the 20, 10 and 5 cents all plain edges.* Another rare lot bought by a certain Chapman for very little over face value – 18s.

(7) Lot 454: *Proofs 50, 20, 10 cents 1870. 50 cents plain edge others grained.* No gold in this lot, but still an interesting grouping. It was sold to Rollin for £1.

(8) Lot 455: *Proofs 50, 20, 10, 5 cents 1880. All grained edge brilliant and rare. From the Montagu Collection.* This lot went to Rollin again, for 9s.

(9) Lot 456: *Proof 20, 10, 5 cents 1890 grained edge. Plus copper pattern $2 1864. This last piece considered to be UNIQUE.* What a grouping of coins! This copper pattern is now held in the National Currency Collection of the Bank of Canada in Ottawa. The lot went to Rollin for £5 15s.

(10) Lot 457: *Copper pattern 20 cents, 5 cents and 1864 1 cent.* This lot went to Rollin for £4 4s.

The Murdoch Sale also included both the $20 and $10 British Columbia gold coins (obtained by Spink for £116 and £53, respectively). It is possible that these coins eventually ended up in the Virgil Brand Collection.

The Murdoch Collection contained no fewer than four 1865 proof Newfoundland $2 gold coins, one of which might be a unique reeded-edge piece, assuming the cataloguer got things right. It had one of the two known 1880 proofs as well as the unique 1864 $2 coin struck in copper. This is an early provenance of the 1864 coin, which is now in Ottawa.

NEW NETHERLANDS SALE, SEPTEMBER 22-23, 1964

The New Netherlands Coin Company was formed in New York City by Moritz Wormser in 1936. It was taken over by his son Charles after his death in 1940. In 1950, the numismatic scholar John J. Ford Jr. joined the company and quickly became a full partner. During the era when the company operated (until 1988), it was one of the most important such companies in the United States, counting among its clients King Farouk of Egypt and the Norwebs. The company was particularly well known for its authoritative and extensively researched auction catalogues.

On the evenings of September 22 and 23, 1964, New Netherlands conducted its fifty-eighth public auction at the Hotel New Weston in New York City. It featured Canadian, Newfoundland, and Maritime coins. Nine lots presented Newfoundland $2 gold coins, but only three were truly memorable.

The most interesting was lot 1048: *Specimen Strike of the Second Type 1870 Two Dollars.* The coin was described as a "'Gem' Mint state coin, undoubtedly made for some special purpose, i.e., a Specimen impression ... the reverse proof-like and obviously struck from a polished die. Almost perfect ..." In describing this lot, New Netherlands pointed out that there were two distinct varieties of the 1870 obverse – one with and one without a dot after "NEWFOUNDLAND." The 1865 coin does have such a dot; the 1872 does not, and the same is true for most 1870s coins. The 1870 coin described by the company is of the same type as the 1872 (that is, without the extra dot). This may be the first instance where this variety was noted. The company

speculated that fewer than 1,500 of the total 10,000 mintage were of the type with three dots.

The coin realized $310, somewhat less than lot 1050, which was a rare uncirculated 1880 coin that sold for $420. The American Numismatic Society retains the auction catalogues of New Netherlands, and notes from the sale indicate that the 1870 coin was bought by Walter L. Holt of Whitman, Massachusetts.

The great interest in the 1870 piece revolved around the question of whether or not it was a real specimen. The description certainly makes it sound like a specimen, but the New Netherlands cataloguers did us a serious disservice by not telling us whether the edge was plain or reeded. If plain, then it is a specimen; if reeded, then it is most probably a first-strike piece. If the coin is a true specimen, then there are a total of four known, two of which are not in museums: the one in the Kingston Collection (ex-Norweb) and this coin (current location unknown).

The New Netherlands catalogue contains a rather poor image of the 1870 coin. Even so, a number of diagnostics are obvious from an examination of this image. The die break to the left of the "A" in "DOLLARS" on the reverse of the coin (see Figure 6-24), which is present on all specimens and patterns of this date, is not apparent on the New Netherlands coin. The specimen in the Kingston Collection also has a bold, wide rim that is not obvious on the coin auctioned by New Netherlands. Other subtle die differences are visible: the shape of the "0" in "1870" seems very different on the two coins, as does the second "L" in "DOLLARS." There seems little doubt that the New Netherlands coin was struck from a different die than the Kingston coin. Most likely, then, it was an early strike and not a specimen coin.

Figure 7-7: The 1885 Newfoundland $2 gold coin in the Perth Collection, graded MS66. The image reproduced here does not do the actual coin justice. It may be the same coin offered in the New Netherlands Sale of 1964 (lot 1053).

(Image: Courtesy of PCGS)

Lot 1050 was a *"very close to Uncirculated Very Rare 1880 Newfoundland Two Dollars."*

This coin was sold for $420 to D.J. Nurein (?) (the name is difficult to decipher in the ledgers), a collector from Melbourne, Florida. This price seems to me to be instructive. I would have expected the 1870 coin to have sold for many times this amount if it had been a true specimen. So the experts at the sale (and there were many of them, including Amon Carter, John Pittman, Saul Hendler, and R. Henry Norweb), who had no doubt viewed the 1870 coin carefully, appear to have concluded that it was not a specimen.

In the description of the 1880 coin, the cataloguers echo something that I had also noted over the years. Many of the 1880 coins that have been examined seem to have some sort of impairment. Most common is a striking flaw on the obverse near Queen Victoria's neck. Coins

of this date often appear abraded, particularly on their reverses, perhaps from long storage in mint bags. The New Netherlands catalogue points out that Spink released a hoard of Newfoundland $2 gold coins (around 1960), and Q. David Bowers indicates in his Norweb Canadian auction catalogue that it was actually New Netherlands that bought this hoard intact.

The last lot of significance is 1053, *"1885. Gem Uncirculated, virtually Superb! ... Date collectors will have a difficult time equaling this low mintage item."* The coin was sold for $100 to the same collector who bought lot 1048. The most impressive 1885 of which I am aware is the one in the Perth Collection, Figure 7-7. Is it possible that these are the same coin? A detailed comparison between them is not possible as New Netherlands did not provide an image of this coin in its catalogue.

COLLECTION FORMED BY A NOBLEMAN, RECENTLY DECEASED

The anonymous "Nobleman" consigner here was Philipp von Ferrary (Count Ferrari), who passed away on May 20, 1917. He was the wealthy son of the Duke and Duchess of Galliera. His Wikipedia entry lists his occupation as "Stamp Collector," as he amassed the finest such collection ever known. His coin collection sale, conducted by Sotheby on March 27-31, 1922, was advertised as a famous and remarkable collection of British and colonial coins, patterns, and proofs.[15] This was not hype; the collection was truly amazing. Lot 636 was a British Columbia pattern $20 in gold (sold for £330 – an extremely high price for the era – to Spink). A single lot (650) contained Canada frosted proofs of 50¢ 1902 (two coins), 1905, 1908 (two coins), and 1911 (two coins), as well as similar holdings for the 25¢, 10¢, and 5¢, all brilliant proofs, and proofs of 10¢ 1858 and 1894 – all this for the "princely" sum of £1 15s. (to Spink).

The Newfoundland $2 gold holdings were in lot 669 (proof 1865, plus currency strikes 1865, 1870, and 1872, all very fine – £4 to Spink) and lot 670 (another proof 1865 together with currency strikes of 1881, 1885, and 1888 – £3 7s. 6d. to Spink).

NORWEB COLLECTION

The Norwebs formed one of the finest collections of US, Canadian, and world coins. Their Canadian and provincial coins were auctioned in Baltimore by Bowers and Merena, Inc., on November 15, 1996.

The collection contained three examples of the 1865 specimen. One of these had a reeded edge (lot 680), and although the Norweb catalogue clearly states that it does not have the full mirror surfaces of the other two examples, and also has a few die mismatches, a case can still be made for its

specimen status. No provenance is given for this coin; could it be the same piece offered as lot 451 in the Murdoch Sale of 1903? The coin went for $5,600 at the Norweb Sale and resides today in an MS66 holder from PCGS in the Perth Collection. Modern grading has asserted that it is not a specimen coin, but today it is the finest known circulation strike piece of this date.

The other Newfoundland $2 specimens in the auction, all bought (or later acquired) by a single Canadian collector, were 1870, 1872, 1880, and a fantastic 1885. In addition, the Norwebs had circulation strike coins of 1870 (two examples), 1880 (from the King Farouk Sale, lot 901), 1881, 1882H, 1885, and 1888, but none of these were listed as uncirculated. Most of these circulation strike coins were probably from the Tennant Collection, which the Norwebs bought in its entirety (via New Netherlands) in 1954. The Bowers and Merena Norweb Sale Canadian catalogue recounts the story of this acquisition.[16] Additional information on this is provided below.

The ultimate lot (741) in the Norweb Sale was the 1865 pattern coin in gold (Bowman 34), which Dr. John Temple bought for $39,600.

More insight into the Norweb $2 Newfoundland gold holdings can be obtained from an analysis of ledgers that were kept by Emery May Norweb over her collecting career between 1937 and 1957. These are currently held by the American Numismatic Society (ANS) in New York City. They were accessed there through one of the ANS cataloguers, John Graffeo, who searched through the ledgers for any entries related to Newfoundland gold coins. The search turned up the acquisition of the Saint John, New Brunswick, collection of Newfoundland gold coins from William B. Tennant (via the New Netherlands Coin Company). The

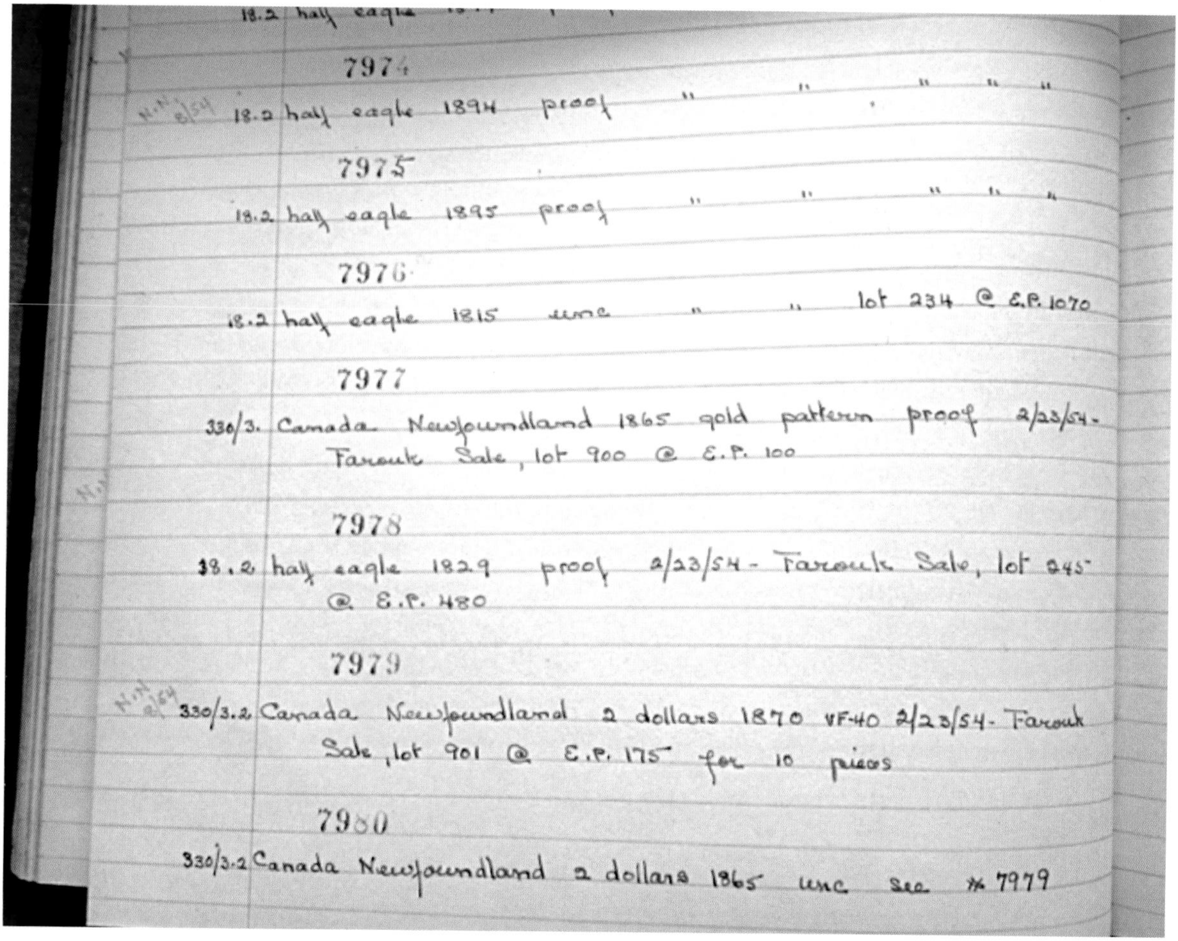

7974

NA. 2/59 18.2 half eagle 1894 proof " " " " " "

7975

18.2 half eagle 1895 proof " " " " "

7976

18.2 half eagle 1815 unc " " lot 234 @ E.P. 1070

7977

330/3. Canada Newfoundland 1865 gold pattern proof 2/23/54. Farouk Sale, lot 900 @ E.P. 100

7978

18.2 half eagle 1829 proof 2/23/54 - Farouk Sale, lot 845 @ E.P. 480

7979

NA. 2/59 330/3.2 Canada Newfoundland 2 dollars 1870 VF-40 2/23/54 - Farouk Sale, lot 901 @ E.P. 175 for 10 pieces

7980

330/3.2 Canada Newfoundland 2 dollars 1865 unc see * 7979

Tennant Collection of Newfoundland gold coins (Norweb ledger entry numbers 9493-9499) contained a complete set in what was termed at that time to be mostly uncirculated grade. Other entries included those from the Farouk Sale (lot 901, total EGP£175) under entries 7979-7987. This was another largely uncirculated set. Thus, the Norwebs had an extensive collection of circulation strike Newfoundland $2 gold coins in addition to their proofs and the single pattern, but many of these were either kept by the family or dispersed before the 1996 auction of the collection (as only a few circulation strike coins were included in the auction).

Figure 7-8: Norweb ledger (entry #7977) cataloguing the purchase of the 1865 pattern Newfoundland $2 gold coin obtained at the Farouk Sale in 1954. Note the purchase price of EGP£100 (= US$310).

(Image: R. Henry Norweb and Emery May Norweb ledgers and auction catalogs, 1867 – ca. 1984, Archives, American Numismatic Society [ANS])

Entries related to the specimen Newfoundland gold coins (the Norwebs would have termed these proofs) proved to be particularly frustrating, however. For some odd reason, none of the specimen gold pieces appear in their ledgers, unless they were miscatalogued and our search did not find them. There are some entries in the Norweb ledgers that might have caused us to miss these coins (for example, some proof Newfoundland cents were catalogued as simply proofs, with no statement about Newfoundland), but several passes through the ledgers could not support the idea that we missed the specimens. The gold specimens are simply not in the ledgers! So it remains somewhat of a mystery from whom, when, and for how much the Norwebs acquired some of these pieces. The provenances of their 1865 (from Virgil Brand) and 1870 (from Spink) specimens are known to some extent, largely due to Dave Bowers, who included, in his catalogue of the collection, notes contained on the paper envelopes enclosing these coins. These provenances are indicated in Appendix 4.

The sole existing proof entry (ledger number 7977) is for the 1865 pattern (Bowman 34) that the Norwebs purchased in the Farouk Sale of 1954 (ledger entry reproduced in Figure 7-8).

PERTH COLLECTION

Perusal of the collections and auctions discussed in this chapter indicates that many of the great collectors had specimens and patterns among their holdings but few held an assemblage of high-grade circulation strike issues. This no doubt attests to the rarity of these coins in pristine condition and may be an indication that the coins circulated widely. The holdings in the British Museum are the great exception to this, of course. The museum acquired its coins in the year of issue directly from the Royal Mint. Virgil Brand had a selection of dates that were listed as uncirculated, but he did not possess a complete set. The Norweb Collection, an amazing assemblage of specimen coins, alas did not include business strike Newfoundland gold coins of high quality, at least those that were auctioned

in 1996. The Pittman Collection had a single low-quality specimen from 1882 and circulation strike coins that, at best, were in the lower grades of uncirculated. Belzberg had two specimens and a complete set in uncirculated coins, but not particularly at the upper levels of mint state. The list goes on.

An exception to this is the fabulous complete set of $2 gold coins found today in the Perth Collection, which was assembled by a Canadian collector with a wonderful eye for superb coins. Almost every coin in this collection is the finest known; his complete type set of Newfoundland coins, consisting of a single coin of the twenty different types issued for Newfoundland, does, in fact, contain the highest-graded coin for every type in the set – a near-impossible feat that takes more than just money.

The $2 gold coins in the Perth Collection are graded as follows; most of these were obtained in 2009, when the owner of the Perth Collection bought the entire collection of circulation strike Newfoundland $2 coins from a Toronto collector.

1865 MS66 – one coin at this grade, finest known
1870 two-dot MS63 – five coins at this grade, 1 finer
1870 three-dot MS62 – three coins at this grade, 1 finer
1872 MS65+ – one coin at this grade, finest known
1880 MS64 – one coin at this grade, finest known
1881 MS66 – two coins at this grade, tied for finest known
1882H MS64 – four coins at this grade, two finer

1885 MS66 – one coin at this grade, none finer
1888 MS64+ – two coins at this grade, none finer

This may be the finest business strike complete collection ever assembled, and it is a delight to view. Among all these coins, the 1885 must rank as one of the most spectacular, if not the most spectacular, circulation strike Newfoundland $2 gold coin in private hands (Figure 7-7).

PITTMAN COLLECTION

John J. Pittman assembled one of the great collections of Canadian and provincial coins.[17] At one point, he owned all of the 1936 dot 1¢ and 10¢ pieces known, and his holdings included very rare specimen sets from the Victoria era through to the reign of Queen Elizabeth II, many of which had been acquired directly from mint employees.

His Newfoundland gold holdings were not in the same class as much of the rest of his collection, however. He did have a complete date set, of which only two were classified as uncirculated, and one specimen coin, an 1882H, that was barely graded SP60.

THE ROOMS

The Rooms houses the provincial archive and museum of Newfoundland and Labrador. During my visit to St. John's in June 2014, the manager of collections and exhibitions, Mark Ferguson, kindly gave me a private showing of the coins. The Rooms obtained these coins by donation from Frances J. Rowe, a very prominent collector of Newfoundland tokens and coins. Anyone interested in these topics should read the excellent book by Rowe and colleagues, *The Currency and Medals of Newfoundland*, which served as an invaluable resource in the preparation of this book.[18] The Rooms' $2 gold collection contains nine circulation strike coins, two dated 1865 plus one of each subsequent date. There is only one 1870 coin, the two-dot variety. The Rooms' coins generally are quite nice, averaging mostly AU. The best coin in the collection is the rare 1880 piece, likely grading about MS60.

ROYAL MINT COLLECTION

The Royal Mint (UK) Collection is currently housed in an attractive new building in Llantrisant, Wales. The collection, as detailed in Chapter 6, contains an 1865, 1870 plain-edge proof, 1870 pattern, 1872, 1880, 1881, 1882H, 1885, 1888 (three examples), a model obverse (no date), and an 1888 model reverse. The 1865 and 1872 through 1888 coins are all circulation strike pieces obtained directly from the Royal Mint at face value in the year they were coined.

RECENT AUCTIONS

Bonhams had an example of the 1865 $2 specimen in its December 16, 2014, auction. It was graded SP62 and carried a high estimate of US$40,000-50,000. Not surprisingly, it did not sell. Heritage Auctions has had a number of high-grade $2 specimen coins in its recent auctions. In 2004, it sold an SP62 example of the 1865 coin for $6,325; on September 14, 2006, it sold a gorgeous SP65 example for $19,550; and on January 3, 2010, it hammered down an SP63 piece for $15,525. It has auctioned two examples of the 1872 in SP65: on January 13, 2003, for $27,025 (from the Belzberg Collection) and June 9, 2005, for $19,550.

For some additional recent public offerings, mainly high-grade circulation strikes, see Table 16 in Appendix 4.

One obvious conclusion regarding the specimen Newfoundland $2 gold coins from this compilation is that the 1865 coin appears to be much more common than any of the other dates. In the auctions and museum holdings noted here, the 1865 appears twenty times (some are certainly duplicate offerings), whereas the other specimens appear extremely rarely (1870, three times; 1872, four times; 1880, two times; 1881, never; 1882H, two times; 1885, once; 1888, two times). It is likely that the proliferation of 1865 coins is the result of broken-up double proof sets that were produced by the Royal Mint in the inaugural year of minting the gold, silver, and copper coins for Newfoundland.

CHAPTER 8

· ·

Hoards of Newfoundland $2 Gold Coins

Final insight into the influence of the gold coins on the economy of late-nineteenth-century Newfoundland can be obtained from analyzing hoards of these coins. When paper money is not highly valued, gold and silver tend to be hoarded. If the precious metal content of a coin exceeds its face value, the coin will be either hoarded or melted. Bank failures often lead to the hoarding of coins composed of precious metals as the populace loses confidence in the banking system. In this case, money is often rapidly withdrawn and hoarded in much the same way as in ancient Greece and Rome. History is replete with stories of hoarding by individuals who trusted only hard money, tried to hide money in order to avoid taxes, or buried or hid stolen coins.

A few recently discovered hoards provide excellent examples of the variety of reasons why people hoard precious objects. The Staffordshire Hoard, unearthed near Hammerwich in central England, consisted of more than four thousand gold weapons ornamented with precious stones. These dated from the early sixth and seventh centuries and were probably the spoils of war buried

in order to keep them safe for recovery at a later date. The Hackney Hoard of US $20 gold coins was discovered in that London borough in 2007. It was originally buried by a Jewish family from Germany during the Second World War when fears of a possible German invasion were high and during a time when the banking system was under stress. The United States has witnessed a number of significant hoards of high-grade coins. For example, the Saddle Ridge Hoard of 1,427 $20 and $10 gold coins, all dated between 1847 and 1894, was found in the Sierra Nevada region of California in 2013. Many of these coins are in high grades – a few up to MS66 (see Chapter 5 for details on the seventy-point grading system) – and perhaps ten or more are the finest known coins for the particular date and mint. The face value of the hoard totalled $27,980, but the numismatic value probably exceeds $10 million. In the early 1990s, the Wells Fargo Hoard, consisting of almost 10,000 US $20 gold coins dated 1908, came to light. This hoard included coins in absolutely remarkable condition, some with grades up to MS69 (that is, almost perfect coins with virtually no visible

Figure 8-1: Duckworth Street, St. John's, pre-1880. The Union Bank of Newfoundland is seen in the centre-right of the picture. It still stands today.

(Image: Digital Archives, Memorial University)

imperfections). There have also been several releases of $1 silver coins from the US government, totalling perhaps as many as 100 million pieces. Lavere Redfield amassed a remarkable hoard of US silver dollars. Born in 1897, he moved to Reno, Nevada, in the late 1930s, became a very successful investor in the stock market, and began buying bags containing one thousand silver dollars from the local banks. In the 1940s and '50s, these could be obtained for face value and his hoard eventually totalled about 400,000 coins, mostly in the higher grades of uncirculated. After Redfield's death, the coins were sold to a dealer for $7.3 million. It is not clear why Redfield hoarded; one possible reason was his distrust of the government and his desire to avoid paying taxes. At one point, he actually served eighteen months in prison for tax evasion.

An important hoard was recently released in Canada. On November 29, 2012, the Royal Canadian Mint and the Bank of Canada made available a hoard of $5 and $10 coins. Apparently, there were 245,000 such coins stored in the bank's vaults since the day they were struck. These were minted in 1912-14, and the First World War disrupted their normal distribution into the commercial stream. About 30,000 specially selected coins (with the fewest nicks and scratches) were actually released for sale to the public. In 2015, the remaining 200,000 or so pieces were melted by the Royal Canadian Mint, yielding approximately 95,586 troy ounces of gold valued at US$113,060,275 on June 12, 2015 (the last day of melting). In total, 35,341 $5 coins were melted together with 179,881 $10 coins, both of which had

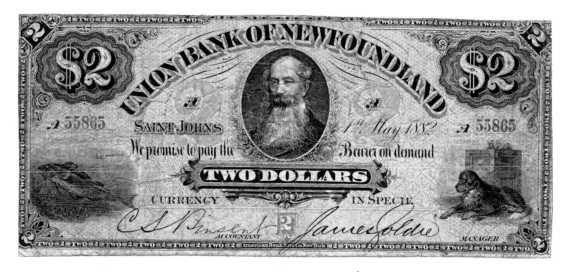

Figure 8-2: Paper money issued by the two major Newfoundland banks
(*Upper*: Union Bank of Newfoundland *Lower*: Commercial Bank of Newfoundland).

(Images: Courtesy of Heritage Coins)

a fine gold content of 0.900.[1]

On December 10, 1894, the banking system of Newfoundland came under extreme pressure. Two of the major banks, the Commercial Bank of Newfoundland and the Union Bank of Newfoundland failed (seen Figure 8-1 for a photograph of this latter bank taken some time

before 1880). These bank failures were largely a result of poor loans made by the boards of these banks, mainly to themselves. Instantly, the existing bank notes from these institutions (Figure 8-2 illustrates examples of these notes prior to devaluation) were deeply discounted. The government of Newfoundland did step in and

Figure 8-3: A $5 note from the Commercial Bank of Newfoundland, stamped with its new value of $1 after the bank failed in December 1894.

passed two acts in 1895 guaranteeing 80¢ on the dollar for the notes from the Union Bank, but only 20¢ for those from the much more poorly run Commercial Bank. Notes were stamped with these new values. Hoarding, mainly of the larger-denomination coins: 20¢, 50¢, and $2, ensued. Figure 8–3 shows an example of a banknote that was devalued. It is a $5 note from the Commercial Bank of Newfoundland that was stamped (in purple) with its new value of $1. Imagine the horror of waking up one morning and realizing that your life savings were only worth 20% of what they were the day before. This must have been keenly felt in impoverished Newfoundland of the 1890s.

The notes from both banks are very scarce today, even though large numbers were in circulation at the time of the bank failures. Eventually, 97.5 percent of the value of a note from the Union Bank was salvaged, but only 22.5 percent from the Commercial Bank.

Shortly after the Newfoundland banks went

out of business, the large Canadian banks – the Bank of Montreal, Bank of Nova Scotia, and Bank of Commerce – arrived on the scene. Canadian currency was adopted in the colony in January 1895, and the well-respected paper money of these institutions was accepted for payment of debts. From the time of the 1863 Act for the Regulation of the Currency until the bank failures in 1894, the exchange rate had been 4.80 Newfoundland dollars to the British pound. The Canadian dollar was valued at $4.86⅔ per pound and this discrepancy had to be adjusted if the Canadian dollar was to be the currency of use in Newfoundland. Viewing the reverse of a Newfoundland $2 gold coin in this light, 200¢ (Canadian) was not equal to 100 pence (it was now devalued to 98 6/10 pence), thus the $2 gold coin could no longer be produced as it had been in the past. Newfoundland $2 gold coins were issued in 1888, and none were minted between 1888 and 1894. Newfoundland continued to mint the smaller coins until it joined Confederation in

Figure 8-4: The exterior of the Palace Theatre in Corner Brook, Newfoundland, in 1949.
It was owned and operated by Joseph Basha.

(Image: Courtesy of Wayne Basha)

1949, but no $2 gold coins could be produced after 1894.

Further insight into possible hoarding of the $2 gold coins can be inferred from a speech given to the Newfoundland House of Assembly by Henry Renouf. Renouf was an opposition member representing St. John's West who played an important role in the anti-Confederation election of 1869. An important insight can be gleaned from his speech to the House regarding the gold coins, as reported in the Newfoundlander newspaper on March 19, 1866, and quoted towards the end of Chapter 2. Renouf detailed the comparative values of all the new coins (1¢ through to 20¢) except for the $2 gold pieces. We can conclude from this that either the gold pieces had not yet arrived in

the colony by the spring of 1866 or they were so infrequently encountered in commerce that no consistent exchange rate could be quoted for them. There is some evidence, however, that the gold coins did circulate eventually, and at a value in excess of the original intended amount in the Currency Act of 1863. Neil Carmichael mentions in his 1960 catalogue that a $2 gold coin was frequently exchanged for a half-sovereign even though the latter should have passed as $2.40 in Newfoundland currency.[2] This is a situation where Gresham's Law should prevail. Simply stated, according to Gresham's Law, a debased money supply will drive from circulation a money supply that has higher value (in this case, the Newfoundland coinage recently struck). The implication here is that the "good money" is then hoarded. So are there hoards of Newfoundland coins just waiting to be discovered?

The only verified hoard of high-grade Newfoundland $2 gold coins known to me is one that surfaced in 2008, the Capital City Hoard. It was dispersed by a Canadian east coast coin dealer and contained just sixteen pieces, all dated 1885. All the coins were in the lower grades of uncirculated condition (MS62 and MS63) and were quite nice overall, with good lustre and only a modest number of abrasions. The dealer uncovered the hoard on a buying trip to St. John's. The seller, Wayne Basha, is the scion of a prominent family from Corner Brook, Newfoundland. The hoard was likely assembled by Wayne's grandfather, Joseph Basha. Joseph was born in Newfoundland in 1888 (the final year that the gold coins were struck), worked as a merchant in St. John's in the 1920s, and passed away in 1952. Joseph's father (Wayne's great-grandfather) had immigrated from Baalbek, Lebanon, sometime in the late 1870s. The Capital City Hoard coins were found in Joseph's safe after he passed away. Joseph's daughter (Wayne's aunt) left the coins to Wayne, who claims that there were other years of the gold coins left in the estate.

In 1936, Joseph built and operated the Palace Theatre in Corner Brook (Figure 8-4). Wayne believes that some of the coins came from people who paid their theatre admissions in gold in the 1930s and 1940s, and also from coins that Joseph bought from other collectors or dealers (he was also an avid coin and stamp collector). It is unlikely that Joseph acquired gold coins via public spending in these later decades, as they had more or less disappeared from circulation after the bank failures of 1894.

Other hoards have probably emerged over time, but I know of no other large dispersals of uncirculated coins. Various websites report the existence of a 1,000-coin hoard from a merchant family living on the west coast of Newfoundland, and another 78 coins from a different source. These coins were all in circulated condition. Other accumulations were just that – gatherings of coins from many sources. An early accumulation was dispersed by Spink around 1960 and acquired in its entirety by the New Netherlands Coin Company. There were several hundred $2 coins in this grouping, including a number of rare 1880 pieces, but almost all, unfortunately, showed signs of mishandling due to their poor method of storage. One hoard surfaced when Stack's auctioned the Amon G. Carter Jr. Family Collection in January 1984. Mr. Carter was apparently quite intrigued with the unique expression of the denomination in three different ways as well as the outstanding design of the coins. The auction contained a total of 141 of these pieces, including two complete sets. There was not one uncirculated coin in the entire hoard, however. Similarly, in the Frontenac Sale (Auctions by Bowers and Merena, Inc., November 20-22, 1991), 77 pieces were offered, with the highest-graded coin being only AU58 – again no mint-state pieces. A group of several hundred coins assembled by a Toronto dealer in the late 1960s and into the early 1970s was shipped to a Swiss bank. At that time, it had become popular among tourists to purchase gold coins while on holidays, particularly in Europe. The Newfoundland gold coin was attractive and of modest cost, and filled the needs of the bank nicely. About twenty years ago, the Bank of Canada sold off the Newfoundland $2 gold coins it had accumulated over time. Between 300 and 400 coins were all bought by a single dealer.

One delightful small hoard, containing a single Newfoundland $2 gold coin, provides an indication of how scarce and varied was the specie circulating in Newfoundland even up to the end of the nineteenth century. The modest hoard of coinage was discovered in 1894. An account first appeared in an article by R.J. Graham[3] and was retold by Dave Bowers in his book on US coin hoards.[4] As related by Graham, an insurance agent working for Mutual Life of New York who attempted to collect a premium from a Newfoundland couple in a remote village was assured that they had no money. When the agent persisted, the man asked his wife to "bring down the stocking." The contents are listed in Table 8, and it was Graham's opinion that these were likely collected surreptitiously via illegal trading with foreign fishing fleets. Whatever their origin, it demonstrates the diversity of coinage that must have circulated in Newfoundland even into the late nineteenth century, well after Newfoundland had its own distinct coinage, and the difficulty that residents must have had in establishing the value of various coins. The insurance premium was actually paid out of this hodgepodge of Spanish-American dollars and German, American, Spanish, Greek, French, Italian, and British coins, together with a single Newfoundland gold coin! Establishing the value of each in a consistent currency must have been an absolute nightmare. For the purposes of the insurance premium, the agent established the values provided in Table 8.

Table 8. 1894 hoard and valuations

COIN (DATE)	VALUE (US$)
1 doubloon	$15.50
1 half doubloon (1780)	$7.75
3 quarter doubloons (1788)	$11.40
1 eight doubloon (1841)	$1.90
2 ten marks (1872)	$4.76
1 US $2.50 gold (1851)	$2.50
1 Newfoundland $2 gold (1872)	$2.00
5 Spanish pieces at 20c (1778)	$1.00
1 Spanish piece (1801)	$0.25
2 Greek drachmas (1822)	$0.366
2 two francs (1871)	$0.72
1 crown (1875)	$0.268
1 mark (1876)	$0.238
3 half-francs (1887)	$0.24
1 eight pence (1822)	$0.16
1 twenty centimes (1867)	$0.05
1 ten centimes (1868)	$0.02
4 two centimes (1878)	$0.04
3 halfpennies (1861)	$0.015

The high exchange values for the Newfoundland gold coins suggests that they should have been hoarded, so it is quite surprising that other hoards of high-grade $2 gold coins have not turned up. It is likely that some hoards do exist out there, tucked away in old dressers, just waiting to be discovered. What has not been uncovered, as far as I know, is a true hoard, where the coins were obtained from a bank at the time of striking and have been kept in more or less pristine condition since that time. Such a grouping is possibly out there somewhere in Newfoundland – but where?

. . . .

EPILOGUE

As a professional astronomer, whenever I have observation time on a major telescope in connection with a particular research project, I always have a few speculative small observations in my back pocket that I plan to execute in case the scheduled observations are completed earlier than expected. These observations often provide the truth-testing for the next important research project to be carried out at the telescope. It has been much the same with the research carried out for this book. While an enormous amount has been learned, a number of unresolved issues remain without closure and could potentially be a rich starting point for future research.

For much of the summer of 2014, some sharp University of British Columbia undergraduate history majors and I searched for coinage stories in Newfoundland newspapers published during the period when the gold coins were first authorized, manufactured and distributed in the colony (between 1863 and 1890). Even though we searched diligently and covered many miles of microfilm (these are still neither indexed nor digitized), no mention whatsoever could be found relating to the gold pieces. It is as though they had never existed. As related in Chapter 2, there were articles on the 1¢ copper coins and extensive reporting of the discussions in the Newfoundland House of Assembly on the introduction of the decimal system into the colony, but absolutely nothing, as far as we could find, on the gold coins themselves. This is a deep mystery for which we have no solid explanation at the moment, except for the possibility that they were extensively hoarded (unlikely) and thus rarely seen in commercial circles, or that they only circulated close to the centre of commerce, St. John's. After all, $2 was a lot of money in those days, about two weeks' salary for a constable in one of the outports. Other evidence seems to suggest that this was not entirely the case, however: (1) they are rarely seen in uncirculated condition (but they are also almost never seen very heavily circulated), and (2) R.W. McLachlan's comment in his book, which was written during the period when the coins were being minted, that "the Newfoundland gold coinage is often met with in circulation in Canada."[5] McLachlan (1845-1926) lived mainly in the Montreal area during the period when these coins were struck and distributed, so he was in a wonderful position to comment on the extent to which they circulated. The Capital City Hoard, if truly accumulated to some extent from people paying in gold throughout the 1930s and 1940s, also implies that the coins circulated widely. So why did the newspapers make no mention of these treasures?

The correspondence between the Newfoundland legislature and the Royal Mint ends abruptly in 1865 and does not resume again until 1869, when the second (1870) issue of coins for Newfoundland was being planned. This critical period should contain numerous documents on the minting, packaging, and shipping of the original issue coins to the colony. Perhaps they are buried somewhere in the UK National Archives or possibly miscatalogued. Their retrieval would provide new insight into the beginnings of circulation of this handsome coinage in the colonies.

Besides the well-documented, almost criminal behaviour related to their crash in 1894, there are a number of hints that the local banks in Newfoundland acted unethically in their forty years of operation. According to the 1870 letter from John Smith to Colonial Secretary John Bemister, the Union Bank of Newfoundland kept on its account all the seigniorage from the manufacture of the Newfoundland coinage (at least for the year 1870). Perhaps the Newfoundland legislature is partially culpable for allowing this source of revenue to slip through its fingers. In addition, the bank added 20 percent to the cost of the coinage and appeared to pass this along to the colony. It should be pointed out that the process Newfoundland underwent in acquiring new coinage was not unique. Before joining confederation in 1873,

Prince Edward Island requested coinage of bronze 1¢ pieces in 1871 and its agent in Britain doubled the bill that the colony paid.

In keeping all the profits from the Newfoundland coinage, it would have been clearly in the interests of the Union Bank to request as much coinage as possible from the Royal Mint as this increased the seigniorage. For many years, the bank's general manager, John W. Smith, was the main adviser to the Newfoundland government on coinage matters. He instructed the government on the amount of coinage required by the colony, as demonstrated by his letter of July 18, 1870 (see Figure 4-13 in Chapter 4). He was clearly in a conflict of interest position. The gold coins were actually produced at a loss, so if fraud had been involved, it would have made no sense for the Union Bank to request very many gold coins. The seigniorage would have been much higher if the colony had been inundated with bronze 1¢ pieces. This may indeed have been the case. From 1865 to 1894, when the banks failed, the number of 1¢ pieces struck for Newfoundland amounted to about 10.4 coins per person, while for significantly wealthier Canada the equivalent number was about 5.2. The number of 5¢ coins was 3.68 per person for Newfoundland, compared with 6.24 for Canada. Thus, Newfoundland seems to have been oversupplied with 1¢ coins relative to Canada, and somewhat undersupplied with 5¢ pieces. Although interesting, this certainly does not prove that the bank was acting improperly; commerce in Newfoundland may simply have required more low-denomination coins.

There are only few provenances known for the rarest and most valuable Newfoundland $2 gold coins. How can we do better than this? Provenances often tell their own story of the history of a coinage, so they are critical to understanding the full picture of the coinage's usage and distribution. Of particular interest here would be the provenances of some of the specimen coins now in the Kingston Collection and earlier held by the Norwebs; and the location of the pattern Bowman 34 coin, how it left the mint, where it was until 1910, and how King Farouk came to acquire it. John J. Ford provided two spectacular patterns to the National Currency Collection of the Bank of Canada in 1973. How did he come to acquire these pieces?

There is much more, of course, but I hope interested readers will formulate their own research projects, see them through to completion, and provide greater insight into this fascinating coinage of Britain's oldest colony.

APPENDICES

Anno Vicesimo-Sexto

VICTORIÆ REGINÆ.

CAP. XVIII.

AN ACT for the Regulation of the Currency.

(Passed 25th March, 1863.)

Be it Enacted by the Governor, Legislative Council and Assembly, in Legislative Session convened as follows :

I.—The denomination of Money in the Currency of this Colony shall be Dollars and Cents, in which Currency the Cent shall be the One Hundredth part of a Dollar ; and all Public Accounts shall be kept, all Public Monies paid and received, all Verdicts received and Judgments entered, and other Legal Proceedings taken, in such Currency.

Denomination of Money, Dollars and Cents.

II.—The British Sovereign of lawful Weight shall be held to be equal to and shall be a Legal Tender and pass Current for Four Dollars and Eighty Cents Currency ; and all parts of the Sovereign shall pass Current and be a Legal Tender in Currency after the like rate, according to the proportion they respectively bear to the Sovereign.

Value of Sovereign.

III.—The Gold Eagle of the United States; coined after the First July, Eighteen Hundred and Thirty-four, and while the Standard of Fineness for Gold Coins then fixed by the Laws of the United States remains unchanged, and weighing Ten Pennyweights Eighteen Grains Troy Weight; shall pass Current and be a Legal Tender for Nine Dollars and Eighty-five Cents Currency ; and all multiples and parts of such Eagle, of like date and proportionate weight; shall pass Current and be a Legal Tender in Currency after the like rate, according to the proportion they respectively bear to the Eagle.

Value of Gold Eagle.

IV.—The Silver Coins of the United Kingdom, while lawfully Current therein, shall pass Current and be a Legal Tender for Sums in Currency

Value of Silver Coins —British.

22

after the rate fixed as aforesaid for the Gold Coins of the United Kingdom, according to the proportion such Silver Coins bear to such Gold Coins : Provided that no Tender in Silver Coin to a greater amount than Ten Dollars shall be valid.

Proviso.

Value of Foreign Gold.

V.—The Foreign Gold Coin called the Doubloon, containing Three Hundred and Sixty-two Grains of pure Gold, shall pass and be a Legal Tender in Currency for Fifteen Dollars and Thirty-five Cents.

Value of Dollars, &c.

VI.—The American, Peruvian, Mexican, Columbian, and old Spanish Dollars, being of the full weight of Four Hundred and Sixteen Grains, and containing not less than Three Hundred and Seventy-three Grains of pure Silver, shall pass Current and shall be a Legal Tender at the rate of One Hundred Cents each ; and the several divisions of such Coins shall pass Current and be a Legal Tender in Currency after the like rate, according to the proportion such divisions shall respectively bear to the Coins of which they are parts. Provided that no Tender of such Coins to a greater amount than Ten Dollars shall be valid.

Proviso.

Government may import Copper or Bronze Coins.

VII —It shall be lawful for the Governor in Council to Obtain and Import such quantity of Copper or Bronze Cents and Half Cents as may be necessary for the purposes of this Act, which Cents and Half Cents shall be a Legal Tender for any amount not exceeding Twenty-five Cents ; and when and after this Act shall have come into operation, the Copper Coinage then in circulation shall be called in, and one half of its circulating value paid to the holder ; and no other Copper or Bronze Coins, other than British Sterling Pence and Half Pence of Bronze, shall pass Current in this Colony. Provided that no Person be entitled to be paid for any such Copper Coins then in circulation until he shall have made and signed, before a Stipendiary Magistrate, an Affidavit setting forth that he had not been in any way concerned in the Importation of such Coin, or of any part thereof, but was in the possession of the same in the ordinary course of his trade or business, on the day on which this Act shall have come into operation.

Amount of Tender in cents and half cents.

Proviso as to copper currency in circulation.

Gold and Silver coins, Dollars, &c., may be struck.

VIII.—Such Gold and Silver Coins, representing Dollars, or multiples or divisions of the Dollar Currency, as Her Majesty shall see fit to direct to be struck for that purpose, shall, by such names, and at such rates, and for such amounts, as Her Majesty, by her Proclamation, shall assign, pass Current and be a Legal Tender in this Colony ; the standard of fineness of such Coins being the same as that now adopted for Coins of the United Kingdom, and their intrinsic value bearing the same proportion to their current value as British Coins respectively bear to their current value under this Act.

Foreign coins may be declared current by Proclamation.

IX.—Her Majesty may at any time declare, by Proclamation, that any other Gold or Silver Coins of any Foreign State shall, when of the weights assigned therein, pass Current and be a Legal Tender at rates in Currency to be assigned to them respectively in such Proclamation, such rates being proportionate to the quantity of pure Gold and Silver contained in such Coins, as compared with the rates of British Coins current under this Act.

X.—Gold Coins Current under this Act shall be a Legal Tender by tale, so long as they shall not want more than two grains of the weight assigned to them by this Act, or by Her Majesty's Proclamation. Provided that in any one payment above Fifty Pounds, the Person paying may pay, or the Person receiving may insist on receiving, the said British Gold Coins by weight, at the rate of Eighteen Dollars and Sixty-nine and a half Cents per ounce Troy, and the said Gold Coins of the United States, by weight, at the rate of Eighteen Dollars Thirty-two and nine-sixteenths of a Cent per ounce Troy.

Gold coins tender by tale, &c. *Proviso:*

XI.—All existing liabilities, whether under Act of the Legislature, Judgment, Rule or Order of a Court of Judicature, or Private Contract, shall be discharged, as follows: The Pound of present Currency by payment of Four Dollars; the Pound of Local Sterling, (equal to Twenty-three Shillings and Twelve-thirteenths of a Penny of present Currency,) by payment of Four Dollars and Sixty-one Cents; and the Pound British Sterling, (equal to Twenty-four Shillings of present Currency,) by payment of Four Dollars and Eighty Cents; and nothing in this Act shall affect the rights of Parties claiming Local Sterling or British Sterling under any Act of the Legislature, or Private Contract, now subsisting.

The Pound currency, 4 Dollars. *Pound Local Sterling 4 Dollars 61 Cents.* *The Pound British, 4 Dollars 80 Cents.*

XII.—In all future Contracts the term Pound shall mean and be equivalent to Four Dollars Currency; and the term Pound Sterling shall mean and be equivalent to Four Dollars and Eighty Cents Currency.

Future contracts. term Pound, 4 dols; Pound Sterling, 4 dollars 80 cents.

XIII —Any Person who shall falsely Make or Counterfeit any Coin resembling, or apparently intended to resemble or pass for, any Gold or Silver Coin Current under or by virtue of this Act or any Proclamation thereunder, or who shall Import into this Colony any such False or Counterfeit Coin, shall be guilty of Felony, and, being convicted thereof, shall be liable, at the discretion of the Court, to Transportation beyond Seas for life, or for any term not less than Seven Years; or to be imprisoned, with hard labour, for any term not exceeding Four Years; and every such offence shall be deemed to be complete, although the Coin so made or Counterfeited shall not be in a fit state to be uttered, or the Counterfeiting thereof shall not be finished or perfected.

Penalty counterfeiting coin.

XIV.—Any Person who shall Tender, Utter, or Put Off any such False or Counterfeit Coin, knowing the same to be False or Counterfeit, shall be guilty of a Misdemeanor, and, being convicted thereof, shall be Imprisoned, with Hard Labour, for any term not exceeding One Year.

Penalty uttering false coin.

XV.—This Act shall not be in force until sanctioned by Her Majesty, nor until a day thereafter to be fixed by Proclamation of His Excellency the Governor, published in the *Royal Gazette.*

Suspending clause.

J. C. Withers, Printer to the Queen's Most Excellent Majesty.

Appendix 2: An Act to Amend the Currency Act (1887)

CAP. IV.

AN ACT to amend Title 25, Chapter 92, of the Consolidated Statutes,
entitled "Of the Currency."

(Passed 18th May, 1887.)

BE it enacted by the Administrator of the Government, the Legislative Council and House of Assembly, in Legislative Session convened, as follows: – *Enacting clause.*

I. – The denomination of Money in the Currency of this Colony shall be Dollars and Cents, in which Currency the Cent shall be One hundredth part of a Dollar, and all Accounts shall be kept, all Moneys paid and received, all Verdicts received and Judgments entered, and other Legal proceedings taken in such Currency. No statement of Account of any debt contracted within this Colony by parties resident within this Colony, shall be binding or valid unless the same shall be rendered, stated or declared in Dollars and Cents. *Denomination of Money to be in Dollars and Cents.*

II. – The British Sovereign of lawful weight shall be held to be equal to, and shall be a legal tender, and pass current for Four Dollars and Eighty Cents, Currency; and all parts of the Sovereign shall pass current and be a legal tender in Currency after the like rate, according to the proportion they respectively bear to the Sovereign. *British Sovereign Legal tender for Four Dollars and Eighty Cents.*

III. – The Gold Eagle of the United States coined after the First July, Eighteen Hundred and Thirty-four, and while the standard of fineness for Gold Coins then fixed by the laws of the United States remains unchanged, and weighing Ten Penny-weights, Eighteen Grains, Troy weight, shall pass current and be a legal tender for Nine Dollars and Eighty-five Cents, Currency; and all multiples and parts of such Eagles of like date and proportionate weight shall pass current and be a legal tender in Currency after the like rate according to the proportion they respectively bear to the Eagle. *Gold Eagle coined after 1834 legal tender for Nine Dollars and Eight-five Cents.*

IV. – The Silver Coins of the United Kingdom, while lawfully current therein, shall pass current and be legal tender for sums in Currency after the rate fixed as aforesaid, for the Gold Coins of the United Kingdom, according to the proportion such Silver Coins bear to such Gold Coins: Provided that no tender in Silver Coin to a greater amount than Ten Dollars shall be valid. *Silver Coins of United Kingdom shall pass current after the aforesaid rate.*

V. – The Governor in Council may obtain and import such quantity of Copper or Bronze Cents as may be necessary for the purposes of this Act, which Cents shall be a legal tender for any amount not exceeding Twenty-five Cents; no other Copper or Bronze Coins other than British Sterling Pence and Half Pence of Bronze, and the said Bronze or Copper Cents imported as aforesaid shall pass current in this Colony. *Governor in Council power to import Coins.*

VI. – Notwithstanding any existing custom or usage, Five of the Copper or Bronze cents obtained or imported as aforesaid, shall be a legal tender in exchange for the Five Cent Silver Coin of this Colony; Ten of the said Cents shall be a legal tender in exchange for the Silver Ten Cent Coin; Twenty of the said Cents a legal tender in exchange for the Silver Twenty Cent Coin; and Twenty-five of the said Cents shall be a legal tender in exchange for the Twenty-five Cent Silver Coin of this Colony, if the Governor in Council should see fit to import and put in circulation Coins of the last denomination. *Five Copper or Bronze Cents to be a legal tender for Five Cent Silver, &c. &c.*

VII. – Such Gold and Silver Coins representing Dollars or multiples or divisions of the Dollar, Currency, as Her Majesty (shall see fit to direct to be struck for that purpose, shall by such names and at such rates, and for such amounts as Her Majesty) by Her Proclamation, *Gold and Silver Coins shall be of same standard of fineness of Coins of United Kingdom.*

shall assign, pass current and be a legal tender in this Colony; the standard of fineness of such Coins being the same as that now adopted for Coins of the United Kingdom, and their intrinsic value bearing the same proportion to their current value as British Coins respectively bear to their current value under this Act.

VIII. — All Gold, Silver, Copper and Bronze Coins, heretofore imported by the Governor in Council into this Colony, shall be a legal tender under this Act. *Coins formerly imported a legal tender.*

IX. — Gold Coins current under this Act shall be a legal tender by tale so long as they shall not want more than two grains of the weight assigned to them by this Act, or by Her Majesty's Proclamations: Provided that in any one payment above Two Hundred Dollars the person paying may pay, or the person receiving may insist on receiving the said British Gold Coins by weight, at the rate of Sixteen Dollars and Sixty-nine Cents, per ounce troy, and the said Gold Coins of the United States by weight at the rate of Eighteen Dollars and Thirty-one Cents per ounce troy. *Weight of Gold Coins, &c.*

X. — Any person who shall falsely make or counterfeit any Coin resembling or apparently intended to resemble, or pass for any Gold or Silver Coin current under or by virtue of this Act, or any Proclamation thereunder, or who shall import into this Colony any such false or counterfeit Coin, shall be guilty of felony, and being convicted thereof shall be liable to be imprisoned with hard labour, for any term not exceeding four years, and every such offence shall be deemed to be complete although the Coin so made or counterfeited shall not be in a fit state to be uttered or the counterfeiting thereof shall not be finished or perfected. *Person counterfeiting any Coin shall be guilty of Felony.* *Penalty, &c.*

XI. — Any person, who shall tender, utter, or put off any such false or counterfeit Coin, knowing the same to be false or counterfeit, shall be guilty of a misdemeanour, and being convicted thereof shall be imprisoned with hard labour for any term not exceeding One Year. *Penalty for uttering.*

— XII. — Chapter Ninety-two of the Consolidated Statutes, entitled "Of the Currency," is hereby repealed. *Repealing Clauses.*

XIII. — This Act shall not come into operation until the First day of January, A.D. Eighteen Hundred and Eighty-eight. *Time of operation.*

Appendix 3: Highest Auction Prices for Newfoundland $2 Gold Coins

Table 9 lists the sixteen highest prices paid for Newfoundland $2 gold pieces at public auction. Many of these coins have subsequently been resold privately, so, except for very recent results, these should generally not be considered current values. If a coin has been auctioned multiple times, I have made an effort to include just the most recent appearance. Additionally, the grade as it appeared when it was auctioned is the one listed in this table. Some of these have been upgraded since then. All prices listed here include the buyer's commission.

Table 9. Highest prices paid for Newfoundland $2 gold coins at public auction as of 2016

DATE	OTHER	GRADE	AUCTION DATE	COMPANY	PRICE
1865	B34	SP63	Apr 2014	Heritage	$102,813
1880	...	SP64	Nov 1996	B&M	$70,400
1885	...	SP66	Nov 1996	B&M	$44,000
1865	...	MS65	Oct 2010	CNC	$33,050
1872	...	SP65	Jan 2006	Heritage	$27,025
1865	...	SP65	Sep 2005	Heritage	$19,550
1872	...	SP65	Jan 2005	Heritage	$19,550
1872	...	MS64	Oct 2010	CNC	$19,475
1881	...	MS64	Jul 2002	Walsh	$18,175
1880	...	MS63	Oct 2010	CNC	$16,525
1881	...	MS64	Jan 2010	Heritage	$16,100
1865	...	SP63	Jan 2010	Heritage	$15,525
1882H	...	MS65	Apr 2005	ANR	$10,925
1870	...	SP64	Nov 1996	B&M	$10,340
1870	...	MS63	Jan 2003	Heritage	$8,625
1880	...	MS62	Apr 2014	Heritage	$7,638

Note: B34 = Bowman 34; B&M = Bowers and Merena; CNC = Canadian Numismatic Company; Walsh = Michael Walsh; ANR = American Numismatic Rarities.

Appendix 4: Provenance of Several Significant Newfoundland $2 Gold Coins

This appendix brings together some of the findings from earlier chapters to summarize provenances and costs (when available) of a few significant coins within the Newfoundland $2 gold series. There are, unfortunately, only a relatively small number of exceptional coins for which a significant provenance can be traced.

Table 10. Provenance of 1864 copper pattern Bowman 31

Number known: 1; Current location: National Currency Collection of the Bank of Canada

DATE	SALE (LOT #)	BUYER	PRICE PAID	COMMENTS
1864				Likely engraved and struck by Wyon in his work-shop
~1885	Acquired by Montagu	Montagu	Unknown	
Mar 1892	Montagu Sale (245)	Rathbone	£3 13s.	First public offering
Jul 1903	Murdoch Sale (456)	Rollin	£5 15s.	Includes 1890 Newfoundland proof set
Jun 1912	Caldecott Sale (367)	Spink	£7 0s.	Last traceable public offering
Before 1973	Unknown	John J. Ford	Unknown	
Since 1973	John J. Ford	Bank of Canada	Unknown	Now permanently in the National Currency Collection of the Bank of Canada

Table 11. Provenance of 1865 pattern Bowman 34

Number known: 1; Current location: Private Canadian collection

DATE	SALE (LOT #)	BUYER	PRICE PAID	COMMENTS
1865		Unknown	8s. 4d.	*
1865-1910	Unknown	Unknown	Unknown	No record of public sales
May 1910	Spink	Unknown	£10	Spink Circular #76006: first public offering
1910-~40	Unknown	Unknown	Unknown	
~1940-54	Unknown	Farouk	Unknown	
Feb 1954	Farouk (900)	Norweb	$332	Sotheby Sale Farouk Collection: Norweb Ledger entry #7977
Nov 1996	Norweb (741)	Temple	$39,600	Norweb Sale, Bowers and Merena Auctions
~2010	Temple	Kingston	$75,000	Private sale
~2011	Kingston	Prager	$75,000	Private sale
Apr 2014	Prager (24275)	Private Canadian	$102,815	Heritage CICF** Sale

* This is the face value of the coin. If the coin had been transferred to either the Royal Mint Museum or the British Museum, this would have been its cost. Although documents related to the transfer of coins from the mint in 1865 are not available, such documents for 1870 indicate that coins were transferred to the museums at face value. However, it was not normal for the museums to acquire pattern coins; their order from the mint was simply for the regular-issue coins.

** Chicago International Coin Fair

Table 12. Provenance of finest known (SP65) 1865 specimen

Total number known: ~10; Current location: Kingston Collection

DATE	SALE (LOT #)	BUYER	PRICE PAID	COMMENTS
Before 1919	Unknown	T. Leon	Unknown	Partner with Brand in Chicago Coin Co., 1907-15
Sep 1919	Private from T. Leon	V. Brand	$11.25	#92779 in Brand Ledgers
Apr 1935			$25.00	Evaluation for Brand Estate
After 1935	Private	New Netherlands	Unknown	Likely Sold by A. or H. Brand*
After 1935	New Netherlands	Norweb	Unknown	**
Nov 1996	Norweb Sale (679)	Campbell	$10,428	
After 1996	Campbell	Canadian collector	Unknown	
2009	Canadian collector	Kingston Collection	Unknown	

*Armin and Horace Brand were Virgil's brothers. After Virgil's death, an evaluation of the estate was carried out in 1935 and the brothers eventually split the Virgil Brand Collection.

** In private communication with Q. David Bowers (cataloguer of the Norweb Canadian Collection), I was informed that the paper envelope containing this coin indicated that it had come from the Brand estate via the New Netherlands Coin Company.

Table 13. Provenance of second-finest known (SP64) 1865 specimen

Total number known: ~10; Current location: Private Canadian collection

DATE	SALE (LOT #)	BUYER	PRICE PAID	COMMENTS
1982 or 1983	CICF	Moore	$17,500	Coin Dealer Charles Moore
1982 or 1983	Moore	Cornwell	$25,000	ICCS owner Brian Cornwell
After 1983	Cornwell	Campbell	Unknown	Coin Dealer Sandy Campbell
After 1983	Campbell	Temple	Unknown	
June 2010	Temple	Private Canadian	$28,000	Sale brokered by Campbell

Note: CICF = Chicago International Coin Fair; ICCS = International Coin Certification Service.

Table 14. Provenance of finest known PCGS (MS66) circulation strike 1865 coin

Total number at this grade: 1; Current location: Perth Collection

DATE	SALE (LOT #)	BUYER	PRICE PAID	COMMENTS
1903	Murdoch (451)	Pinnock	£1 10s.	This provenance uncertain; lot also included plain-edge 1865 specimen*
1996	Norweb (680)	Campbell	$5,600	**
After 1996	Campbell	Canadian collector	Unknown	Private sale
2009	Canadian collector	Perth Collection	Unknown	Part of complete $2 gold collection

* It is possible that this coin came from the Murdoch Sale because in that sale an 1865 coin was catalogued as a grained-edge proof. Lot 680 in the Norweb Sale was catalogued as a possible reeded-edge specimen, implying that this might be the same coin.

** In the Norweb Sale, the cataloguer suggested that this coin could possibly be a specimen. Recent grading has indicated that it is a first strike and not a specimen.

Table 15. Provenance of only known 1870 specimen outside of a museum

Total number known: 3;* Current location: Kingston Collection

DATE	SALE (LOT #)	BUYER	PRICE PAID	COMMENTS
Jan 1894	Spink (fixed)	Unknown	£6	Spink Circular Jan 1894 #11803A
1940s or '50s	Spink	Norweb	Unknown	Spink to Norweb by private treaty**
Nov 1996	Norweb (682)	Canadian collector	$10,340	Norweb Sale, Bowers and Merena Auctions
2009	Canadian collector	Kingston Collection	Unknown	

* It has been indicated here that only three are known and that this is the only 1870 specimen not in a museum. However, see the discussion in Chapter 7 on the New Netherlands Sale of 1964, which may indicate that there could be a fourth one out there somewhere.

** In private communication, Q. David Bowers (cataloguer of the Norweb Canadian Collection) wrote that the paper envelope containing this coin indicated that it came from Spink in the 1940s or 1950s. However, there is no entry in the Norweb ledgers for this coin.

Table 16. Provenance of only known 1880 specimen outside of a museum

Total number known: 2; Current location: Kingston Collection

DATE	SALE (LOT #)	BUYER	PRICE PAID	COMMENTS
1880	Royal Mint	Melbourne Mint	Face value	2 coins for 1880 Melbourne International Exhibition
~1880	Melbourne Mint	Wilhemj (?)	Very little	In trade for almost worthless ancients*
After 1880	Wilhemj	Anderson	Unknown	This transaction unverified
1880–93?	Anderson Collection	Unknown	Unknown	Anderson (Master of Melbourne Branch of Royal Mint)
1895?	Anderson?	Murdoch	Unknown	Likely through some intermediary
Jul 1903	Murdoch Sale (452)	Rollin	£1 14s.	Lot also included 1865 specimen $2 gold coin
Apr 1937	Spink (fixed)	Norweb?	£3	Spink Circular, April 1937, #60532**
Nov 1996	Norweb (688)	Canadian collector	$70,400	Bowers and Merena auction
2009	Canadian collector	Kingston Collection	Unknown	

* See further discussion on Melbourne Museum Collection in Chapter 7.

** It is not clear whether the Norwebs acquired this coin from the Spink circular or at some later date.

Table 17. Provenance of finest known PCGS (MS65) circulation strike 1882H coin

Total number at this grade: 1; Current location: Private Canadian collection

DATE	SALE (LOT #)	BUYER	PRICE PAID	COMMENTS
Before 1944	Unknown	Colonel Flanagan*	Unknown	
Mar 1944	Flanagan (255)	Eliasberg	$6.50	Stack's Colonel John W. Flanagan Auction
Apr 2005	Eliasberg (1324)	US dealer	$10,925	Sold by American Numismatic Rarities
January 2008	Kroisos (3450)	Private Canadian	$3,220	Stack's Auction

* Flanagan was a very famous US coin collector. In 1944, when most of his collection was sold, the US government seized his example of a 1933 US $20 gold coin that it claimed was not legal to own.

NOTES

Prologue

[1] James Powell, "British Colonies in North America: The Early Years (pre-1841)," in *A History of the Canadian Dollar* (Ottawa: Bank of Canada, 2005), http://www.bankofcanada.ca/wp-content/uploads/2010/07/pre-1841.pdf.

[2] Library and Archives Canada, "Newfoundland, Rutherford Brothers, One halfpenny token, 1846," http://www.coinsandcanada.com/tokens-medals-articles.php?article=newfoundland,-rutherford-brothers,-one-halfpenny-token,-1846&id=340.

[3] Stanley Lebergott, "Wage Trends, 1800-1900," in *Trends in the American Economy in the Nineteenth Century* (Princeton, NJ: Princeton University Press, 1960), 449-500, http://www.nber.org/chapters/c2486.

Chapter 1 - A Brief History of Newfoundland

[1] S.J. McCuaig, "Current Research," Newfoundland Department of Mines and Energy Geological Survey, Report 03-1 (St. John's: Government of Newfoundland and Labrador, 2003), 279-92.

[2] The first two paragraphs of this section draw on information found in Ralph Pastore, "First Arrivals," Newfoundland and Labrador Heritage, http://www.heritage.nf.ca/aboriginal/first.html (last modified January 2012).

[3] *Royal Commission on Renewing and Strengthening Our Place in Canada: Research Volume I* (St. John's: Government of Newfoundland and Labrador, 2003), 3.

[4] J.V. Wright, *A History of the Native People of Canada: Volume 1 (10,000-1,000 B.C.)* (Quebec: Canadian Museum of Civilization, 1995), 178.

[5] "L'Anse Amour National Historic Site of Canada," Canada's Historic Places, http://www.historicplaces.ca/en/rep-reg/place-lieu.aspx?id=14130.

[6] Ibid.

[7] Ibid.

[8] *Royal Commission on Renewing and Strengthening Our Place in Canada*, 4.

[9] Newfoundland Historical Society, *A Short History of Newfoundland and Labrador* (St. John's: Boulder Publications, 2008), 10.

[10] Ibid., 16.

[11] Ibid.

[12] *Royal Commission on Renewing and Strengthening Our Place in Canada*, 3.

[13] Newfoundland Historical Society, *A Short History of Newfoundland and Labrador*, 18.

[14] Ralph Pastore, "The Beothuk," Newfoundland and Labrador Heritage, http://www.heritage.nf.ca/aboriginal/beothuk.html (last modified 1997).

[15] "The Beothuk," http://www.heritage.nf.ca/aboriginal/beothuk.html.

[16] See Sean T. Cadigan, *Newfoundland and Labrador: A History* (Toronto: University of Toronto Press, 2009), 32.

[17] Ibid., 26.

[18] Ibid.

[19] Ibid., 28.

[20] Rev. M. Harvey, *Newfoundland in 1897 Being Queen Victoria's Diamond Jubilee Year and the Four Hundredth Anniversary of the Discovery of the Island by John Cabot* (London: Sampson Low, Marston and Company, 1897), 1, 4, https://archive.org/stream/cihm_05210#page/4/mode/2up.

[21] Cadigan, *Newfoundland and Labrador*, 31.

[22] Ibid.

[22] Ibid., 29.

[24] Harvey, *Newfoundland in 1897*, 15.

[25] Ibid.

[26] Ibid.

[27] Ibid., 40.

[28] Ibid., 41.

[29] Ibid., 46.

[30] Ibid., 46-47.

[31] Ibid., 33.

[32] Ibid., 61.

[33] Ibid.

[34] Ibid.

[35] Tim Lambert, "Brief History of Ireland in the 18th Century," http://www.localhistories.org/ireland18th.html (last modified 2013).

[36] Ibid.

[37] Cadigan, *Newfoundland and Labrador*, 62.

[38] Ibid.

[39] The rest of this paragraph draws from Cadigan, *Newfoundland and Labrador*, 62.

[40] Ibid., 64.

[41] Mary Mulcahy, RSM, "The Catholic Church in Newfoundland: The Pre-Emancipation Years," CCHA Historical Studies 52 (1985): 5-34.

[42] Cadigan, *Newfoundland and Labrador*, 80.

[43] Ibid., 84.

[44] Ibid., 85.

[45] Ibid., 88.

[46] Ibid., 89.

[47] Ibid., 83.

[48] Ibid.

[49] Ibid., 102.

[50] Ibid., 119.

[51] This paragraph draws from the webpage "Newfoundland Currency and Banking Institutions," http://visitnewfoundland.ca/currency.html.

[52] Cadigan, *Newfoundland and Labrador*, 125.

[53] Ibid.

[54] Ibid., 127.

[55] Ibid., 130.

[56] Ibid., 142

[57] Ibid., 150–52.

[58] Ibid., 152.

[59] Ibid.

[60] Newfoundland and Labrador Heritage, "The Confederation Election of 1869," http://www.heritage.nf.ca/law/election.html (last modified 1997).

[61] New Zealand Ministry for Culture and Heritage, "Becoming a Dominion – Dominion Status," New Zealand History, http://www.nzhistory.net.nz/culture/dominion-day/becoming-dominion (last modified September 3, 2014).

[62] Cadigan, *Newfoundland and Labrador*, 177.

63 Veterans Affairs Canada, "The Opening Day, Battle of the Somme, 1916," http://www.veterans.gc.ca/eng/remembrance/memorials/overseas/first-world-war/france/beaumonthamel/somme#n2 (last modified October 23, 2014).

64 Newfoundland and Labrador Heritage, "Newfoundland and Labrador in the First World War," http://www.heritage.nf.ca/greatwar/articles/somme.html (last modified April 2015).

65 This paragraph and the next draw from James K. Hiller, *Confederation: Deciding Newfoundland's Future 1935-1949* (St. John's: Newfoundland Historical Society, 1998), 2-3.

66 Ibid., 4.

67 Ibid., 5.

68 Ibid.

69 Ibid.

70 Ibid., 6.

71 Ibid., 7.

72 Ibid., 23.

73 Ibid., 54.

Chapter 2 – A Snapshot of Newfoundland in 1865

1 Statistics Canada, *2006 Census of Population* (Ottawa: Government of Canada, 2008), https://www12.statcan.gc.ca/census-recensement/2006/index-eng.cfm.

2 Royal Newfoundland Constabulary, "Salary," http://www.rnc.gov.nl.ca/careers/salary.

3 James Powell, "British Colonies in North America: The Early Years (pre-1841)," in *A History of the Canadian Dollar* (Ottawa: Bank of Canada, 2005), http://www.bankofcanada.ca/wp-content/uploads/2010/07/pre-1841.pdf.

Chapter 4 – Circulation Strike Newfoundland $2 Gold Coins

1 R.W. McLachlan, "Canadian Numismatics," *The Gazette* (Montreal), 1886.

2 C.F. Rowe, Robert J. Graham, and James A. Haxby, *The Currency and Medals of Newfoundland* (Toronto: Numismatic Education Society of Canada, 1983), 51.

3 James O. Sweeny, *A Numismatic History of the Heaton Mint* (Birmingham: Birmingham Mint, 1981), 114.

4 A more complete discussion can be found in Rowe et al., *The Currency and Medals of Newfoundland*, 49, 62.

5 James A. Haxby, *A Guide Book of Canadian Coins and Tokens*, 1st ed. (Atlanta: Whitman Publishing, 2012), 17.

6 J. Richard Becker, *The Decimal Coinage of Nova Scotia, New Brunswick and Prince Edward Island* (Acton, MA: Beacon Publishing, 1975), 58.

7 Rob Turner, The 1858 Cents of Provincial Canada (Fountain Valley, CA: The Author, 2007), 31-35.

8 Dictionary of Canadian Biography, vol. 12 (1891-1900) (Toronto/Laval: University of Toronto/Université Laval, 1966).

9 Ibid.

10 Ibid.

11 Rowe et al., *The Currency and Medals of Newfoundland*, 57.

12 Haxby, *A Guide Book of Canadian Coins and Tokens*, 89.

13 Rowe et al., *The Currency and Medals of Newfoundland*.

14 P.N. Breton, *Illustrated History of Coins and Tokens Relating to Canada* (Montreal: P.N. Breton and Company, 1894), 194.

15 Robert Chalmers, *A History of Currency in the British Colonies* (London: HMSO, 1893).

16 Neil Carmichael, *Canada Coin Catalogue*, 7th ed. (Toronto: Carmichael's Stamp and Coin Company, 1960).

[17] Ibid., 44.

[18] James Atkins, *The Coins and Tokens of the Possessions and Colonies of the British Empire* (London: B. Quaritch, 1889).

[19] Joseph Leroux, *Numismatic Atlas of Canada*, 1st ed. (Montreal: Jos. Leroux, 1883).

[20] Rowe et al., *The Currency and Medals of Newfoundland*, 34.

Chapter 5 – Extant Populations of Newfoundland Gold Coins

[1] R.W. McLachlan, "Canadian Numismatics," *The Gazette* (Montreal), 1886,114.

Chapter 6 – Specimens and Patterns

[1] Bowers and Merena Inc., eds., *Norweb Collection of Canadian and Provincial Coins: Auctions by Bowers and Merena Inc.* (Baltimore: Norweb Collection, 1996) 48.

[2] R.W. McLachlan, "Canadian Numismatics," *The Gazette* (Montreal), 1886.

[3] Fred Bowman, *Canadian Patterns* (Ottawa: Canadian Numismatic Association, 1957).

[4] W. K. Cross, *Canadian Coins: A Charlton Standard Catalogue*, 59th ed. (Toronto: Charlton International, 2005).

[5] C.F. Rowe, Robert J. Graham, and James A. Haxby, *The Currency and Medals of Newfoundland* (Toronto: Numismatic Education Society of Canada, 1983), 51.

[6] Fred Bowman, "Canada's Ten Rarest Coins," *Canadian Numismatic Journal* 14, 7+8 (July-August 1969): 229-30.

[7] Harvey Richer, "Canadian Coins in the British and Ashmolean Museums," *Canadian Numismatic Journal* 23, 1 (January 1978): 5-11.

[8] H.W.A. Linecar, "A Catalogue of Coins and Tokens in the British Museum, 1959," *Canadian Numismatic Journal* 5, 1+2 (January-February 1960): 7-11.

[9] Richer, "Canadian Coins in the British and Ashmolean Museums."

[10] William. J. Hocking, *Catalogue of the Coins, Tokens, Medals, Dies and Seals in the Museum of the Royal Mint*, 2 vols. (London: Wyman and Sons, 1906, 1910), 1: 311, 2: 126-27.

[11] Bowman, *Canadian Patterns*.

[12] Hocking, *Catalogue of the Coins, Tokens, Medals*.

[13] David L. Ganz, *Rare Coin Investing: An Affordable Way to Build Your Portfolio* (Iola, WI: Krause Publications, 2010).

[14] Bowers and Merena Inc., *Norweb Collection of Canadian and Provincial Coins*.

[15] Richer, "Canadian Coins in the British and Ashmolean Museums."

[16] Hocking, *Catalogue of the Coins, Tokens, Medals*.

[17] Leonard Forrer, *The Wyons* (London: Spink and Son, 1917).

[18] Rowe et al., *The Currency and Medals of Newfoundland*, 51.

[19] Many of the coins listed here are not included in Hocking's Catalogue of Coins, Tokens, Medals, indicating that his inventory was either incomplete or that the museum obtained these pieces after 1906. Note that "1870 – obverse bust in beaded circle" is included in Hocking's book.

[20] R.W. McLachlan, *A Descriptive Catalogue of Coins, Tokens and Medals Issued in or Relating to the Dominion of Canada and Newfoundland* (Montreal: The Author, 1886).

[21] Ibid., 114.

[22] Ibid.

[23] Ibid.

[24] Ibid., 115

[25] Bowman, "Canada's Ten Rarest Coins."

[26] John McKay-Clements, "Canada's Ten Rarest

Coins," *Canadian Numismatic Journal* 14, 7+8 (July-August 1969): 228 (reprinted from Ontario Numismatist, March 1969).

[27] James A. Haxby, *A Guide Book of Canadian Coins and Tokens*, 1st ed. (Atlanta: Whitman Publishing, 2012), 89.

[28] Rowe et al., *The Currency and Medals of Newfoundland*, 51.

[29] Graham Esler, "The History of the National Currency Collection," *Canadian Numismatic Journal* 49, 7 (September 2004): 347-58.

Chapter 7 – Great Auctions and Collections of Newfoundland Gold Coins

[1] "The Belzberg Collection of Canadian Coinage, New York, January 13, 2003, Heritage Auctions."

[2] Harvey Richer, "Canadian Coins in the British and Ashmolean Museums," *Canadian Numismatic Journal* 23, 1 (January 1978): 5-11.

[3] "Catalogue of the Collection of Coins and Tokens of the British Possessions & Colonies formed by J. B. Caldecott, Esq. who is relinquishing this series, which will be sold by auction by Messrs. Sotheby, Wilkinson & Hodge At Their House, No. 13, Wellington Street, Strand, W.C. (London), on Tuesday, the 11th of June 1912, and Two Following Days, at One O'clock Precisely."

[4] "The Amon G. Carter, Jr. Family Collection of United States Gold, Silver & Copper Coins, Foreign Coins. January 18-21, 1984. Auctioned by Stacks, New York City."

[5] "The Louis E. Eliasberg Sr. Collection of World Gold Coins and Medals, April 18-19 2006, American Numismatic Rarities in Conjunction with Spink, Helmsley Park Lane Hotel, New York City."

[6] "Catalogue of the Valuable Collection of Coins and Tokens of the British Possessions and Colonies, in Gold, Silver, Copper, &c. Including many Patterns and Proofs, the Property of Lieut.-Colonel H. Leslie Ellis, F.S.A. F.R.G.S. &c. who is relinquishing this series, Sotheby, Wilkinson & Hodge, At Their House, No. 13 Wellington Street, Strand, W.C. (London), On Wednesday, the 18th day of June, 1902, and following Day, at One O'clock Precisely" (emphasis added).

[7] British Museum, http://www.britishmuseum.org/.

[8] "The Frontenac Sale, Auctions by Bowers and Merena, Inc. November 20-22 1991, New York City."

[9] John Sharples, "The Numismatic Collection of the Museum of Victoria," *Journal of the Numismatic Association of Australia* 2 (1986): 37-52, http://www.numismatics.org.au/pdfjournal/Vol2/Vol%202%20Article%203.pdf.

[10] Ibid., 41.

[11] Joseph Jacobs and Goodman Lipkind, "Montagu, Hyman," in *Jewish Encyclopedia* (n.d.), http://jewishencyclopedia.com/articles/10953-montagu-hyman.

[12] "Catalogue of the Very Important & Valuable Collection of Patterns and Proofs in Gold, Silver, Bronze, Tin &c for the Coinages of the Possessions and Colonies of the British Empire, formed by H. Montagu, Esq. F.S.A. &c. Sotheby, Wilkinson & Hodge, At Their House, No. 13 Wellington Street, Strand, W.C. (London), Tuesday, the 3rd day of May 1892, and Following Day at One O'clock Precisely."

[13] *British Numismatic Society*, http://www.britnumsoc.org.

[14] "Catalogue of the Valuable Collection of Coins and Medals the Property of the Late John G. Murdoch Esq. Member of the Numismatic Society of London which will be sold by auction by Messrs. Sotheby, Wilkinson & Hodge At Their House,

No. 13, Wellington Street, Strand, W.C. (London), Fourth Part. The Coins and Tokens of the British Colonies and Dependencies. America and the European Continent. 21st of July 1903, Quarto, pp 107, 1233 lots, 10 superb plates."

[15] "Catalogue of the Famous & Remarkable Collection of British and Colonial Coins, Patterns & Proofs From George III to the Present Day formed by A Nobleman, Recently Deceased. Which will be sold by Auction by Messrs Sotheby, Wilkinson & Hodge at the Large Galleries 34 & 35 New Bond Street, W.(1), on Monday, the 27th of March, 1922 and Four Following Days at One O'clock Precisely."

[16] "The Norweb Collection, Auctions by Bowers and Merena, Inc., November 15, 1996, Baltimore, Maryland."

[17] "The John J. Pittman Collection, Part Three, August 6-8, 1999, Rosemont, Illinois. David Akers Numismatics, Inc."

[18] C.F. Rowe, Robert J. Graham, and James A. Haxby, *The Currency and Medals of Newfoundland* (Toronto: Numismatic Education Society of Canada, 1983).

Chapter 8: Hoards of Newfoundland $2 Gold Coins

[1] Jeff Starck, "Top Ten Stories of 2015: Canada Melts Thousands of Historic Gold Coins," Coin World, http://www.coinworld.com/news/world-coins/2015/12/top-10-stories-of-2015--canada-gold-coin-melt--coin-melt.html.

[2] Neil Carmichael, *Canada Coin Catalogue*, 7th ed. (Toronto: Carmichael's Stamp and Coin Company, 1960).

[3] R.J. Graham, "An Old Newfoundland Savings Hoard," *Canadian Numismatic Association Journal* 31, 7 (July-August 1986): 316-17.

[4] Q. David Bowers, American Coin Treasures and Hoards (Bowers and Merena Galleries, 1997), 131.

[5] R.W. McLachlan, "Canadian Numismatics," *The Gazette* (Montreal), 1886.

Credit for map in background of front cover: Wikipedia Commons.

Credits for coin images at the beginning of each chapter:

Prologue: National Currency Collection of the Bank of Canada
Ch 1: Image courtesy of Heritage Coins
Ch 2: Image courtesy of National Currency Collection of the Bank of Canada
Ch 3: Image courtesy of National Currency Collection of the Bank of Canada
Ch 4: Image courtesy Museums Victoria (Australia)
Ch 5: Image courtesy Museums Victoria (Australia)
Ch 6: Image courtesy PCGS
Ch 7: Image courtesy of the Trustees of the British Museum
Ch 8: Image courtesy PCGS
Epilogue: National Currency Collection of the Bank of Canada

BIBLIOGRAPHY

"The Amon G. Carter, Jr. Family Collection of United States Gold, Silver & Copper Coins, Foreign Coins. January 18-21, 1984. Auctioned by Stacks, New York City."

Atkins, James. *The Coins and Tokens of the Possessions and Colonies of the British Empire.* London: B. Quaritch, 1889.

"The Belzberg Collection of Canadian Coinage, New York, January 13, 2003, Heritage Auctions."
Bowers and Merena Inc., eds. *Norweb Collection of Canadian and Provincial Coins: Auctions by Bowers and Merena Inc.* Baltimore: Norweb Collection, 1996.

Bowman, Fred. "Canada's Ten Rarest Coins." *Canadian Numismatic Journal* 14, 7+8 (July-August 1969): 229-30.

—. *Canadian Patterns.* Ottawa: Canadian Numismatic Association, 1957.

Breton, P. N. *Illustrated History of Coins and Tokens Relating to Canada.* Montreal: P.N. Breton and Company, 1894.

British Museum, http://www.britishmuseum.org/.

British Numismatic Society. http://www.britnumsoc.org. Last modified 2013.

Cadigan, Sean T. *Newfoundland and Labrador: A History.* Toronto: University of Toronto Press, 2009.

Caldecott, J. B. Esq. "Catalogue of the Collection of Coins and Tokens of the British Possessions & Colonies. Auctions by Sotheby, Wilkinson & Hodge. June 11, 1912. London."

Carmichael, Neil. *Canada Coin Catalogue*. 7th ed. Toronto: Carmichael's Stamp and Coin Company, 1960.

"Catalogue of the Famous & Remarkable Collection of British and Colonial Coins, Patterns & Proofs From George III to the Present Day formed by A Nobleman, Recently Deceased. Which will be sold by Auction by Messrs Sotheby, Wilkinson & Hodge at the Large Galleries 34 & 35 New Bond Street, W.(1), on Monday, the 27th of March, 1922 and Four Following Days at One O'clock Precisely."

Cross, W. K. *Canadian Coins: A Charlton Standard Catalogue*. 59th ed. Toronto: Charlton International, 2005.

Chalmers, Robert. *A History of Currency in the British Colonies*. London: HMSO, 1893.

Dictionary of Canadian Biography. Vol. 12, 1891-1900. Toronto/Laval: University of Toronto/Université Laval, 1966.

Ellis, Leslie H., Lieut.-Colonel. "Catalogue of the Collection of Coins and Tokens of the British Possessions and Colonies, in Gold, Silver, Copper &c. Including Many Patterns and Proofs. Auctions bySotheby, Wilkinson & Hodge. June 18, 1902. London."

Esler, Graham. "The History of the National Currency Collection." *Canadian Numismatic Journal* 49, 7 (September 2004): 347-58.

Forrer, Leonard. The Wyons. London: Spink and Son, 1917.

"The Frontenac Sale. Auctions by Bowers and Merena, Inc. November 20-22, 1991. New York City."

Ganz, David L. *Rare Coin Investing: An Affordable Way to Build Your Portfolio*. Iola, WI: Krause Publications, 2010.

Graham, R.J. "An Old Newfoundland Savings Hoard." *Canadian Numismatic Association Journal* 31, 7 (July-August 1986): 316-17.

Harvey, Rev. M. *Newfoundland in 1897 Being Queen Victoria's Diamond Jubilee Year and the Four Hundredth Anniversary of the Discovery of the Island by John Cabot*. London: Sampson Low, Marston and Company, 1897.

Haxby, James A. *A Guide Book of Canadian Coins and Tokens.* 1st ed. Atlanta: Whitman Publishing, 2012.

Hiller, James K. *Confederation: Deciding Newfoundland's Future 1935-1949.* St. John's: Newfoundland Historical Society, 1998.

Hocking, William. J. *Catalogue of the Coins, Tokens, Medals, Dies and Seals in the Museum of the Royal Mint.* 2 vols. London: Wyman and Sons, 1906, 1910.

Jacobs, Joseph, and Goodman Lipkind. "Montagu, Hyman." *Jewish Encyclopedia* (n.d.), http://jewishencyclopedia.com/articles/10953-montagu-hyman.

"The John J. Pittman Collection, Part Three. August 6-8, 1999. Rosemont, Illinois. David Akers Numismatics, Inc."

Lambert, Tim. "Brief History of Ireland in the 18th Century." http://www.localhistories.org/ireland18th.html. Last modified 2013.

"L'Anse Amour National Historic Site of Canada." Canada's Historic Places, http://www.historicplaces.ca/en/rep-reg/place-lieu.aspx?id=14130.

Lebergott, Stanley. "Wage Trends, 1800-1900." In *Trends in the American Economy in the Nineteenth Century.* Princeton, NJ: Princeton University Press, 1960. http://www.nber.org/chapters/c2486.

Leroux, Joseph. *Numismatic Atlas of Canada.* 1st ed. Montreal: Jos. Leroux, 1883.

Library and Archives Canada. "Newfoundland, Rutherford Brothers, One halfpenny token, 1846." http://www.coinsandcanada.com/tokens-medals-articles.php?article=newfoundland,-rutherford-brothers,-one-halfpenny-token,-1846&id=340.

Linecar, H.W.A. "A Catalogue of Coins and Tokens in the British Museum, 1959." *Canadian Numismatic Journal* 5, 1+2 (January-February 1960): 7-11.

"The Louis E. Eliasberg Sr. Collection of World Gold Coins and Medals. April 18-19, 2006. American Numismatic Rarities in Conjunction with Spink, Helmsley Park Lane Hotel, New York City."

McCuaig, S.J. "Current Research." Newfoundland Department of Mines and Energy Geological Survey, Report 03-1 (St. John's: Government of Newfoundland and Labrador, 2003).

John McKay-Clements, "Canada's Ten Rarest Coins," *Canadian Numismatic Journal* 14, 7+8 (July-August 1969): 228

McLachlan, R.W. "Canadian Numismatics----" *The Gazette* (Montreal), 1886.

—. *A Descriptive Catalogue of Coins, Tokens and Medals Issued in or Relating to the Dominion of Canada and Newfoundland.* Montreal: The Author, 1886.

Montagu, H., Esq. "Catalogue of the Very Important & Valuable Collection of Patterns and Proofs in Gold, Silver, Bronze, Tin &c for the Coinages of the Possessions and Colonies of the British Empire. Auctions by Sotheby, Wilkinson & Hodge. May 3, 1892. London."

Mulcahy, Mary, RSM. "The Catholic Church in Newfoundland: The Pre-Emancipation Years." CCHA *Historical Studies* 52 (1985): 5-34.

Newfoundland and Labrador Heritage. "Newfoundland and Labrador in the First World War." http://www.heritage.nf.ca/greatwar/articles/somme.html. Last modified April 2015.

—. "The Confederation Election of 1869." http://www.heritage.nf.ca/law/election.html. Last modified 1997.

"Newfoundland Currency and Banking Institutions." http://visitnewfoundland.ca/currency.html. Newfoundland Historical Society. *A Short History of Newfoundland and Labrador.* St. John's: Boulder Publications, 2008.

New Zealand Ministry for Culture and Heritage. "Becoming a Dominion – Dominion Status." New Zealand History, http://www.nzhistory.net.nz/culture/dominion-day/becoming-dominion. Last modified September 3, 2014.

"The Norweb Collection. Auctions by Bowers and Merena, Inc. November 15, 1996. Baltimore, Maryland."

Pastore, Ralph. "First Arrivals." Newfoundland and Labrador Heritage, http://www.heritage.nf.ca/aboriginal/first.html. Last modified January 2012.

—. "The Beothuk," Newfoundland and Labrador Heritage, http://www.heritage.nf.ca/aboriginal/beothuk.html. Last modified 1997.

Powell, James. "British Colonies in North America: The Early Years (pre-1841)." In *A History of the Canadian Dollar*. Ottawa: Bank of Canada, 2005. http://www.bankofcanada.ca/wp-content/uploads/2010/07/pre-1841.pdf.

Richer, Harvey. "Canadian Coins in the British and Ashmolean Museums." *Canadian Numismatic Journal* 23, 1 (January 1978): 5-11.

Rowe, C. Francis, Robert J. Graham, and James A. Haxby. *The Currency and Medals of Newfoundland*. Toronto: Numismatic Education Society of Canada, 1983.

Royal Commission on Renewing and Strengthening Our Place in Canada: Research Volume I. St. John's: Government of Newfoundland and Labrador, 2003.

Royal Newfoundland Constabulary. "Salary." http://www.rnc.gov.nl.ca/careers/salary.html.

Sharples, John. "The Numismatic Collection of the Museum of Victoria." *Journal of the Numismatic Association of Australia* 2 (1986): 37-52. http://www.numismatics.org.au/pdfjournal/Vol2/Vol%202%20Article%203.pdf.

Smallwood, Joseph Robert, ed. *The Book of Newfoundland*. 6 vols. St. John's: Newfoundland Book Publishers, 1937.

Starck, Jeff. "Top Ten Stories of 2015: Canada Melts Thousands of Historic Gold Coins." Coin World, http://www.coinworld.com/news/world-coins/2015/12/top-10-stories-of-2015--canada-gold-coin-melt--coin-melt.html.

Statistics Canada. *2006 Census of Population*. Ottawa: Government of Canada, 2008. https://www12.statcan.gc.ca/census-recensement/2006/index-eng.cfm.

Sweeny, James O. *A Numismatic History of the Heaton Mint*. Birmingham: Birmingham Mint, 1981.

Turner, Rob. *The 1858 Cents of Provincial Canada*. Fountain Valley, CA: The Author, 2007.

Veterans Affairs Canada. "The Opening Day, Battle of the Somme, 1916." http://www.veterans.gc.ca/eng/remembrance/memorials/overseas/first-world-war/france/beaumonthamel/somme#n2. Last modified October 23, 2014.

Wright, J.V. *A History of the Native People of Canada: Volume 1 (10,000-1,000 B.C.)*. Quebec: Canadian Museum of Civilization, 1995.

INDEX

HARVEY RICHER is professor of astronomy at the
University of British Columbia in Vancouver, Canada.
He has published over 140 scientific papers in peer-
reviewed journals and is one of the largest Canadian
users of the Hubble Space Telescope. Professor Richer
was the 2014 recipient of the Carlyle S. Beals Award
of the Canadian Astronomical Society given for
lifetime achievement. Recently he was made a Fellow
of the Royal Society of Canada, the foremost academic
society in the country.

He has been a coin collector since the time (at age 8)
he and his brother discovered a large one-cent coin
of Queen Victoria under a rock in a vacant lot in
Montreal. He lives in Vancouver with his wife and has
two adult children that are scattered at opposite sides
of the globe. Neither of his two young grandchildren
have as yet caught the collecting bug.